Literature-Based Activities for Integrating Mathematics with Other Content Areas, Grades K–2

Robin A. Ward

RICE UNIVERSITY

PEARSON

Boston New York San Francisco
Mexico City Montreal Toronto London Madrid Munich Paris
Hong Kong Singapore Tokyo Cape Town Sydney

Series Editor: Kelly Villella Canton
Series Editorial Assistant: Christine Pratt Swayne
Marketing Manager: Danae April
Production Editor: Paula Carroll
Editorial Production Service: Kathy Smith Editorial Production
Composition Buyer: Linda Cox
Manufacturing Buyer: Linda Morris
Interior Design and Composition Services: Schneck-DePippo Graphics
Cover Administrator: Linda Knowles
Cover Designer: Elena Sidorova
Director of Professional Development: Alison Maloney

For related titles and support materials, visit our online catalog at www.ablongman.com.

Between the time website information is gathered and then published, it is not unusual for some sites to have closed. Also, the transcription of URLs can result in typographical errors. The publisher would appreciate notification where these errors occur so that they may be corrected in subsequent editions.

Cataloging in Publication Data on file at the Library of Congress

ISBN–13: 978-0-205-53040-3
ISBN–10:   0-205-53040-0

Printed in the United States of America

10 9 8 7 6 5 4 3 2 1   11 10 09 08

Allyn & Bacon
is an imprint of

www.pearsonhighered.com

Contents

CHAPTER 2

Literature-Based Mathematics and Social Studies Activities   *67*

CHAPTER **3**

Literature-Based Mathematics and Visual Arts Activities *123*

About the Author

After earning a Bachelor's degree in math/physics from Immaculata College and a Master's of Arts degree in mathematics from Villanova University, Robin worked as an aerospace engineer and systems programmer. Prompted by a growing interest in teaching mathematics she pursued a PhD in mathematics education from the University of Virginia. Since graduating with her doctorate, Robin has spent ten years working as a professor of mathematics education at California Polytechnic State University and the University of Arizona. A devoted mathematics teacher educator, she sought and received numerous grants from NASA, NSF, and the U.S. Department of Education, all geared toward improving K–12 teachers' mathematical and pedagogical knowledge. A two-time recipient of a Stanford-ASEE fellowship, she partnered with the NASA Dryden Flight Research Center to develop web-based materials for K–12 teachers that showcase the work of NASA scientists. In 2005, the University of Arizona's College of Education bestowed upon her the Outstanding Teaching Award. Robin has written numerous articles and has presented many professional development workshops and talks at national conferences on improving mathematics pedagogy and using children's literature to enhance the teaching and learning of K–8 mathematics.

Robin lives in Houston with her husband, Chris DelConte, and two young daughters, Sienna and Sophia Arabella. There she pursues her passion for improving K–12 teachers' mathematical and pedagogical knowledge as the Associate Director of Curriculum Integration at the Rice University School Mathematics Project. In addition, she gives professional development workshops for local teachers and integrated mathematics-art classes for Pre-Kindergarten–Grade 8 students.

Acknowledgments

I would like to thank the many elementary and middle school teachers whose ideas served as the basis for many of the integrated activities included in this book. I also thank my former students who allowed me to use the classroom as a laboratory for my ideas on how to integrate children's literature into the teaching and learning of mathematics. Their active participation in literature-based classroom activities and their candid responses shared in their reflections assisted me in formulating and fine-tuning many of the ideas presented in this book.

Also, I'd like to acknowledge and thank Dawn Corso, my dear friend and colleague, for her insight and spirited efforts during the initial design phases of this book.

I am also grateful for the thoughtful comments and feedback on this book series from the reviewers lined up by Allyn and Bacon: Tammy Brown, Denver Public Schools; Karen Caldwell, John Early Paideia Middle School; Linda Cole, Barrie School; Bethany Dannelly, Hampton Roads Academy; Amanda Guinn, Monroe County Community Schools-University School; Cheri Howard, Fairbanks North Star Borough School District; Tim Linnet, Maywood Middle School; Kris O'Clair, Denver Public Schools; Lorel Preston, Westminster College; E. Elaine Rafferty, Charleston County School District; Ellen Szecsy, Math Consultant; Alexandra Thompson, Devon Elementary School; Karen Ward, Centennial Middle School.

Thank you to my other friends and colleagues spread far and wide, who supported me in a variety of immeasurable ways during this book endeavor and who continue to inspire me, namely, Gina Bernitt, Michelle Bickman, Andy Chan, Elaine Chin, Winnie Doyle, Shirley Fisher, Gassia Gerges, Mary

Beth Gilbert, Therese Grahn, my friends at JMH, Cynthia Johnson, Ingrid Johnson, the Kinerk family, Lori Levitt, the Livengood family, Michelle Lozano, Nicole O'Fiesh, Sheryl O'Neill, Diana Perdue, Patricia Reedy-Deserio, Gazala Siddiqui, Sheila Tobias, and Fred and Nancy Utter.

Finally, a huge thank you to my husband, parents, family, and two daughters. Sienna and Sophia Arabella, Mommy is all done!

Literature-Based Activities for Integrating Mathematics with Other Content Areas, Grades, K–2

Introduction

Reading in the mathematics classrooms? Absolutely! Integrating children's literature into the teaching and learning of mathematics, however, is more than just reading a book to students. By exploring picture books and reading works of fiction, nonfiction, and poetry, students can engage in worthwhile and stimulating mathematical activities that encourage them to communicate their ideas verbally or through drawing or writing. In short, mathematics can be viewed as "a vehicle for thinking, a medium for creating, and a language for communicating" (Kleiman, 1991, p. 48). In addition, using children's literature requires students to listen and comprehend—two vital skills needed for academic success. Thus, the goal of integrating children's literature into the teaching and learning of mathematics is to improve the overall literacy of students.

Using Children's Literature to Teach Mathematics

Integrating children's literature into the teaching and learning of mathematics is gaining momentum. In fact, a growing body of research and anecdotal evidence documents the potential and power of using children's literature in mathematics classrooms (Avery & Avery, 2001; Burns, 1995; Burns & Sheffield, 2004; Capraro & Capraro, 2006; Carr, Buchanan, Wentz, Weiss, & Brant, 2001; Draper, 2002; Hellwig, Monroe, & Jacobs, 2000; Hunsader, 2004; Johnson & Giorgis, 2001; Leitze, 1997; Leu, Castek, Henry, Coiro, & McMullan, 2004; MacGregor & Price, 1999; Monroe & Livingston, 2002; Moyer, 2000; Schiro,

1997; Ward, 2003, 2004a, 2004b, 2004c, 2005, 2006a, 2006b; Ward & Muller, 2006; Whitin & Whitin, 1996, 2004; Whitin & Wilde, 1992, 1995; Young, 2001). Because many mathematical ideas and concepts are abstract or symbolic in nature, children's literature offers teachers the opportunity to present and discuss these ideas and concepts within the context of a story, using illustrations, prose, and more informal, familiar language. This, in turn, can make the learning of mathematics less intimidating and more engaging, especially for students whose first language is not English. Further, using children's literature to teach mathematics provides students with additional opportunities, encouragement, and support for speaking, writing, reading, and listening in mathematics classes.

Johnson & Giorgis (2001) agree that interacting with children's literature "encourages delight, nurtures curiosity and wonderment, and invites readers to discover things never experienced before" (p. 204). Additionally, shapes can be more readily understood through clear visuals in picture books, while number relationships can spark new interests when the facts are incorporated into fiction, poetry, and visually enticing illustrations. Because children's literature can be used to initiate a discussion on a social issue, introduce a theme, trigger a round of creative writing, or strengthen an appreciation for poetry, even secondary teachers are discovering the therapeutic and instructional value of this genre (Avery & Avery, 2001). In fact, it has been noted that picture books used in the mathematics and science curricula that relate content to the real world are beneficial for students' understanding of specific concepts and may encourage them to seek a career in the sciences (Carr et al., 2001). Additionally, many pieces of children's literature can be appreciated at different grade levels and can provide strategic opportunities for students to engage in problem solving.

Many national educational organizations, such as the National Council of Teachers of Mathematics (NCTM), the National Council of Teachers of English (NCTE), and the International Reading Association (IRA) also advocate that preK–8 mathematics teachers regularly integrate children's literature into their teaching because of its many benefits. For example, in its *Principles and Standards for School Mathematics* (NCTM, 2000), NCTM asserts that "students who have opportunities, encouragement, and support for speaking, writing,

reading, and listening in mathematics classes reap dual benefits: they communicate to learn mathematics, and they learn to communicate mathematically"
(p. 60). NCTE (1996), noted for its history of commitment to the teaching of
literature in connection with the teaching of reading and English/language arts,
advocates the extensive use of children's and adolescent's literature throughout
the reading and writing curriculum and as a valuable source in content-area
studies. The NCTE further endorses preparing and certifying teachers with
strong content and pedagogical knowledge of children's and/or adolescent's
literature. Finally, in its position statement, IRA (2006) recognizes excellent
reading teachers as those who are familiar with children's literature and who
include a wide variety of fiction and nonfiction genres (such as storybooks,
novels, and biographies) in their teaching.

Teaching Using an Integrated Approach

Gaining equal momentum is the movement by preK–8 teachers to integrate their teaching across content areas with the goal of building connections between and among the various subject matters taught in school.
Organizations such as NCTM, the National Council for the Social Studies
(NCSS), the National Research Council (NRC), and the Music Educators
National Conference (MENC) support an integrated approach to teaching. For
example, in its *Curriculum Standards for the Social Studies,* NCSS (1994) states
that "a social studies perspective is academically sound, multidisciplinary, and
integrative" (pp. xvii–xviii). The *National Science Education Standards* (NRC,
1996) offer that "school science and mathematics programs should be coor-
dinated so that students learn the necessary mathematical skills and concepts
before and during their use in the science program" (p. 214). Similarly, MENC
(1994) has identified as its goal for the *National Standards for Arts Education* to
"help students make connections between concepts and across subjects," as the
learning tasks defined by these standards serve as "bridges among the arts disciplines, and finally as gateways from the arts to other areas of study" (p. 13).
NCTM (2000) echoes these same sentiments and advocates that students'

mathematical experiences at all levels include opportunities for connections to other subject areas and disciplines, especially because mathematics permeates music and art content, and is used in science, the social studies, and other fields of study. Finally, the National Middle School Association (NMSA, 1995) argues that the school curriculum needs to be integrative in order to help young adolescents make sense out of their life experiences and connect school experiences to their daily lives outside of the classroom.

The benefits of an integrated curriculum, which recognizes that the subjects within the curriculum are connected to each other and to the real world, have been noted by several educational philosophers, curriculum theorists, and others (Beane, 1993, 1995, 1997; Bruner, 1977; Dewey, 1924, 1933; Drake & Burns, 2004; Gelineau, 2003; Howey, 1996; Jacobs, 1989; Kim, Andrews, & Carr, 2004; McDonald & Fisher, 2006; Schwartz & Pollishuke, 2005; Vars, 1997; Wortham, 1996). Beane (1997) notes that for many students, the separate subject approach offers a "disconnected and incoherent assortment of facts and skills. There is no unity, no real sense to it all" (p. 42). Gardner (1997) also recognizes that students need to explicitly see connections and nonconnections between domains of knowledge, or else generalization and transfer will not occur. Beane (1993, 1995, 1997) as well as others (Jacobs, 1989; Vars, 1997) advocate for integrated curriculum models because they center on the problems and interests of young adolescent learners and serve as a valuable lens for understanding student thinking (Perkins, 1989). According to Wortham (1996), "An integrated curriculum crosses subject areas. …[T]he intent is to construct meaningful bridges to show connections in development and learning" (p. 330). Thus, curriculum integration is often achieved through the design of integrated thematic units or through the study of a topic.

A growing body of literature continues to document the effectiveness of integrated curriculum on student achievement (Arhar, 1997; Cornett, 2003; Davies, 1992; Drake, 1998; Drake & Burns, 2004; National Association for Core Curriculum, 2000; Vars, 1996, 1997; Vars & Beane, 2000; Watts, 2004) and its ability to increase student motivation, elicit higher order thinking, and build stronger interpersonal skills (Vars, 1997). Several scholars argue that an integrated curriculum is warranted, as a truly integrated curriculum enables teachers and their students to make connections between real life and their classroom learning experiences (Bailey, 2000; Caskey, 2001; Caskey & Johnston, 1986). Further, an integrated curriculum engages teachers, stimulates students, and energizes classroom learning environments (Meinbach, Fredericks, & Rothlein, 2000).

Using Children's Literature Combined with an Integrated Approach to Teaching

Given that more and more teachers are turning to children's literature as a means to enliven and demystify the study of mathematics, and given that teachers are striving to build rich connections for students by using an integrated approach to teaching, this book was written to address these two merging efforts. This book series is divided into three volumes for the following grade bands: K–2, 3–5, and 6–8. Within each of these grade-specific volumes are three chapters of classroom-tested activities. The first chapter in each series articulates literature-based activities that integrate mathematics and science; Chapter 2 contains literature-based activities that integrate mathematics and the social studies; and Chapter 3 describes literature-based activities that integrate mathematics and the visual arts.

Each of the chapters opens with a brief overview, articulating the connection between mathematics and the specific content area (whether it be science, social studies, or the visual arts), followed by a list of the concepts and skills featured in the literature-based activities. A matrix follows, which lists each piece of children's literature used in that chapter's integrated activities, and which identifies other relevant cross-curricular concepts and skills. The collection of literature-based activities follows next.

Featured in many of the literature-based activities in this book are book pairs and, in some cases, book trios: that is, two or three pieces of children's literature that work powerfully together when teaching an integrated lesson. Also, several biographies are featured as well as works of nonfiction and poetry.

The format of each activity is as follows:

Book title (along with the name(s) of the author(s), publisher, and ISBN number)

Overview of Book (brief overview of the story line of each book or poem featured in the activities)

Mathematical Concepts and Skills (list of the mathematical concepts and skills serving as the focus of the activities)

Content-Area Concepts and Skills (list of the content-area concepts and skills serving as the focus of the activities)

Overview of Activities (brief description of the activities to follow)

National Mathematics Standards (mathematical expectations of students as defined by NCTM)

National Standards for the Content Area (content-area expectations of students as defined by NRC, NCSS, or MENC)

Materials (list of necessary materials)

Description of Activities (step-by-step procedure describing how to implement the literature-based activities)

Assessment (considerations and questions to ask when assessing student understanding of the concepts and skills presented in activities; see the appendix for more assessment ideas and rubrics)

Activity Extensions (description of potential follow-up activities)

Cross-Curricular Connections (brief description of related, follow-up activities for other content areas)

Related Children's Literature (list of other pieces of children's literature that feature the same or similar concepts and skills presented in the activities)

Related Instructional Resources (list of resources useful to the teacher)

Related Websites (list of websites pertinent to the concepts and skills presented in the activities)

Worksheets/Handouts (if applicable)

Located at the end of the book is an extensive bibliography of over three hundred pieces of children's literature cited throughout this book as well as over one hundred citations of instructional resources that will support the teacher. Additionally, an appendix includes several assessment tools and rubrics useful in evaluating students' performance, skills, and abilities as they engage in the literature-based activities.

Finally, a word of advice: Prior to implementing the integrated, literature-based explorations articulated in this book, read through the entire activity *before* class to assess whether you need to modify or delete any steps in the activities due to student accommodations, lack or substitution of materials, limited resources or space, prior preparation of materials, or other reasons. Do not feel as though these activities are scripted! Use your judgment and pedagogical ingenuity to take tangents as deemed appropriate and to capitalize on those teachable moments. The ultimate goal is to maximize student understanding and to make the teaching and learning of mathematics and the other content areas come to life.

The author hopes that the interdisciplinary, literature-based activities presented in this book will provide readers with the information, resources, and confidence to make the teaching and exploration of mathematics, science, social studies, and the visual arts more meaningful, cohesive, interactive, and exciting to learners.

Helpful Hints

For teachers who are incorporating children's literature into their teaching for the first time, consider these suggestions:

- Situate your audience so that all students can clearly hear you and easily see the pages and illustrations during the read-aloud of each.

- Take time to stop and allow students to ask questions about the text or illustrations in the book. Take advantage of those teachable moments when insightful questions are asked!

- Read each piece of children's literature in its entirety *prior* to implementing the accompanying activities so that you are familiar with the story line and so you can anticipate questions from students.

- In some of the activities featured in this book, the author suggests that only excerpts from a piece of children's literature be read. If, depending on your audience, you deem it appropriate to read the book in its entirety, then do so. You know your students best.

Regarding Assessment

NCTM (1989, 2000) advocates that student assessment be integral to instruction, that teachers use multiple means of assessment, and that all aspects of mathematical knowledge (confidence, attitude, problem-solving abilities, and so on) be assessed. Examples of multiple means of assessment include observations, interviews and questions, student journal entries, portfolios, student self-evaluations, and peer evaluations. Thus, toward the end of each activity in this book, several questions are included under the heading, Assessment. Consider posing these questions as a means to assess students' understanding of the concepts and mastery of the skills presented in each of the literature-based activities.

Included in the appendix are several assessment tools and rubrics a teacher might employ as a means to better assess students as they engage in the literature-based activities. Other helpful assessment resources are included at the end of this book in the Assessment Resources section.

Literature-Based Mathematics and Science Activities

The Mathematics-Science Connection

Science encompasses many domains including life science, physical science, and earth and space science. It can be described as the study and exploration of our world, our universe, our environment, and other phenomena. In studying science, students should not memorize facts but, instead, be encouraged to think, observe, hypothesize, reason, communicate, and problem-solve, activities NCTM (1989, 2000) and NRC (1996) strongly advocate. Recognizing the interplay between mathematics and science, the German mathematician Carl Gauss once stated that "mathematics is the Queen of the Sciences." Given the strong interconnectedness between mathematics and science, a mounting movement continues to support the integration of mathematics and science in the classroom curriculum (Basista & Mathews, 2002; Cobb, 2000; Johnson & Giorgis, 2001, Kaser, 2001; Moyer, 2000; Putnam & Borko, 2000; Roth & McGinn, 1998). One of the best ways for young learners to increase their knowledge and understanding of their world to make sense out of nature's sometimes complicated phenomena and today's advanced technological society is to integrate children's literature into the study of science and mathematics.

"Children's literature can help young learners make sense out of nature and today's advanced technological society."

This chapter articulates a variety of literature-based activities that integrate concepts and skills used and learned in the study of mathematics with those in science. While engaged in these activities, students will discover and gain practice with such mathematics concepts and skills as counting, numerals, number name, skip counting, multiples, grouping (Number and Operations Standard); geometric and numeric patterns, pattern recognition, cause-and-effect relationships, dependence, sorting, classification, Venn diagrams (Algebra Standard); symmetry (Geometry Standard); linear measurement, capacity, volume, size (Measurement Standard); and tallying, data collection and interpretation, bar graphs, line graphs, pictographs (Data Analysis and Probability Standard).

Science concepts and skills featured in this chapter include scientific inquiry (Science as Inquiry, Content Standard A); position and motion of objects (Physical Science, Content Standard B); characteristics of organisms, life cycles of organisms, animals, animal parts and their functions, animal homes and habitats, parts of a plant, the five senses, the human skeleton (Life Science, Content Standard C); change of seasons, movement of the earth on its axis and about the sun, weather, wind, clouds (Earth and Space Science, Content Standard D); understanding about science and technology (Science and Technology, Content Standard E); pollution, recycling, and environmental awareness (Science in Personal and Social Perspectives, Content Standard F); and science as a human endeavor (History and Nature of Science, Content Standard G).

The integrated literature-based activities also provide students with many opportunities to predict, estimate, problem-solve, and reason (Problem Solving and Reasoning and Proof Standards) as well as communicate and use various representations to organize, record, model, and interpret mathematical ideas (Communication and Representation Standards). Further, students will discover and explore real-life applications of mathematics and science and careers in mathematics and science (Connections Standard).

Remember to check the appendix for assessment ideas and samples of assessment rubrics.

Matrix of Mathematics and Science Activities

BOOK TITLE	MATHEMATICAL CONCEPTS AND SKILLS	SCIENCE CONCEPTS AND SKILLS	SOCIAL STUDIES CONCEPTS AND SKILLS	VISUAL ARTS CONCEPTS AND SKILLS
Counting in the Garden; The Reason for a Flower	counting, numerals, number name, measurement	parts of a plant	explore a biography of Johnny Appleseed, farms and farming	create a handprint flower, create garden artwork using petals or plants as crayons, explore van Gogh's sunflowers or O'Keeffe's flower masterpieces
What Comes in 2's, 3's, & 4's?; My Five Senses	counting, skip counting, multiples, grouping, geometric and numeric patterns	five senses	explore a biography of Helen Keller or Ludwig van Beethoven	artists' renditions of the five senses
If You Give a Moose a Muffin; What If?	pattern recognition, cause-and-effect relationships, dependence, measurement, length	life cycles of organisms, scientific inquiry	location of grasslands, jungles, rain forests; exploration of a biographical piece	Vincent van Gogh's paintings of sunflowers
A Hippopotamusn't and Other Animal Poems; Zoo-ology; What Do You Do with a Tail Like This?	sorting, classification, Venn diagrams	characteristics of organisms, animals, animal parts and their functions	geographic location of animal habitats	coloring, patterning, and camouflage in animal skin
Let's Fly a Kite; The Cloud Book	symmetry, line symmetry in shapes, patterns	clouds, wind, position and motion of objects	exploration of a biographical piece	artists' renditions of windy scenes, seasons, and the weather
Dem Bones; The Skeleton Inside You	measurement, length, counting, estimation	human skeleton, bones, joints	fossils, archaeology, and extinct animals	create skeleton art
House for Birdie; Animals in Their Homes	capacity, volume, measurement, size	animal homes and habitats	importance of home and friendship	Audubon's renditions of birds

BOOK TITLE	MATHEMATICAL CONCEPTS AND SKILLS	SCIENCE CONCEPTS AND SKILLS	SOCIAL STUDIES CONCEPTS AND SKILLS	VISUAL ARTS CONCEPTS AND SKILLS
The Earth and I; Where Does the Garbage Go?; Recycle! A Handbook for Kids	counting, measuring, tallying, data collection and interpretation, graphing (bar graphs or line graphs)	pollution, recycling, environmental awareness	causes and impact of other types of pollution	create watercolor paintings of the Earth
Winter; Spring; Summer; Fall; Sunshine Makes the Seasons	prediction, data collection and interpretation, pictographs, bar graphs	change of seasons, characteristics of the seasons, movement of the Earth on its axis and about the sun, weather	global weather	artists' renditions of seasons and weather
What Is a Scientist?	real-life applications of mathematics, careers in mathematics and science	careers in science and technology, nature and applications of science and technology	scientists' contributions to community and/or world, exploration of a biographical piece	create a self-portrait of one's future career

Counting in the Garden (2005)

by Kim Parker

Orchard Books, ISBN #0439694523

The Reason for a Flower (1999)

by Ruth Heller

Penguin Young Readers, ISBN #0698115597

Overview of Books: In *Counting in the Garden,* count from one to ten as you search for various colorfully camouflaged animals hiding in the garden. Then, in *The Reason for a Flower,* enjoy colorful illustrations and rhyming text explaining the parts of plants and their functions.

Mathematical Concepts and Skills: counting, numerals, number name, measurement

Science Concepts and Skills: parts of a plant

Overview of Activities: Using an illustrated garden, students count from one to ten while connecting the number name to its corresponding numeral. Students grow plants, measure their growth, and sketch and identify plant parts.

National Mathematics Standards (2000): Students in preK–2 should "count with understanding and recognize 'how many' in sets of objects." They should also "connect number words and numerals to the quantities they represent, using various physical models and representations" (Number and Operations Standard) (p. 392). Students in preK–2 should "recognize the attributes of length" and be able to "use tools to measure" (Measurement Standard) (p. 398).

National Science Standards (1996): Students in grades K–4 should develop an understanding of the characteristics of organisms and understand that "each plant or animal has different structures that serve different functions in growth, survival, and reproduction" (Life Science, Content Standard C) (p. 129).

Materials: fast-growing seeds (e.g., marigold seeds), potting soil, plastic spoons, small flower pots or egg cartons

Description of Activities:

1. Engage students in a discussion about gardens. Ask questions like these: What is a garden? What grows in a garden? Where might you see a garden? What is needed to maintain a garden?

2. Read *Counting in the Garden*. With each page, point to the numeral shown, let students say the number aloud, and ask one student to locate and count each animal that is hiding in the garden of flowers.

3. Read the book again and ask students to listen carefully and to raise their hands when they hear the name of a part of a plant (e.g., two turtles meeting in the *leaves*, six ladybugs tiptoeing along a *stem*, nine inchworms inching toward the *petals*, etc.).

4. Describe the parts of a plant: the seed, root, stem, leaves, flower, and fruit, and each part's purpose. Read all or select pages from *The Reason for a Flower*, which illustrates various parts of a plant. Consider viewing some of the pictures and information posted on the Flower and Plant Parts websites listed below.

5. Students plant their own class garden by planting fast-growing flower seeds (e.g., marigolds) or sunflower seeds (which sprout in one week, become a small seedling after two weeks, and grow approximately two feet tall after a month). Students tend to the plants daily and measure and record their growth. Discuss the importance of water and light in the growth of a plant.

6. Once the plants have grown, students sketch their plants and identify their parts.

Assessment:

- Did students participate in a discussion about gardens?
- Did students correctly identify and say the number name and count the hidden number of hidden animals?
- Did students' plants grow successfully?
- Did students accurately measure and record their plant's growth?
- Did students sketch and identify the parts of a plant?

Activity Extensions:

- Explore and discuss the differences between fruit and vegetables using *Eating the Alphabet* (Ehlert, 1993).

- In *The Reason for a Flower*, the author introduces the terms *carnivore* and *herbivore*. Begin a unit on animals and what they eat.

- Read and enjoy poems about planting and gardens, such as "Spaghetti Seeds" (Prelutsky, 1996) and "The Cherries Garden Gala" (Prelutsky, 1984).

Cross-Curricular Connections:

Visual Arts

- Visit the Handprint Flower website and let students create a flower using green construction paper (leaves), any color construction paper (flower/petals), and a green pipecleaner (stem). Tie three short pieces of brown yarn to the bottom of the pipecleaner, serving as the roots.

- Students create their own garden of color by smearing petals of flowers (e.g., roses, marigolds, or pansies) or plants (e.g., blueberries, spinach, beets, or carrots) onto heavy cardstock.

- Explore the sunflowers of Vincent van Gogh or the flower masterpieces of Georgia O'Keeffe.

Social Studies

- Explore a biography of Johnny Appleseed.

- Begin a unit on farms and farming.

Related Children's Literature

Brandenburg, A. (1963). *The story of Johnny Appleseed.* New York: Aladdin.

Bunting, E. (2000). *Flower garden.* San Diego: Harcourt Children's Books.

Carle, E. (1999). *The tiny seed.* New York: Simon & Schuster Books for Young Readers.

Cave, K. (2002). *One child, one seed: A South African counting book.* New York: Holt.

Cole, H. (1997). *Jack's garden.* New York: HarperTrophy.

Cole, J. (2001). *The magic school bus plants seeds: A book about how living things grow* (Magic school bus series). New York: Scholastic.

Crews, L. (2000). *This is the sunflower.* New York: Scholastic.

Ehlert, L. (1990). *Growing vegetable soup.* San Diego: Harcourt Children's Books.

Ehlert, L. (1993). *Eating the alphabet.* San Diego: Harcourt Children's Books.

Ehlert, L. (2001). *Planting a rainbow.* San Diego: Harcourt Children's Books.

Fowler, A. (2001). *From seed to plant.* New York: Scholastic.

Gibbons, G. (1993). *From seed to plant.* New York: Holiday House.

Glaser, O. (1997). *Round the garden.* New York: Scholastic.

Heller, R. (1999). *Plants that never ever bloom.* New York: Penguin Young Readers.

Heller, R. (1999). *The reason for a flower.* New York: Penguin Young Readers.

Holub, J. (2001). *Vincent van Gogh: Sunflowers and swirly stars.* New York: Grosset & Dunlap.

Jordan, H. (1992). *How a seed grows.* New York: HarperCollins.

Keller, H. (2001). *Growing like me.* San Diego: Harcourt.

Krauss, R. (1989). *The carrot seed.* New York: HarperCollins.

Mannis, C. (2002). *One leaf rides the wind: Counting in a Japanese garden.* New York: Scholastic.

Pallotta, J. (1992). *The icky bug counting book.* Watertown, MA: Charlesbridge.

Pallotta, J. (1998). *The butterfly counting book.* New York: Scholastic.

Parker, K. (2005). *Counting in the garden.* New York: Orchard Books.

Pfeffer, W. (2004). *From seed to pumpkin.* New York: HarperCollins.

Pomeroy, D. (1996). *One potato: A counting book of potato prints.* San Diego: Harcourt Brace.

Prelutsky, J. (1984). *The new kid on the block.* New York: Scholastic.

Prelutsky, J. (1996). *A pizza the size of the sun.* New York: Scholastic.

Royston, A. (1998). *How plants grow.* Chicago: Heinemann Library.

Venezia, M. (1989). *van Gogh* (Getting to know the world's greatest artists series). Chicago: Children's Press.

Venezia, M. (1993). *Georgia O'Keeffe* (Getting to know the world's greatest artists series). Chicago: Children's Press.

Worth, B. (2001). *Oh say can you seed?* New York: Random House.

Related Instructional Resources

Burnie, D. (2004). *Plant* (Eyewitness Books series). New York: Dorling Kindersley.

Kalman, B. (2000). *What is a plant?* New York: Crabtree.

Tocci, S. (2001). *Experiments with plants.* New York: Children's Press.

Related Websites

Flower Crafts
> http://www.enchantedlearning.com/crafts/flowers/

Flower and Plant Parts
> http://www.hhmi.org/coolscience/vegquiz/plantparts.html
> http://www.kinderplans.com/content.cfm?pageid=169
> http://www.kinderplans.com/admin/images/partsofflower.pdf
> http://www.theteachersguide.com/plantsflowers.htm

Gardening for Kids
> http://gardeninglaunchpad.com/kids.html
> http://flowergardens.suite101.com/article.cfm/five_fun_flowers_for_kids_garden
> http://eartheasy.com/grow_gardening_children.htm

Georgia O'Keeffe
> http://www.okeeffemuseum.org/indexflash.php

Handprint Flower
> http://www.enchantedlearning.com/crafts/flowers/handprintflower/

Vincent van Gogh
> http://www.vangoghgallery.com/

What Comes in 2's, 3's, & 4's? (1990)

by Susan Aker

Simon & Schuster Children's Publishing, ISBN #0671792474

My Five Senses (1989)

by Aliki Brandenburg

HarperCollins, ISBN #006445083X

Overview of Books: Find out about all the things in a child's everyday world that come in twos, threes, and fours by reading the book *What Comes in 2's, 3's, & 4's?* Then, learn facts about the five senses in *My Five Senses*.

Mathematical Concepts and Skills: counting, skip counting, multiples, grouping, geometric and numeric patterns

Science Concepts and Skills: five senses

Overview of Activities: Students gain practice counting and viewing a variety of examples of objects from everyday life that come in twos, threes, and fours. Students also gain practice skip counting using a hundreds board while noticing and predicting numeric and geometric patterns. Then students discuss the five senses and identify which sense (or senses) is used when experiencing an object.

National Mathematics Standards (2000): Students in preK–2 should "count with understanding and recognize 'how many' in sets of objects." They should also "connect number words and numerals to the quantities they represent, using various physical models and representations" (Number and Operations Standard) (p. 392). Students in preK–2 should "recognize, describe, and extend patterns such as sequences of sounds and shapes or simple numeric patterns and translate from one representation to another" (Algebra Standard) (p. 394).

National Science Standards (1996): Students in grades K–4 should develop an understanding of the characteristics of organisms and understand that "humans and other organisms have senses that help them detect internal and external cues" (Life Science, Content Standard C) (p. 129).

Materials: hundreds boards, clear-colored counters, pictures of various objects, 4" × 6" index cards, Popsicle sticks, crayons or markers, tape or glue

Description of Activities:

1. Ask students to think of or look around the classroom and see if they notice any objects grouped in twos, threes, or fours (e.g., two shoes in a pair, two doors, twins, three windows, four students per table, etc.).

2. Read *What Comes in 2's, 3's, & 4's?* Allow students to first notice and then count what they see two of (or three of, or four of) on select pages.

3. Distribute a hundreds board and clear-colored counters to students. Assist students in learning how to skip count by twos by counting aloud and, while doing so, placing a clear counter on each multiple of two on the hundreds board (up to twenty) as it is spoken. After all the multiples of two (up to twenty) are covered, look at the numbers covered by the clear counters and count again aloud by twos (e.g., 2, 4, 6, 8, . . .), reinforcing how to skip count by twos.

4. Ask students to notice what geometric and/or numeric patterns they see in the covered numbers. (Geometrically, the multiples of two create a checkerboard pattern; numerically, all the covered numbers are even and they all end in a 0, 2, 4, 6, or 8.)

5. Clear the hundreds board. Students skip count by threes (up to thirty) and then by fours (up to forty). Repeat the above steps in which students say the numbers aloud as they cover them with a clear counter. Students then look for and identify geometric and numeric patterns in the covered multiples.

6. Students skip count by fives up to forty. What numeric and geometric patterns do students see? (Geometrically, if one skip counts by five, the resulting pattern on the hundreds board is two vertical columns; numerically, all the multiples of five end in a 0 or 5.) Challenge students to think of things that come in groups of fives (e.g., five sides on a pentagon, five points on a star, five cents in a nickel, five fingers on a hand, etc.). Describe to students how we have five senses. Ask students if they know what their senses are and to describe each one.

7. Read *My Five Senses*. On page 21, the author describes how sometimes we use more than one sense when experiencing an object. When reading the following pages (pages 22 and 24), ask students to identify which sense(s) they think they use when engaged in the activities described by the author.

8. Give each student five index cards and five Popsicle sticks. Students sketch pictures of each of the five senses (an eye for sight; an ear for hearing; a nose for smell, a mouth or tongue for taste; a hand for touch) on their cards and label each card with the name of the corresponding sense. Students tape or glue the index cards to the top of a Popsicle stick.

9. Show pictures (either hand-drawn or images from a magazine or the Internet) of various objects. Students indicate which sense(s) they use when experiencing each object by holding up the appropriate Popsicle stick(s). Examples of pictures might include a fire alarm ringing (hearing), a chirping bird (sight, hearing), smoke coming from a chimney (sight, smell), a croaking frog (sight, hearing, touch), peeling an orange (sight, touch, smell, taste), a flower (sight, smell, touch), eating an apple (sight, hear, smell, touch, and taste).

10. Challenge students to think of objects that would require someone to use one, two, three, four, or all five senses. Students explain their thinking for their choices.

11. Students describe what it would be like to *not* have use of one or more senses.

Assessment:

- Did students name or identify objects grouped in twos, threes, fours, and fives?

- Did students correctly skip-count using the hundreds board?

- Did students recognize geometric and numeric patterns in the multiples of two, three, four, and five?

- Did students participate in a discussion about the five senses?

- Did students correctly guess what sense(s) they might use as they viewed each picture?

- Did students identify objects that require the use of one or more of their senses?

- Did students describe what it would be like to not have use of one or more of their senses?

Activity Extensions:

- Explore various animals and their keen senses (e.g., owls have keen sight, bats have keen hearing, etc.).

- Read the poem "Senses" in *A Light in the Attic* by Shel Silverstein (1981).

Cross-Curricular Connections:

Visual Arts

- Explore pages 46-47 in *A Child's Book of Art* (Micklethwait, 1993), which display masterpieces that capture each of the five senses.

Social Studies

- Explore a biography of an individual (Helen Keller, Ludwig van Beethoven, etc.) who did not have use of one or more senses, but still accomplished great things.

Related Children's Literature

Adler, D. (1992). *A picture book of Helen Keller.* New York: Holiday House.

Aker, S. (1990). *What comes in 2's, 3's, & 4's?* New York: Simon & Schuster Children's Publishing.

Brandenburg, A. (1989). *My five senses.* New York: HarperCollins.

Cole, J. (1999). *The magic school bus explores the senses* (Magic school bus series). New York: Scholastic.

Cristaldi, K. (1996). *Even Steven and odd Todd.* New York: Scholastic.

Giganti, P. (1988). *How many snails?* New York: Greenwillow Books.

Giganti, P. (1992). *Each orange had 8 slices: A counting book.* New York: Scholastic.

Lundell, M. (1995). *A girl named Helen Keller.* New York: Scholastic.

Micklethwait, L. (1993). *A child's book of art: Great pictures: first words.* New York: Dorling Kindersley.

Miller, M. (1998). *My five senses.* New York: Simon & Schuster's Children's Publishing.

Murphy, S. (2001). *Missing mittens.* New York: HarperCollins.

Murphy, S. (2003). *Double the ducks.* New York: HarperCollins.

Pallotta, J. (2001). *Underwater counting: Even numbers.* Watertown, MA: Charlesbridge.

Pallotta, J. (2005). *Ocean counting: Odd numbers.* Watertown, MA: Charlesbridge.

Rachlin, A. (1994). *Beethoven* (Famous children series). Hauppauge, NY: Barron's Educational Series.

Rius, M., Parramon, J., & Puig, J. (1985). *Hearing* (The five senses series). Hauppauge, NY: Barron's Educational Series.

Rius, M., Parramon, J., & Puig, J. (1985). *Sight* (The five senses series). Hauppauge, NY: Barron's Educational Series.

Rius, M., Parramon, J., & Puig, J. (1985). *Smell* (The five senses series). Hauppauge, NY: Barron's Educational Series.

Rius, M., Parramon, J., & Puig, J. (1986). *Taste* (The five senses series). Hauppauge, NY: Barron's Educational Series.

Rius, M., Parramon, J., & Puig, J. (1986). *Touch* (The five senses series). Hauppauge, NY: Barron's Educational Series.

Silverstein, S. (1981). *A light in the attic.* New York: HarperCollins.

Venezia, M. (1996). *Ludwig van Beethoven* (Getting to know the world's greatest composers series). Chicago: Children's Press.

Related Instructional Resources

Levine, S., & Johnstone, L. (2003). *First science experiments: Super senses*. New York: Sterling.

Levine, S., & Johnstone, L. (2005). *First science experiments: Nature, senses, weather, & machines*. New York: Sterling.

Related Websites

Five Senses

> http://faculty.washington.edu/chudler/chsense.html
> http://edtech.kennesaw.edu/web/5senses.html
> http://freda.auyeung.net/5senses/
> http://www.preschoolrainbow.org/5senses.htm

Helen Keller Biography

> http://www.afb.org/braillebug/helen_keller_bio.asp

Ludwig van Beethoven Biography

> http://www.lvbeethoven.com/Bio/BiographyDeafness.html

If You Give a Moose a Muffin (1991)

by Laura Numeroff

HarperCollins, ISBN #0060244054

What If? (1999)

by Jonathan Shipton

Dial Books for Young Readers, ISBN #0803723903

Overview of Books: In *If You Give a Moose a Muffin*, readers will discover the hilarious domino effect of giving a moose a muffin. Then, in *What If?*, readers will keep asking themselves "What if?" as they turn the pages of this book, following a young boy on his imaginary journey as he climbs a sunflower as tall as a skyscraper and encounters a daring young girl.

Mathematical Concepts and Skills: pattern recognition, cause-and-effect relationships, dependence, measurement, length

Science Concepts and Skills: life cycles of organisms, scientific inquiry

Overview of Activities: Students explore the pattern and concept of cause-and-effect and then predict and discover what factors contribute to plant growth by growing sunflower plants under three different conditions. Students also measure and record plant growth.

National Mathematics Standards (2000): Students in preK–2 should "recognize, describe, and extend patterns such as sequences of sounds and shapes or simple numeric patterns and translate from one representation to another" (Algebra Standard) (p. 394). Students in preK–2 should "recognize the attributes of length" and be able to "compare and order objects according to these attributes." Students should also "use tools to measure" and "develop common referents for measures to make comparisons and estimates" (Measurement Standard) (p. 398).

National Science Standards (1996):

Students in grades K–4 should develop understandings that "organisms have basic needs (… plants require air, water, nutrients, and light)," and "organisms can survive only in environments in which their needs can be met." Students should develop understandings that "plants and animals have life cycles that include being born, developing into adults, reproducing, and eventually dying" (Life Science, Content Standard C) (p. 129). Also, as a result of activities, students should "develop abilities to do scientific inquiry" and "develop understanding about scientific inquiry" (Science as Inquiry, Content Standard A) (p. 121).

Materials:

half-pint milk cartons (or small containers), potting soil, sunflower seeds, cardboard box, water, paper, crayons

Description of Activities:

1. Read *If You Give a Moose a Muffin*. After students begin noticing the cause-and-effect patterning in events, ask them to predict what might happen next before reading the next page.

2. Introduce the concept of cause-and-effect by explaining how one event can trigger the occurrence of another event. For example, if it rains, then you will need an umbrella. If you are very sick, then you will see a doctor. Relate this idea of dependence and cause-and-effect to the book, explaining how specific events resulted after giving a moose a muffin. Ask students to give examples of a cause-and-effect situation using an if-then sentence (e.g., If I win the contest, then I will receive a ribbon; If I do not eat lunch, then I will be hungry; etc.).

3. Read *What If?* Let students predict what might occur next with each successive "what if" prompt.

4. In the story, *What If?*, a boy awakens to find a sunflower growing outside of his window as tall as a skyscraper. Ask students, "What if we wanted a plant to grow? What would a plant need to grow?" Engage students in a discussion in which they conjecture and discuss what a plant needs if they want it to grow.

5. Break students into three groups. Each group grows sunflower plants under one of the following three conditions:

   - Condition #1: water but no light. (These plants will be placed in a covered cardboard box or unlit room but will be watered.)
   - Condition #2: light but no water. (These plants will be placed near a light source but receive no water.)
   - Condition #3: water and light. (These plants will be placed near a light source and receive water.)

6. Students make predictions about the growth of their sunflower plants by writing a response and/or creating an illustration. For example, students growing a sunflower plant under Condition #1 (water but no light) should respond to the prompt, "What if a plant has water but no light?" Repeat for the other two groups growing plants under Conditions #2 and #3. Students share their predictions with the class.

7. On a daily basis, students make and record in their journals observations of their plants in terms of their growth and appearance. After a period of time, students discuss what condition(s) allowed the sunflower plants to grow. Were their predictions accurate?

8. Based on the results of their experiment, students write responses and/or create supporting illustrations to the question, "What if we want a plant to grow?"

9. Revisit the concept of cause-and-effect. Students sit in a circle. Ask students, "What if you climbed to the top of a sunflower as tall as a skyscraper? Then . . ." One by one, students take a turn and add on to the prior student's story, similar to what was done in *If You Give a Moose a Muffin* and *What If?*

Assessment:
- Did students make reasonable predictions of what might happen during the reading of *If You Give a Moose a Muffin*?

- Did students provide examples of cause-and-effect relationships using an if-then sentence?

- Did students identify needs of a plant?

- Did students successfully grow sunflower plants under the various conditions?

- Did students create correct illustrations showing the results of their experiment?

Activity Extensions:

- Ask students to respond to the question (either orally, in writing, or via an illustration) posed at the end of *What If?*: "What if you landed on a secret door and behind it there were steps . . ."

- Read and enjoy the poem "What if" in *A Light in the Attic* by Shel Silverstein (1981) and the poem "If" in *A Pizza the Size of the Sun* by Jack Prelutsky (1996).

- Demonstrate the importance of sunlight for plants by creating a maze using a cardboard box and cardboard for dividers. Punch holes in the dividers. Place an already-growing, small bean plant at one end of the maze. Shield the maze from light by covering all of it, except for one hole at the opposite end of the box from where the plant is located. Water the plant, perhaps in a dark room to keep light out. Over time, the plant will grow toward the end of the maze, toward the light source.

Cross-Curricular Connections:

Visual Arts

- Explore the paintings of sunflowers created by Vincent van Gogh.

Social Studies

- Locate on a map such areas as grasslands, jungles, rain forests, and so on.

- Explore a biographical piece (i.e., Johnny Appleseed, Vincent van Gogh), and place this figure's life in a larger historical context.

Related Children's Literature

Brandenburg, A. (1963). *The story of Johnny Appleseed.* New York: Aladdin.

Charman, A. (2003). *I wonder why trees have leaves and other questions about plants.* Boston: Houghton Mifflin.

Holub, J. (2001). *Vincent van Gogh: Sunflowers and swirly stars.* New York: Grosset & Dunlap.

Marzollo, J. (1996). *I'm a seed.* New York: Scholastic.

McCallum, A. (2005). *Beanstalk: The measure of a giant.* Watertown, MA: Charlesbridge

Numeroff, L. (1985). *If you give a mouse a cookie.* New York: HarperCollins.

Numeroff, L. (1991). *If you give moose a muffin.* New York: HarperCollins.

Numeroff, L. (1998). *If you give a pig a pancake.* New York: HarperCollins.

Numeroff, L. (2005). *If you give a pig a party.* New York: HarperCollins.

Prelutsky, J. (1996). *A pizza the size of the sun.* New York: Scholastic.

Schaefer, L. (2000). *This is the sunflower.* New York: Scholastic.

Shipton, J. (1999). *What If?* New York: Dial Books for Young Readers.

Silverstein, S. (1981). *A light in the attic.* New York: HarperCollins.

Venezia, M. (1989). *Vincent van Gogh* (Getting to know the world's greatest artists series). Chicago: Children's Press.

Wyatt, V. (2000). *Wacky plant cycles.* New York: Mondo.

Related Instructional Resources

Burnie, D. (2004). *Plant* (Eyewitness books series). London: Dorling Kindersley.

Levine, S., & Johnstone, L. (2005). *First science experiments: Nature, senses, weather, & machines.* New York: Sterling.

Spilsbury, L. (2002). *Plant parts* (Life of plants series). Portsmouth, NH: Heinemann.

Unwin, M. (1993). *Science with plants* (Science activities series). Tulsa, OK: EDC.

Related Websites

Laura Numeroff's Website
http://www.lauranumeroff.com/kids_fun/index.htm

Plant Activities for the Classroom
http://www.proteacher.com/110013.shtml
http://www.kidsgardening.com/
http://gardeninglaunchpad.com/kids.html
http://www.global-garden.com.au/gardenkids_grow1.htm

Recipe for an Ecosphere
http://spaceplace.nasa.gov/en/kids/earth/wordfind/

Vincent van Gogh Gallery
http://www.vangoghgallery.com/painting/sunflowerindex.html

A Hippopotamusn't and Other Animal Poems (1990)

by J. Patrick Lewis

Dial Books for Young Readers, ISBN #0140552731

Zoo-ology (2002)

by Joelle Jolivet

Roaring Brook Press, ISBN # 0761318941

What Do You Do with a Tail Like This? (2003)

by Steve Jenkins and Robin Page

Houghton Mifflin, ISBN #0618256288

Overview of Books: Enjoy a variety of poems about members of the animal kingdom humorously depicted in *A Hippopotamusn't and Other Animal Poems*. In the 2-foot high oversized book, *Zoo-ology*, readers encounter all kinds of animals categorized into eclectic groups such as black and white, underground, and spots and stripes. Then, in *What Do You Do with a Tail Like This?*, explore the amazing things for which animals use their eyes, ears, tails, and other parts of their body. The closing pages of *Zoo-ology* and *What Do You Do with a Tail Like This?* both reveal fascinating secrets about each of the animals appearing in the colorfully illustrated books.

Mathematical Concepts and Skills: sorting, classification, Venn diagrams

Science Concepts and Skills: characteristics of organisms, animals, animal parts and their functions

Overview of Activities: Students enjoy poetry about and illustrations of various animals, which highlight their unique characteristics. Students then discern characteristics and features of animals while gaining practice with sorting, classifying, and using Venn diagrams. Students discover how certain parts of animals serve various functions. Students create an illustration of an animal and identify its different characteristics.

National Mathematics Standards (2000):

Students in preK–2 should "sort, classify, and order objects by size, number, and other properties" (Algebra Standard) (p. 394).

National Science Standards (1996):

Students in grades K–4 should develop an understanding of characteristics of organisms, life cycles of organisms, and organisms and their environments. Students should understand that "each plant or animal has different structures that serve different functions in growth, survival, and reproduction" and that many characteristics of organisms "result from an individual's interactions with the environment." "Inherited characteristics of organisms" include the color of flowers and the number of limbs of an animal (Life Science, Content Standard C) (p. 129).

Materials:

white construction paper, crayons or markers, scissors, hula-hoops (or two large pieces of string), 9" × 12" colored posterboard, blank Venn diagram for each student (see website below)

Description of Activities:

1. Read select poems from *A Hippopotamusn't and Other Animal Poems*, setting the stage for the upcoming activity in which students identify and sort animals into their respective families and according to their features and characteristics.

2. Prior to class, using a sticky note, cover up the category labeled "In the trees" on page 17 of *Zoo-ology*. Allow students to view the animals appearing on pages 16 and 17 and to guess what all these animals have in common. Students should explain their reasoning and specify the features and characteristics they noticed about the various animals that support their guess. Reveal that the author categorized these animals as animals "in the trees." Ask students what other animals might belong on this page (e.g., bird or monkey) and which ones would not (e.g., rabbit or shark). If desired, share some of the animal facts about the "in the trees" animals found at the end of *Zoo-ology*.

3. Ask students to continue viewing pages 16 and 17 and to think of ways to sort the animals into smaller groups by noticing features of the animals, such as their skin, legs, or wings. Students might sort animals into subgroups such as animals with long tails, animals with fur, animals with four legs, animals that fly, and so on.

4. Using white construction paper and crayons or markers, students sketch and color an animal of their choice and cut it out. View their sketches noting potential grouping schemes. Place a hula-hoop (or large string shaped into a circle) on the floor. Without telling students, decide on a sorting scheme and ask three or four students whose animal possesses this certain characteristic (e.g., four legs) to place their animals inside the hula-hoop. Students look at the animals placed inside the hula-hoop and try to determine what the sorting scheme is. (Explain how the hula-hoop represents a set or group of like things.) Assist students in determining the sorting scheme by also selecting students whose animal does *not* possess the particular characteristic (e.g., the animal does *not* have four legs) and place that animal *outside* of the hula-hoop, noting that this animal does *not* possess the same characteristic as the animals inside the hula-hoop.

5. Place two hula-hoops on the floor side by side, but not overlapping. Mentally select two characteristics of the students' animals that would result in an overlap (e.g., animals with four feet *and* animals that live in the jungle). Announce the two categories. Ask students to place their animals in the hula-hoop indicated as "animals with four feet" or in the hula-hoop indicated as "jungle animals." See if students realize that the hula-hoops must overlap since some students will have animals with four feet that *also* live in the jungle (e.g., a tiger, but not a toucan). Pose questions to ensure that students can correctly interpret a Venn diagram (e.g., Which animals have four feet? Which animals live in the jungle? Which animals live in the jungle *and* have four feet? If an animal has four feet and lives in the jungle, where on the diagram does it reside? Where on the Venn diagram would an animal with two feet that does *not* live in the jungle reside?).

6. Challenge individual students to create a Venn diagram on the floor of the class by sorting the animals into two intersecting (or two nonintersecting) groups, and then letting the other students determine the sorting scheme. Or, students create their own Venn diagram using the blank Venn diagram website below.

7. Students mount their animals onto a 9" × 12" colored posterboard and record at least three of the animal s characteristics by which it could be sorted (e.g., has stripes, has fur, has fins, etc.). Engage students in a discussion about the purpose or function of these features (e.g., stripes serve to camouflage the animal, fur keeps it warm, fins help it to swim, etc.).

8. Read *What Do You Do with a Tail Like This?* Let students view the partially drawn illustrations of the five animals on various pages in the book and guess what animal is pictured. Students should then guess and describe what function the part of the animal illustrated serves. Consider providing students with additional information about each animal located at the end of the book.

Assessment:

- Did students discern attributes and features of the various animals?

- Did students identify ways to sort the animals into smaller groups?

- Did students correctly construct and interpret a Venn diagram?

- Did students create and color an illustration of an animal and list its characteristics?

- Did students offer reasonable explanations for the purpose and functions of various animal parts?

Activity Extensions:

- Students play Who am I? Students give successive hints (e.g., It lives underwater; it does not have fins, etc.) about a particular animal and its features, challenging students to guess it.

- Locate five (or more) interesting animal facts appearing at the end of *Zoo-ology* and list them on a sheet of paper along with five (or more) animal names. Students match the name of the animal to the animal fact.

Cross-Curricular Connections:

Visual Arts
- Discern coloring, patterning, and camouflage in animal skin.

Social Studies
- Use maps to identify the location of the habitats of some of the animals discussed in class.

Related Children's Literature

Cole, J. (2000). *The magic school bus explores the world of animals* (Magic school bus series). New York: Scholastic.

Florian, D. (2001). *Lizards, frogs, and polliwogs.* Orlando, FL: Voyager Books.

Giganti, P. (1988). *How many snails?* New York: Greenwillow Books.

Jenkins, S. (1995). *Biggest, strongest, fastest.* Boston: Houghton Mifflin.

Jenkins, S. (2004). *Actual size.* Boston: Houghton Mifflin.

Jenkins, S. (2006). *Almost gone: The world's rarest animals.* New York: Scholastic.

Jenkins, S., & Page, R. (2003). *What do you do with a tail like this?* Boston: Houghton Mifflin.

Jenkins, S., & Page, R. (2005). *I see a kookaburra!* Boston: Houghton Mifflin.

Jolivet, J. (2002). *Zoo-ology.* New Milford, CT: Roaring Brook Press.

Jolivet, J. (2005). *Almost everything.* New Milford, CT: Roaring Brook Press.

Lesser, C. (1999). *Spots: Counting creatures from sea to sky.* San Diego: Harcourt Brace.

Lewin, B. (1980). *Animal snackers.* New York: Scholastic.

Lewis, J. (1999). *A hippopotamusn't and other animal poems.* New York: Dial Books for Young Readers.

Otto, C. (1996). *What color is camouflage?* New York: HarperCollins.

Pallotta, J. (2006). *Snakes: Long longer longest.* New York: Scholastic.

Pluckrose, H. (1995). *Sorting.* New York: Children's Press.

Schwartz, D. (1999*). If you hopped like a frog.* New York: Scholastic.

Sendak, M. (1988). *Where the wild things are.* New York: HarperCollins.

Trapanzi, I. (1992). *What am I? An animal guessing game.* New York: Whispering Coyote.

Wells, R. (1995). *What's smaller than a pygmy shrew?* Morton Grove, IL: Whitman.

Wormell, C. (2004). *Teeth, tails, & tentacles: An animal counting book.* Philadelphia: Running Press.

Related Instructional Resources

Dorling Kindersley. (1998). *DK nature encyclopedia.* London: DK Children.

Hare, T. (2005). *Animal fact file: Head-to-tail profiles of more than 90 mammals.* New York: Checkmark Books.

Kudlinski, K. (1991). *Animal tracks and traces.* New York: Franklin Watts.

National Geographic Society. (2000). *National Geographic animal encyclopedia.* Hanover, PA: National Geographic Children's Books.

Parsons, J. (2000). *Children's illustrated encyclopedia.* London: DK Children.

Twist, C. (2005). *Reptiles and amphibians dictionary: An A to Z of cold-blooded creatures.* New York: Scholastic.

Related Websites

Animal Facts

      http://www.indianchild.com/amazing_facts.htm

      http://www.quia.com/cm/1000.html

      http://www.bbc.co.uk/education/mathsfile/shockwave/games/animal.html

      http://lsb.syr.edu/projects/cyberzoo/a_list.html

      http://www.factmonster.com/ipka/A0768508.html

      http://sunsite.berkeley.edu/KidsClick!/midanim.html

      http://www.kidsplanet.org/factsheets/map.html

      http://www.wildlifeart.org/ArtTales/index.html

      http://www.sandiegozoo.org/animalbytes/index.html

      http://www.worldalmanacforkids.com/explore/animals.html

Blank Venn Diagram

      http://home.att.net/%7Eteaching/graphorg/venn.pdf

Introducing the Venn Diagram

      http://www.readwritethink.org/lessons/lesson_view.asp?id=378

Virtual Manipulatives—Venn diagram

      http://nlvm.usu.edu/en/nav/frames_asid_153_g_2_t_1.html?open=instructions

      http://nlvm.usu.edu/en/nav/frames_asid_187_g_2_t_1.html?open=instructions

      http://nlvm.usu.edu/en/nav/frames_asid_269_g_1_t_1.html?open=instructions

Activities Featuring Geometry

Let's Fly a Kite (2000)

by Stuart Murphy

HarperCollins, ISBN #0064467376

The Cloud Book (1975)

by Tomie de Paola

Holiday House, ISBN #0823405311

Overview of Books: Explore the concept of symmetry in *Let's Fly a Kite,* as a family builds a kite and heads to the beach, only to encounter many other real-life examples of line symmetry. Then, discover the many types and appearance of clouds in *The Cloud Book.*

Mathematical Concepts and Skills: symmetry, line symmetry in shapes, patterns

Science Concepts and Skills: clouds, wind, position and motion of objects

Overview of Activities: Students explore the symmetry in objects and in kites and create a symmetrically colored kite using watercolor. Students sketch and learn about various types of clouds as well as observe and identify clouds in the sky. Students observe and discuss the motion and position of a kite in flight.

National Mathematics Standards (2000): Students in preK–2 should "recognize and create shapes that have symmetry" (Geometry Standard) (p. 396). Students in preK–2 should "recognize, describe, and extend patterns such as sequences of standard shapes" (Algebra Standard) (p. 394). Students in preK–2 should "recognize and apply mathematics in contexts outside of mathematics" (Connections Standard) (p. 402).

National Science Standards (1996):

Students in grades K–4 should develop an understanding of changes in earth and sky. Students should understand "weather changes from day to day and over the seasons. Weather can be described by measurable quantities such as temperature, wind direction and speed, and precipitation" (Earth and Space Science, Content Standard D) (p. 134). Students in grades K–4 should develop an understanding that the "position and motion of objects can be changed by pushing or pulling" and that the "position of an object can be described by locating it relative to another object or the background" (Physical Science, Content Standard B) (p. 127).

Materials:

images of symmetric objects (e.g., butterfly, face, kite, etc.), paper cutout of a kite, 9" × 12" blue construction paper, watercolor paints, white chalk, ribbon, cotton balls, glue, kite

Description of Activities:

1. Show students several examples of photos or images of objects that are symmetric (see the Symmetry in Animals website for examples). Ask students to look at your face (or a classmate's). What do they notice about the left-hand side of the face? The right-hand side? What do they notice about the left side of their bodies compared to the right side of their bodies? Facilitate a discussion leading students to see how each object is symmetric, meaning that if you folded a picture of the object in half (or drew a line through the middle of an object), the image on one side is the exact (or mirror) image of the other. Ask students to look for examples of objects in the classroom that have symmetry (e.g., door, window, their desk, etc.).

2. Give each student a large paper cutout of a kite using the Kite Outline website listed below. Students determine whether the kite is symmetric by folding it in half to see if both sides are identical. Students will find that a kite is symmetric if folded along its longer diagonal but not symmetric (that is, asymmetric) if folded along its shorter diagonal.

3. Show students the colorful illustrations of kites on the opening and final pages of *Let's Fly a Kite*, encouraging them to see the symmetry in the shapes of the kites as well as in the symmetric colored patterns appearing on the kites.

4. Read *Let's Fly a Kite*. Challenge students to look for pictures of objects in the book that are symmetric as the story unfolds.

5. Using the large paper cutout of a kite from step #2, students paint one side of it using watercolors, fold it along the longer crease, and then open it up. Students will see a symmetrically colored kite. Let kites dry for use later. Students can tie colorful ribbon to the tail of their kite if desired.

6. Describe how a windy day is the perfect type of day to fly a kite. Explain to students that wind brings changes in the weather as the wind pushes clouds along.

7. Engage students in a discussion about clouds. What are clouds? What do clouds look like? What are they made of? Are clouds different colors? Where do clouds come from?

8. Give students a piece of 9" × 12" blue construction paper and white chalk. Fold the paper in half vertically and then in half horizontally, creating four regions. Using the white chalk, students label the top left region as, "Clouds in the Sky."

9. Begin reading *The Cloud Book,* which defines what clouds are in its beginning pages and then names the three main types of clouds (cirrus, cumulus, and stratus). Students use the white chalk and record three cloud names—cirrus, cumulus, and stratus—in the remaining three regions on their paper.

10. Read the author's description (but do not show the illustration) of a cirrus cloud (i.e., "white and feathery . . ."). Stop reading and, using the white chalk, students make a sketch of what they think a cirrus cloud looks like in the region labeled "cirrus." Then, share the author's illustrations with the students. How accurate were their sketches?

11. Read the pages describing cumulus and stratus clouds, after which students make a sketch of each of these clouds, based on the author's description, in the appropriately labeled regions on the paper. Compare their sketches to the author's. How accurate were their sketches?

12. Continue reading all or select pages of *The Cloud Book*. Show the illustrations after reading the descriptions of the other types of clouds featured in the book.

13. On a new piece of 9" × 12" blue construction paper, students glue their watercolor kites. Glue cotton balls onto the blue construction paper, around the kites, representing clouds in a blue sky. Create a mural on a classroom wall by hanging their artwork in a rectangular array. Let students observe and discuss the patterns and symmetry they see in the kites.

14. On a frequent basis, allow students to observe and record the clouds they see in the sky at the start and end of each class day.

15. On a breezy day, fly a kite outside and let students observe its motion. Engage students in a discussion about the motion and movement of the kite. How is the kite moving (up? down?, etc.)? Where in the sky is the kite located? What forces are acting on the kite? How does the kite stay in the air?

Assessment:

- Did students notice the symmetry in the images and illustrations?
- Did students locate other objects in the classroom with line symmetry?
- Did students see that a kite has one line of symmetry?
- Did students create and see patterns and symmetry in the watercolor kites?
- Did students participate in the discussion about clouds?
- Did students sketch the three types of clouds?
- Did students record accurate observations about the clouds they observed?
- Did students participate in a discussion about a kite's motion?

Activity Extensions:

- Distribute paper cutouts of various shapes to students (precut prior to class). Students fold each shape in search of lines of symmetry. Students will find that some shapes have exactly one line of symmetry (e.g., isosceles triangle or trapezoid), some have more than one line of symmetry (e.g., square, rectangle, or circle) and some have no lines of symmetry (e.g., parallelogram or scalene triangle).
- Enjoy the poem "Strange Wind" in *A Light in the Attic* by Shel Silverstein (1981).

Cross-Curricular Connections:

Visual Arts

- Explore the work of artists who captured windy scenes (e.g., Van Gogh's *Wheat Fields under Threatening Skies,* Winslow Homer's *The Coming Storm,* etc.).

- View pages 38–41 in *A Child's Book of Art* (Micklethwait, 1993), which display masterpieces illustrating the seasons and weather.

Social Studies

- Explore biographies of scientists and other historical figures who experimented with kites (e.g., Benjamin Franklin, the Wright Brothers, etc.).

Related Children's Literature

Birmingham, D. (1988). *M is for mirror*. Norfolk, UK: Tarquin.

Chorao, K. (2001). *Shadow night*. New York: Dutton Children's Books.

de Paola, T. (1975). *The cloud book*. New York: Holiday House.

DeWitt, L. (1991). *What will the weather be?* New York: HarperCollins.

Gibbons, G. (1989). *Monarch butterfly*. New York: Scholastic.

Gibbons, G. (1990). *Weather words and what they mean*. New York: Holiday House.

Holub, J. (2001). *Vincent van Gogh: Sunflowers and swirly stars*. New York: Grosset & Dunlap.

Hopkins, L. (1995). *Weather: Poems for all seasons*. New York: HarperCollins.

Hutchins, P. (1993). *The wind blew*. New York: Simon & Schuster Children's Publishing.

Metzger, S. (2003). *The little snowflake*. New York: Scholastic.

Murphy, S. (2000). *Let's fly a kite*. New York: HarperCollins.

Roca, N. (2004). *Fall*. Hauppauge, NY: Barron's Educational Series.

Roca, N. (2004). *Spring*. Hauppauge, NY: Barron's Educational Series.

Roca, N. (2004). *Summer*. Hauppauge, NY: Barron's Educational Series.

Roca, N. (2004). *Winter*. Hauppauge, NY: Barron's Educational Series.

Siddals, M. (1998). *Millions of snowflakes*. New York: Scholastic.

Silverstein, S. (1981). *A light in the attic*. New York: HarperCollins.

Related Instructional Resources

Dorros, A. (1990). *Feel the wind*. New York: HarperCollins.

Guerra, R. (2004). *The kite making handbook*. Devon, UK: David & Charles.

Hunt, L. (1971). *25 kites that fly*. Mineola, NY: Dover.

Levine, S., & Johnstone, L. (2005). *First science experiments: Nature, senses, weather, & machines*. New York: Sterling.

Mack, L. (2004). *Weather* (Eye wonder series). New York: Dorling Kindersley.

Martin, J. (1998). *Snowflake Bentley*. Boston: Houghton Mifflin.

Micklethwait, L. (1993). *A child's book of art: Great pictures first words*. New York: Dorling Kindersley.

Pelham, D. (2000). *Kites*. New York: Overlook TP.

Reed, B. (1987). *Easy-to-make decorative paper snowflakes*. London: Dover.

Simon, S. (193). *Weather*. New York: HarperCollins.

Sitomer, M., & Sitomer, H. (1970). *What is symmetry?* New York: Crowell.

Related Websites

Clouds

http://eo.ucar.edu/webweather/cloud3.html
http://www.urbanext.uiuc.edu/weather/2.html
http://www.wildwildweather.com/clouds.htm

Interactive Symmetry

http://www.adrianbruce.com/Symmetry/
http://www.adrianbruce.com/Symmetry/game/whiteboard-activity4.html

Kite Outline

http://www.fastq.com/%7Ejbpratt/education/theme/kitepatterns.pdf

Kite Resources for Teachers

http://webtech.kennesaw.edu/jcheek3/kites.htm
http://www.gombergkites.com/nkm/index.html
http://classroom.kitingusa.com/resources.htm
http://www.skratch-pad.com/kites/make.html

Make Snowflakes

http://www.kinderart.com/seasons/dec7.shtml
http://snowflakes.lookandfeel.com/
http://pbskids.org/zoom/activities/sci/snowflake.html

Symmetry

http://www.bbc.co.uk/schools/gcsebitesize/maths/shape/symmetryrev2.shtml
http://regentsprep.org/Regents/math/symmetry/Photos.htm

Symmetry in Animals

http://www.adrianbruce.com/Symmetry/4.htm
http://www.adrianbruce.com/Symmetry/3.html

Symmetry in Faces

http://www.adobe.com/education/digkids/lessons/symmetry.html

Symmetry in Shapes

http://www.adrianbruce.com/Symmetry/9.htm

Virtual Manipulatives Library—Reflections

http://nlvm.usu.edu/en/nav/frames_asid_206_g_1_t_3.html?open=activities

Activities Featuring Measurement

Dem Bones (1996)

by Bob Barner

Chronicle Books, ISBN #0811808270

The Skeleton Inside You (1989)

by Philip Balestrino

HarperCollins, ISBN #0064450872

Overview of Books: Sing the familiar song about how our bones are connected to other bones in *Dem Bones,* while also learning facts about the human skeleton. Then, in *The Skeleton Inside You,* discover a world of facts about your bones and skeleton.

Mathematical Concepts and Skills: measurement, length, counting, estimation

Science Concepts and Skills: human skeleton, bones, joints

Overview of Activities: Students learn facts about, compare, and discuss the number of bones located in various parts of the human skeleton. Students measure specific bones and record these measurements on a handmade sketch of a human skeleton.

National Mathematics Standards (2000): Students in preK–2 should "recognize the attributes of length" and be able to "compare and order objects according to these attributes." Students should also "use tools to measure" and "develop common referents for measures to make comparisons and estimates." Students should "understand how to measure using nonstandard and standard units" (Measurement Standard) (p. 398). Students in preK–2 should "count with understanding and recognize 'how many' in sets of objects." They should also "connect number words and numerals to the quantities they represent, using various physical models and representations" (Number and Operations Standard) (p. 392).

National Science Standards (1996):

Students in grades K–4 should develop an understanding of the characteristics of organisms and understand that "each plant or animal has different structures that serve different functions in growth, survival, and reproduction" (Life Science, Content Standard C) (p. 129).

Materials: 9" × 12" posterboard, black crayons or markers, measuring tapes

Description of Activities:

1. Engage students in a discussion about the human body and how the skeleton is made up of many bones. Ask them to point to certain bones (e.g., leg bone, skull, backbone, etc.). Can they point to and name any other bones? What are bones made of? Are bones hard or soft? How many bones do they think are in the human skeleton?

2. Introduce the book *Dem Bones,* and "sing" the text that describes how one bone is connected to another bone. Ask students to point to the particular bone mentioned in the lyrics as you sing.

3. Revisit *Dem Bones,* this time reading the facts about the different bones in the human body listed on various pages. For those pages that list the number of bones located in that part of the body (e.g., on the page describing the foot bone, the author tells us that twenty-two bones are in the foot), ask students to touch that part of the body, feel and count how many bones are under their skin, and then make a guess as to how many bones are in that specific part of their body. Take some guesses and then disclose the actual number given in the book. Students might record this information in their journals or the teacher might record the information of the board.

4. At the end of the book, compare the recorded number of bones in various parts of the body. Ask such questions as: Are there more bones in your head bone or in your backbone? In which part of the skeleton are the most bones located? The least? As students answer, they point to that specific part of their bodies.

5. Read all or select pages from *The Skeleton Inside You* as a means to supply additional information about the human skeleton. Distribute a copy of page 7 to all students so they can see a complete illustration of the human skeleton and its bones as you discuss additional facts (e.g., page 10 informs readers that the human skeleton contains 206 bones; page 11 sums the number of bones in one's arms and hands; page 17 illustrates how your bones grow as you grow; pages 27–28 describes how bones meet at joints, etc.). An illustration of a skeleton also appears at the end of *Dem Bones* on pages 17–18.

6. On 9" × 12" posterboard, students make an outline in black of a skeleton, using the illustration appearing on page 7 of *The Skeleton Inside of You* as a guide (or obtain an image using one of the Human Skeleton websites below). Using measuring tapes, students work in pairs to measure and record on their skeleton poster the lengths of their various bones (e.g., thigh bone, tibia, backbone, humerus, radius, head bone, etc.).

7. Students compare and discuss their skeletal measurements. Which bone measured longest? Was this the longest bone for everyone in the class? Which bone was the shortest? How many inches longer (or how many times longer) was your thighbone compared to your tibia?

Assessment:
- Did students participate in a discussion about bones and the human skeleton?

- Did students estimate and record the number of bones in various parts of the body?

- Did students create an illustration of a skeleton and accurately measure and compare the lengths of various bones?

Activity Extensions:
- Read *How Big Is a Foot?* (Myller, 1990). Students trace their foot on a piece of paper, measure it, and cut it out. Students estimate how many of their feet long certain objects are in the classroom (e.g., the chalkboard, bookcase, the teacher's desk, etc.). Are all students' measurements the same (i.e., is each object measured the same number of feet long)? Why or why not? Are their feet longer or shorter than an actual foot (measuring 12 inches)?

- Bring in an actual x-ray and discuss how x-rays provide us with a picture of our bones.

Cross-Curricular Connections:

Visual Arts

- Using a large piece of butcher paper, trace the outline of each student and then students sketch the bones (drawn to scale) in their skeleton.

- Using 9" × 12" black construction paper and glue, students create a skeleton using various pasta noodles (e.g., angel hair pasta for arm bones, linguine noodles for thigh bone, macaroni for the ribs, shells for hip bone, orzo for toes, etc.). When making their skeletons, students should try to find a type of pasta that matches the size and shape of each bone and should also try to show the correct number of bones located in various parts of the skeleton.

Social Studies

- Embark on a unit on fossils, archaeology, and extinct animals.

Related Children's Literature

Arnold, T. (2000). *Parts*. New York: Puffin Books.

Arnold, T. (2005). *More parts*. New York: Puffin Books.

Arnold, T. (2007). *Even more parts*. New York: Puffin Books.

Balestrino, P. (1989). *The skeleton inside you*. New York: HarperCollins.

Barner, B. (1996). *Dem bones*. San Francisco: Chronicle Books.

Cumbaa, S. (2006). *The bones book and skeleton*. New York: Workman.

Myller, R. (1990). *How big is a foot?* New York: Random House.

Parker, S. (2004). *The human body* (100 things you should know about series). New York: Barnes & Noble Books.

Sacks, J. (2004). *Magic skeleton: Human body*. New York: Sterling.

Simon, S. (2000). *Bones: Our skeletal system*. New York: HarperCollins.

Turnbull, S. (2005). *Your body* (Usborne beginners series). New York: Scholastic.

Related Instructional Resources

Berger, M., & Berger, G. (1998). *Why don't haircuts hurt? Questions and answers about the human body*. New York: Scholastic.

The Book Studio. (2004). *Big book of the human body*. Kettering, UK: Book Studio.

Farndon, J. (2002). *1000 facts on human body*. New York: Barnes & Noble Books.

Studio Book. (2006). *Big book of the human body*. New York: Dorling Kindersley.

Related Websites

Human Skeleton

http://library.thinkquest.org/10030/human.htm
http://www.stemnet.nf.ca/CITE/skeletal.htm
http://www.enchantedlearning.com/subjects/anatomy/skeleton/Skelprintout.shtml

Virtual Body

http://www.ehc.com/vbody.asp

House for Birdie (2004)

by Stuart Murphy

HarperCollins, ISBN #0060523530

Animals in Their Homes (2006)

by Sonia Goldie

Lark Books, ISBN #1579909205

Overview of Books: In *House for Birdie,* explore the concept of capacity (and friendship) as some feathered friends help their bird companion find a home that fits him perfectly. Then, discover the variety of homes that provide shelter and protection to animals in *Animals in Their Homes.*

Mathematical Concepts and Skills: capacity, volume, measurement, size

Science Concepts and Skills: animal homes and habitats

Overview of Activities: Students explore the concept of capacity by viewing and sketching birdhouses for birds of varying sizes. Students also identify which boxes would best fit their own stuffed animal and why. Students explore the variety of homes used by animals for shelter and protection.

National Mathematics Standards (2000): Students in preK–2 should "recognize the attributes of length, volume, weight, area, and time" and be able to "compare and order objects according to these attributes." Students should also "use tools to measure" and "develop common referents for measures to make comparisons and estimates" (Measurement Standard) (p. 398).

National Science Standards (1996):

NCSS

Students in grades K–4 should develop an understanding of the characteristics of organisms, life cycles of organisms, and organisms and their environments. Students should understand that "organisms can survive only in environments in which their need can be met" (Life Science, Content Standard C) (p. 129).

Materials: several boxes of varying sizes, students' stuffed animals, copy of birdhouses appearing on page 31 in *House for Birdie,* images of animals' homes and habitats, crayons or markers

Description of Activities:

1. Read *A House for Birdie*. As the story unfolds, ask students why each birdhouse is a perfect fit for the bird pictured, encouraging them to notice and describe the bird's size (how tall, how long, how wide, etc.) before reading the accompanying text.

2. Illustrated at the end of the story on page 31 is a picture of all five birds in their new birdhouses. Point to a specific birdhouse and ask whether another bird would fit inside of it. Students should explain their reasoning.

3. Copy one of the last pages in *A House for Birdie*, which pictures several empty birdhouses. Students sketch a picture of a bird that would fit into each house perfectly. Students share their illustrations with the class and explain their drawings.

4. Introduce to students the concept of volume, or capacity, which is a measure of how much a three-dimensional object can hold (i.e., volume or capacity indicates how much fits inside). Explain that knowing the size or dimensions (i.e., its length [how long], width [how wide], and depth [how deep]) of a box or a container determines how much it can fit inside.

5. On a table, set out several boxes that vary in size along with several of the students' stuffed animals. Ask the students which box fits their stuffed animal best. Encourage them to explain their reasoning, focusing on how tall, how long, or how wide their stuffed animal is and why it would (or would not) fit into a particular box.

6. Describe how birds not only use birdhouses for homes, but also build nests for homes. Ask students if they have ever seen a nest and what it looks like. If possible, bring in a nest to show students. Show images of nests for a small bird (e.g., swallow) and an eagle (very large nest), encouraging students to notice the size difference in the birds and thus, the size difference in their nests. Engage students in a discussion regarding in what other homes animals live (e.g., a turtle's home is its shell, beavers build dams around their lodge, moles burrow underground in tunnels, etc.).

7. Prior to class, preview *Animals in Their Homes*. This book is divided into categories of animals (e.g., animals that burrow and thus build underground houses, birds and the various types of nests various species build, animals that build houses on the water, animals that build clever homes, and animals that carry their homes with them). Select particular animals to discuss. Before reading the accompanying text in the book,

engage students in a discussion about what they think a particular animal's house looks like, why it is designed as such, how big or small it is, how it reflects the size of the animal, and so on. Discuss the ways in which each home serves to protect and provide shelter for the animal. Show photos and descriptions of each animal's home. Compare and contrast how each animal builds its home.

8. Students make an illustration of a particular animal's home and list at least two facts about it. Students share their work with the class.

Assessment:

- Did students articulate why or why not a bird would fit into a particular sized birdhouse?

- Did students make accurate sketches of birds fitting into each birdhouse?

- Did students articulate whether their stuffed animal would fit into a box and why?

- Did students participate in discussions about animal homes?

- Did students create an illustration of their animal's home and list facts about it?

Activity Extensions:

- On a table, place three containers, varying in size. Using a measuring cup, students estimate and record how many cupfuls of birdseed (or rice) fit into each container. Students then use the measuring cup to fill each container, recording the number of cupfuls it took. Students compare their measurements to their estimations.

- Begin a discussion about what a habitat is: an animal's living place. Explore a variety of animal habitats in *I See a Kookaburra!* (Jenkins & Page, 2005). On each page, allow students to "spy" the animals hiding within the illustrations. Then share additional facts about each animal and about each habitat located at the end of the book.

Cross-Curricular Connections:

Visual Arts

- Explore the work of John James Audubon, famous for his paintings of birds in their habitats.

Social Studies

- Discuss the importance of home in terms of it providing shelter and safety, but also as a place where a family unites.

- Discuss the importance of friendship, helping others in need, and working cooperatively to accomplish a goal.

Related Children's Literature

Blackstone, S. (2006). *How big is a pig?* Cambridge, MA: Barefoot Books.

Brown, C. (1998). *Animal at homes.* Lanham, MD: Rinehart.

Brown, S. (2003). *Professor Aesop's the crow and the pitcher.* Berkeley, CA: Tricycle Press.

Cole, J. (1995). *The magic school bus hops home: A book about animal habitats* (Magic school bus series). New York: HarperCollins.

Goldie, S. (2006). *Animals in their homes.* New York: Lark Books.

Hoban, T. (1997). *Is it larger? Is it smaller?* New York: Greenwillow Books.

Jenkins, S., & Page, R. (2005). *I see a kookaburra!* Boston: Houghton Mifflin.

Kalman, B. (1994). *Animal homes.* New York: Crabtree.

Lewis, J. (1990). *A hippopotamusn't and other animal poems.* New York: Dial Books for Young Readers.

Maze, S. (2006). *Peaceful moments in the wild: Animals and their homes.* Potomac, MD: Moonstone Press.

Murphy, S. (1999). *Room for Ripley.* New York: HarperCollins.

Murphy, S. (2002). *Bigger, better, best!* New York: HarperCollins.

Murphy, S. (2004). *A House for Birdie.* New York: HarperCollins.

Murphy, S. (2004). *Mighty Maddie.* New York: HarperCollins.

Nicolson, J. (2006). *Animal architects.* Crows Nest, NSW: Allen & Unwin.

Pluckrose, H. (1995). *Capacity.* New York: Scholastic.

Pluckrose, H. (1995). *Size.* New York: Scholastic.

Russo, M. (2000). *The big brown box.* New York: Greenwillow Books.

Shipman, W. (1994). *Animal architects: How animals weave, tunnel, and build their remarkable homes.* Mechanicsburg, PA: Stackpole Books.

Squire, A. (2001). *Animal babies.* New York: Children's Press.

Squire, A. (2002). *Animal homes.* New York: Scholastic.

Stewart, D. (2002). *Animal builder.* New York: Scholastic.

Related Instructional Resources

Burnie, D. (2005). *Animal. The definitive visual guide to the world's wildlife*. New York: Scholastic.

Greenaway, T. (2004). *Jungle* (Eyewitness book series). New York: Dorling Kindersley.

Macquitty, M. (2004). *Desert* (Eyewitness book series). New York: Dorling Kindersley.

Macquitty, M. (2004). *Ocean* (Eyewitness book series). New York: Dorling Kindersley.

Parker, S. (2004). *Mammals* (Eyewitness book series). New York: Dorling Kindersley.

Parker, S. (2004). *Seashore* (Eyewitness book series). New York: Dorling Kindersley.

Robinson, W. (1999). *Animal architects: How birds build their amazing homes*. Farmington Hills, MI: Blackbirch Press.

Robinson, W. (1999). *Animal architects: How insects build their amazing homes*. Farmington Hills, MI: Blackbirch Press.

Robinson, W. (1999). *Animal architects: How mammals build their amazing homes*. Farmington Hills, MI: Blackbirch Press.

Robinson, W. (1999). *Animal architects: How shell-makers build their amazing homes*. Farmington Hills, MI: Blackbirch Press.

Robinson, W. (1999). *Animal architects: How spiders and other silkmakers build their amazing homes*. Farmington Hills, MI: Blackbirch Press.

Wilkes, A. (2003). *Animal homes* (Kingfisher young knowledge series). Boston: Kingfisher.

Related Websites

Animal Habitats

http://www.uen.org/utahlink/activities/view_activity.cgi?activity_id=3792
http://library.advanced.org/11922/habitats/habitats.htm
http://library.thinkquest.org/11234/
http://www.worldalmanacforkids.com/explore/animals4.html#6
http://www.enchantedlearning.com/biomes/

Animal Homes

http://www.kidport.com/RefLib/Science/AnimalHomes/AnimalHomes.htm
http://www.units.muohio.edu/dragonfly/houses/
http://www.enchantedlearning.com/subjects/animals/matching/homes/index.shtml
http://www.uen.org/utahlink/activities/view_activity.cgi?activity_id=3804
http://www.suelebeau.com/animalhomes.htm

Interactive Capacity

http://www.abc.net.au/countusin/games/game15.htm
http://www.activescience-gsk.com/games/index.cfm?module=2

John James Audubon

http://www.audubon.org/bird/boa/BOA_index.html
http://www.artcyclopedia.com/artists/audubon_john_james.html

Activities Featuring Data Analysis and Probability

The Earth and I (1994)

by Frank Asch

Scholastic, ISBN #0590897527

Where Does the Garbage Go? (1994)

by Paul Showers

HarperCollins, ISBN #0064451143

Recycle! A Handbook for Kids (1992)

by Gail Gibbons

Little, Brown, ISBN #0316309435

Overview of Books: Enjoy the friendship shared between a boy and his planet in *The Earth and I*. In *Where Does the Garbage Go?*, find out exactly where the garbage goes: from the landfill, to the incinerator, to the recycling center. Then, learn everything you wanted to know about recycling in Gibbons's fact-filled book, *Recycle! A Handbook for Kids*.

Mathematical Concepts and Skills: counting, measuring, tallying, data collection and interpretation, graphing (bar graphs or line graphs)

Science Concepts and Skills: pollution, recycling, environmental awareness

Overview of Activities: Students engage in a discussion about pollution and recycling and the impact of both on the environment. Students then measure, count, tally, graph, and analyze how much trash they generate in the classroom daily and over the course of one week.

National Mathematics Standards (2000): Students in preK–2 should "pose questions and gather data about themselves and their surroundings" and "represent data using concrete objects, pictures, and graphs." Students should also "describe parts of the data and the set of data as a whole to determine what the data show" (Data Analysis and Probability Standard) (p. 400).

54

National Science Standards (1996):

Students in grades K–4 should develop an understanding that the "supply of many resources is limited" and that "resources can be extended through recycling and decreased use." Students should develop an understanding that "changes in environments can be natural or influenced by humans" and that "pollution is a change in the environment that can influence health, survival, or activities of organisms, including humans" (Science in Personal and Social Perspectives, Content Standard F) (p. 140).

Materials: Our Weekly Trash Totals poster, large trash bag, scale

Description of Activities:

1. Read *The Earth and I*. At the end of the story, ask students why the earth and the boy became sad in the story. How can they keep the earth happy?

2. Begin a discussion about pollution and recycling. Ask such questions as: What types of pollution are there (e.g., air, water, noise, land, etc.)? How does pollution affect the environment and Earth? What does it mean to litter? Where is our garbage taken after it is picked up? What does it mean to recycle? What types of materials are recyclable? How can recycling improve our environment? What does the recycle symbol look like?

3. Read all or select pages from *Where Does the Garbage Go?*

4. Place a large trash bag at the front of the room. Ask students to estimate and record how many items get thrown out in one day and to estimate how many pounds of garbage the class generates in one week. Students explain their reasoning.

5. On the board, near the trash bag, create a list of typical classroom items students might dispose of (e.g., paper, cups, broken pencils or crayons, etc.). Every time a student throws something out, he or she places a tally mark next to the name of the item disposed of. (If necessary, take time to explain how to tally. That is, students make a vertical line next to the item's name and when a fifth item is thrown out, draw a diagonal line through the existing group of four vertical lines. This makes summing easy, as you can count the groups of tallies by fives.) Students should not place food or other perishable materials in the trash bag since the bag will be opened up and re-used every day for one week.

6. At the end of each day, count up the tallies next to each item and record the totals on a poster entitled Our Weekly Trash Totals. Let students examine the data. How many total pieces of garbage did the class generate for that day? Was it greater than, less than, or equal to their predictions? What item was thrown out most often? Least often?

7. Tie the bag shut and open it up the next morning. Over the course of the rest of the week, each time an item is thrown out, students should place a tally mark next to the item's name written on the board above the trash bag. At the end of each day, the tally marks should be counted and recorded on the Our Weekly Trash Totals poster.

8. At the end of one week, let students view the data and discuss it. Are they surprised at how much trash they collected? On what day was the most trash collected? The least?

9. Weigh the trash bag. Are they surprised at how much their weekly trash weighs? How accurate were their estimations for the weight of the trash at the end of one week? How heavy do they think a bag of trash would weigh after two weeks? A month?

10. Using graph paper (or using the Create a Graph website) younger students create a bar graph and older students create a line graph of the data appearing on the poster, Our Weekly Trash Totals. Students examine and interpret the data and their graphs. On what day were the most trash items collected? The least? How do you know this? On what day was the most paper collected? The least? What item was placed most often in the trash overall? On any particular day?

11. Read select pages as well as some of the facts listed at the end of *Recycle! A Handbook for Kids*. Students examine the list of items that were thrown out. Which items are recyclable? How would the weight of the trash be impacted if they recycled select materials? Begin a discussion on how recycling can positively impact our environment.

12. Over the course of the next week or month, place recyclable materials in a separate trash bag and continue to collect, graph, and discuss additional desired data.

13. Encourage other teachers to recycle in their classrooms and encourage students to recycle at home.

Assessment:
- Did students participate in discussions about pollution and recycling?
- Did students make accurate predictions about the collection of trash items?
- Did students accurately tally, graph, and interpret the trash data?

Activity Extensions:
- Students predict, measure, and record the amount of trash their classroom or school creates in a month.
- Begin a recycling program at your school.

Cross-Curricular Connections:

Visual Arts
- Students fold a piece of large paper in half. On the left-hand side of the paper, students make a watercolor painting or colored illustration of a clean Earth; on the right-hand side, a polluted Earth.

Social Studies
- Explore and discuss the causes and impact of other types of pollution (water, air, noise, etc.).

Related Children's Literature

Asch, F. (1994). *The earth and I.* New York: Scholastic.

Gibbons, G. (1992). *Recycle! A handbook for kids.* Boston: Little, Brown.

Gibbons, G. (1995). *Planet Earth/Inside out.* New York: Morrow Books.

Green, J. (1992). *Why should I recycle?* Hauppauge, NY: Barron's Educational Series.

Leedy, L. (2000). *The great trash bash.* New York: Holiday House.

Marzollo, J. (2001). *I am planet Earth.* New York: Scholastic.

Robinson, F. (1995). *Recycle that!* New York: Scholastic.

Schnetzler, P. (2004). *Earth Day birthday.* Nevada City, CA: Dawn.

Showers, P. (1994). *Where does the garbage go?* New York: HarperCollins.

Related Instructional Resources

Donald, R. (2001). *Recycling.* New York: Children's Press.

Hall, E. (2005). *Recycling.* Farmington Hills, MI: Kidhaven Press.

Hunter, R. (2001). *Pollution and conservation.* Austin, TX: Raintree Steck-Vaughn.

Maass, R. (2000). *Garbage.* New York: Holt.

Parsons, J. (2000). *Children's illustrated encyclopedia.* London: DK Children.

Ross, K. (1995). *Every day is Earth Day.* Brookfield, CT: Millbrook Press.

Royston, A. (1999). *Recycling.* Austin, TX: Raintree Steck-Vaughn.

Twist, C. (2005). *Reptiles and amphibians dictionary: An A to Z of cold-blooded creatures.* New York: Scholastic.

Related Websites

Create a Graph Online
   http://nces.ed.gov/nceskids/createagraph/

Environmental Protection Agency
   http://www.epa.gov/kids/garbage.htm
   http://www.epa.gov/osw/

Landfill
   http://www.howstuffworks.com/landfill.htm

Recycling
   http://www.ecy.wa.gov/programs/swfa/kidspage/
   http://www.kidsrecycle.org/index.php

Winter (The Seasons Series) (2004)

by Nuria Roca

Barron's Educational Series, ISBN #0764127314

Spring (The Seasons Series) (2004)

by Nuria Roca

Barron's Educational Series, ISBN #0764127330

Summer (The Seasons Series) (2004)

by Nuria Roca

Barron's Educational Series, ISBN #0764127357

Fall (The Seasons Series) (2004)

by Nuria Roca

Barron's Educational Series, ISBN #0764127292

Sunshine Makes the Seasons (2005)

by Franklyn Branley

HarperCollins, ISBN #0060592059

Overview of Books: The four books, *Winter, Spring, Summer,* and *Fall,* delight in the celebration of the four seasons by viewing illustrations and reading text that evoke the moods of and depict activities related to each of the four seasons. Then, discover how the motion of the earth results in the four seasons in *Sunshine Makes the Seasons.*

Mathematical Concepts and Skills: prediction, data collection and interpretation, pictographs, bar graphs

Science Concepts and Skills: change of seasons, characteristics of the seasons, movement of the earth on its axis and about the sun, weather

Overview of Activities: Students develop lists of vocabulary words that describe each season. Students then take a class vote to determine the class's favorite season and create and interpret pictographs and/or bar graphs. Students explore how the earth's movement around the sun and its tilt result in the change of seasons. Students create their own illustration of each season.

National Mathematics Standards (2000):

Students in preK–2 should "pose questions and gather data about themselves and their surroundings" and "represent data using concrete objects, pictures, and graphs" (Data Analysis and Probability Standard) (p. 400).

National Science Standards (1996):

Students in grades K–4 should develop an understanding of the objects in the sky and changes in the earth and sky. Students should understand that "weather changes from day to day and over the seasons" (Earth and Space Science, Content Standard D) (p. 136).

Materials: 1" graph paper (see website below), stickers (representing each season) or colored linking cubes (one color for each season) or crayons, one orange, Popsicle stick, nail, flashlight, black marker, 9" × 12" white construction paper

Description of Activities:

1. Divide students into groups of four. Students peruse one of Roca's books on the seasons (*Winter, Spring, Summer,* or *Fall*). One student in each group should slowly turn the pages while all students focus on the illustrations in the book, and not necessarily the text.

2. Record the words, WINTER, SPRING, SUMMER, and FALL on the board. Under each season, ask students who viewed that season's book to state a word that reminds them of that season (e.g., winter: cold, snow, blizzard; spring: rain, puddles, flowers). Encourage students to recall the pictures they just viewed in their group's book to assist them. Record their words on the board under the season's name.

3. Ask students to view the list of words that describe each season and to predict what the class's favorite season might be. Students explain their reasoning.

4. Take a class vote in which students identify their favorite season. Record the total number of students who voted for each season above the words WINTER, SPRING, SUMMER, and FALL on the board.

5. Students create a graph of the data. Younger students might create a pictograph by placing stickers in vertical columns (using 1″ graph paper—see website below) to represent the season data (a sun for summer, a snowflake for winter, a leaf for fall, a flower or bird for spring). Or, students might create a bar graph using colored linking cubes (yellow for summer, white for winter, orange for fall, and green for spring) to create the bars or by coloring in squares on 1″ graph paper.

6. Students interpret their graphs. What season was the class's favorite? How can you tell this from your graph? Did this match your prediction? How many more students prefer summer to winter? Do the same number of students like two seasons? What season was least preferred? Encourage students to justify their reasoning.

7. Engage students in a discussion in which they offer reasons and explanations for the change in seasons.

8. Read all or select pages from *Sunshine Makes the Seasons*, which describes why we have seasons. Demonstrate why we have seasons by implementing the experiment beginning on page 12. Insert a Popsicle stick into the center of an orange, acting as the axis on which the earth rotates. Using a black marker, mark the North and South Poles. Darken the room and let one student hold the orange (the earth) on the stick and another student hold the flashlight (acting as the sun). Keep the flashlight shining on the orange at all times. The student holding the orange on the stick walks around the light source (the sun), keeping the orange (the earth) positioned straight up and down. Students will notice that half of the earth is lit; the other is in darkness.

9. Tilt the orange to replicate how the earth is tilted on its axis. Keep slowly walking around the flashlight. As the earth circles the sun, different parts of the earth are closer to the sun than others. This, in turn, affects the amount of light and heat the earth receives from the sun, which dictates the season.

10. Read page 27 in *Sunshine Makes the Seasons*, which describes how opposite seasons occur in the northern and southern halves of the earth, due to the tilting of the earth. When the North Pole is tipped toward the sun, the South Pole is tipped away from the sun. Thus, it is summer in the northern hemisphere but winter in the southern hemisphere. The opposite case holds true.

11. Explain that there are twelve months in one year (which is the amount of time it takes the earth to revolve around the sun) and that each season lasts about three months. Record on the board the months associated with each season (winter: December, January, February; spring: March, April, May; summer: June, July, August; fall: September, October, November).

12. Students fold a 9" × 12" piece of white construction paper in half and then half again, creating four regions. Students label each region with the names of the seasons. Students sketch and color their own interpretation of each season, with a focus on the words heard in the books and those discussed in class. Students share their work. Hang students work on a wall for all to enjoy.

Assessment:

- Did students provide words that accurately depict the seasons?

- Did students correctly graph and interpret the season data?

- Did students offer reasonable explanations for the changes in the seasons?

- Did students notice how portions of the orange were lit (or were in darkness) at various times, indicating seasons?

- Did students create an accurate illustration of all four seasons?

Activity Extensions:

- Read *Weather Words and What They Mean* (Gibbons, 1990). As you read each word, students respond with what season is best described by the word (e.g., flurries for winter, wind for spring or fall, etc.).

- Using a globe and a lamp, demonstrate how the earth rotates on its axis, creating day and night.

Cross-Curricular Connections:

Visual Arts

- View pages 38–41 in *A Child's Book of Art* (Micklethwait, 1993), which display masterpieces illustrating the seasons and weather.

Social Studies

- Indicate on a map of the world which places experience all or a few seasons and which receive mostly rain, snow, sun, etc.

Related Children's Literature

Bader, B. (2003). *All aboard math reader: Graphs*. New York: Grosset & Dunlap.

Branley, F. (1997). *Down comes the rain*. New York: HarperCollins.

Branley, F. (2005). *Sunshine makes the seasons*. New York: HarperCollins.

Gibbons, G. (1990). *Weather words and what they mean*. New York: Holiday House.

Hopkins, L. (1995). *Weather: Poems for all seasons*. New York: HarperCollins.

Leedy, L. (2005). *The great graph contest*. New York: Holiday House.

Micklethwait, L. (1993). *A child's book of art: Great pictures first words*. New York: Dorling Kindersley.

Prelutsky, J. (2006). *It's snowing! It's snowing: Winter poems*. New York: HarperCollins.

Roca, N. (2004). *Fall*. Hauppauge, NY: Barron's Educational Series.

Roca, N. (2004). *Spring*. Hauppauge, NY: Barron's Educational Series.

Roca, N. (2004). *Summer*. Hauppauge, NY: Barron's Educational Series.

Roca, N. (2004). *Winter*. Hauppauge, NY: Barron's Educational Series.

Sipiera, P. (1999). *Seasons* (True book series). New York: Scholastic.

Williams, J. (2005). *How does the sun make weather?* Berkeley Heights, NJ: Enslow.

Related Instructional Resources

Levine, S., & Johnstone, L. (2005). *First science experiments: Nature, senses, weather, & machines*. New York: Sterling.

Mackenzie, F. (1995). *Weather and seasons*. New York: Sterling.

Oliver, C. (2004). *The weather* (100 things you should know about series). New York: Barnes & Noble Books.

Related Websites

Free Online Graph Paper
   http://incompetech.com/beta/linedGraphPaper/easy.html
   http://www.enchantedlearning.com/math/graphs/graphpaper/

Interactive Weather Word Search
   http://www.apples4theteacher.com/word-finds/weather-words.html

The Seasons
   http://www.kathimitchell.com/seasons.htm
   http://www.christiananswers.net/kids/edn-seasons.html
   http://www.youthonline.ca/crafts/seasons.shtml

Activities Featuring Connections

What Is a Scientist? (1988)

by Barbara Lehn

HarperCollins, ISBN #0761312986

Overview of Book: Through the use of text and photographs, discover what a scientist is, what a scientist does, the tools they use, the questions they ask, the math they use, and the activities in which they engage.

Mathematical Concepts and Skills: real-life applications of mathematics, careers in mathematics and science

Science Concepts and Skills: careers in science and technology, nature and applications of science and technology

Overview of Activities: Students learn about, discuss, and observe what scientists do and the math they use in their jobs. Students generate a list of things they would like to study and then learn the name of the scientist that studies such things. Students make a sketch of themselves as a particular type of scientist and articulate the math and science skills or knowledge they would need to be successful in this job.

National Mathematics Standards (2000):

Students in preK–2 should "recognize and apply mathematics in contexts outside of mathematics" (Connections Standard) (p. 402). Students should also "communicate their mathematical thinking coherently and clearly to peers, teachers, and others" (Communication Standard) (p. 402).

National Science Standards (1996):

NCSS

Students in grades K–4 should develop an understanding of science as a human endeavor and that "many people choose science as a career and devote their entire lives to studying it." Students should understand that both "men and women have made a variety of contributions throughout the history of science and technology" (History and Nature of Science, Content Standard G) (p. 141). Students should also develop understandings about science and technology and understand that "people have always had questions about their world. Science is one way of answering questions and explaining the natural world." Students should understand that people have "invented tools and techniques to solve problems" and that "tools help scientists make better observations, measurements, and equipment for investigations." Students should understand that "women and men of all ages, backgrounds, and groups engage in a variety of scientific and technological work" (Science and Technology, Content Standard E) (p. 138).

Materials: 9" × 12" white paper or posterboard, crayons or markers

64

Description of Activities:

1. Engage students in a discussion about careers as a scientist. Ask students: What is a scientist? What skills and qualities would you need to be a successful scientist? Do you know anyone who is a scientist? If possible, ask a scientist to come speak to the students.

2. Read *What Is a Scientist?* Ask students to pay careful attention to the photos in the books showing what scientists do. When appropriate, discuss how many of the pictures show scientists performing mathematics (e.g., measuring, counting, sorting, testing predictions, etc.).

3. Ask students what they would like to study if they were scientists. On the board, create a two-column list, recording the name of the item a student would like to study and, next to it, record the name of the scientist who would study such a thing (e.g., rocks [geologist], ocean life [marine biologist], animals [zoologist], plants [botanist], insects [entomologist], butterflies [lepidopterist], stars and planets [astronomer], etc.).

4. On pieces of 9" × 12" white paper or posterboard, students write, "I want to be a . . . ," where they complete the prompt with the names of the scientists they would like to be. Using crayons or markers, students make sketches of themselves as these scientists, showing the uniforms they might wear, the tools they might use, the labs or environments in which they would work, etc. At the bottom of the sketches, students record what math and science skills or knowledge they would use in these jobs.

Assessment:

- Did students engage in discussions about what scientists do, the tools they use, etc.?
- Did students respond to the writing prompt and create sketches of themselves as future scientists?

Activity Extensions:

- Read *ABC of Jobs* (Priddy, 2003) and find out what other people in our community use mathematics and science in their jobs and who contribute to the betterment of society.

Cross-Curricular Connections:

Visual Arts

- Visit the What Do You Want to Be? interactive website and select a career, put on a uniform, and then print and color it.

Social Studies

- Discuss how scientists (e.g., doctors, astronauts, etc.) help and contribute their knowledge and skills to our community and/or world.
- Explore a biographical piece of a scientist who helped our community and/or world (e.g., Jonas Salk, Marie Curie, Louis Pasteur, etc.).

Related Children's Literature

Barton, B. (1988). *I want to be an astronaut*. New York: HarperCollins.

Bredeson, C. (2003). *Astronauts*. New York: Children's Press.

Cohen, J. (2000). *You can be a woman engineer*. Culver City, CA: Cascade Pass.

Ghez, A., & Cohen, J. (2006). *You can be a woman astronomer*. Culver City, CA: Cascade Pass.

Hayward, L. (2001). *A day in the life of a doctor*. London: Dorling Kindersley.

Kalman, B. (1997). *Community helpers from A to Z*. New York: Crabtree.

Kupchella, R. (2004). *Girls can! Make it happen*. Golden Valley, MN: Tristan.

Lehn, B. (1988). *What is a scientist?* New York: HarperCollins.

McAlary, F., & Cohen, J. (2001). *You can be a woman marine biologist*. Culver City, CA: Cascade Pass.

Miller, M. (1990). *Who uses this?* New York: Greenwillow Books.

Priddy, G. (2003). *ABC of jobs*. New York: Scholastic.

Sis, P. (1996). *Starry messenger*. New York: Farrar Strauss Giroux.

Thompson, V., & Cohen, J. (2001). *You can be a woman marine biologist*. Marina del Ray, CA: Cascade Pass.

Thompson, V., & Cohen, J. (2001). *You can be a woman zoologist*. Marina del Ray, CA: Cascade Pass.

Related Instructional Resources

Chipman, D., Florence, M., & Wax, N. (1998). *Cool women*. Chicago: Girl Press.

Marzollo, J. (1994). *My first book of biographies: Great men and women every child should know*. New York: Scholastic.

Saunders, H. (1988). *When are we ever gonna have to use this?* Palo Alto, CA: Seymour.

VanCleave, J. (2004). *Scientists through the ages*. Hoboken, NJ: Wiley.

Weldon, A. (1998). *Girls who rocked the world: Heroines from Sacagawea to Sheryl Swoopes*. Hillsboro, OR: Beyond Words.

Related Websites

Career Information
http://www.bls.gov/k12/
http://www.kids.gov/k_careers.htm
http://www.kathimitchell.com/careers.htm
http://www.enchantedlearning.com/classroom/K1/occupations.shtml

What Do You Want to Be?
http://www.econedlink.org/lessons/em207/flash/activity1.html

Literature-Based Mathematics and Social Studies Activities

The Mathematics–Social Studies Connection

Social studies encompasses many disciplines including anthropology, archaeology, economics, geography, history, law, philosophy, political science, psychology, religion, and sociology. Social studies also draws on "appropriate content from the humanities, mathematics, and natural sciences" (NCSS, 1994, p. vii). According to the National Council for the Social Studies (1994), the primary purpose of teaching social studies is to enable learners to become informed consumers and skilled decision makers working toward the public good in a culturally diverse, democratic society coexisting in an interdependent world. Further, exemplary social studies programs prepare students to acquire, organize, interpret, and communicate information; process data and draw conclusions; and generate and assess alternative approaches to problem solving and making decisions (NCSS, 1994). These same skills of thinking, observing, hypothesizing, reasoning, communicating, and problem solving are skills the National Council of Teachers of Mathematics advocates in its *Principles and Standards for School Mathematics* (NCTM, 2000).

A growing body of research and anecdotal evidence documents the power of teaching social studies and mathematics in an integrated fashion, in particular by using children's literature (Butzow & Butzow, 2006; Donoghue, 2001;

"Children's literature enables students to explore the many themes of social studies while learning about mathematics and statistics."

Fredericks, 1991, 2000; Gallavan, 2001; Martinez & McGee, 2000; McCoy, 2003; Moss, 2003; Rose, 2000; Thompson & Holyoke, 2000; Ward, 2004b; Whitin & Whitin, 2004). Further, works of fiction and nonfiction offer a lens for students to see, understand, and experience their world. By integrating children's literature into one's teaching, students can explore the

many themes of social studies (such as culture, economics, and geography) while learning the mathematics and statistics that support and define these themes.

This chapter articulates a variety of literature-based activities that integrate concepts and skills used and learned in the study of mathematics with those in social studies. While engaged in these activities, students will discover and gain practice with such mathematics concepts and skills as counting, skip counting, ordinal numbers, more than, less than, equal to, addition, multiples, patterns in multiples, money, coin value, adding coins (Number and Operations Standard); numeric and geometric pattern creation and recognition, writing number sentences (Algebra Standard); geometric shapes and patterns, perspective, visualization, spatial reasoning, drawing shapes, lines, and angles (Geometry Standard); telling time (Measurement Standard); and data creation and interpretation, bar graphs, pie charts (Data Analysis and Probability Standard).

Social studies concepts and skills featured in this chapter include African culture, people, language, clothing, animals, and geography; Hmong culture, traditions, art, and people; folktales and storytelling; historical aspects of money, its role, purpose, and value; timelines; distinguishing features on a globe, world time zones, map interpretation and creation; qualities of a leader and the duties and responsibilities of the president; the American flag, its symbolism, patriotism, and loyalty; U.S. history facts; civic duties and responsibilities; working for a common good, loyalty to family and community, careers, the specialized role of individuals in the community; and values and characteristics of a community and family.

The integrated literature-based activities also provide students with many opportunities to predict, estimate, problem-solve, and reason (Problem Solving and Reasoning and Proof Standards) as well as communicate and use various representations to organize, record, model, and interpret mathematical ideas (Communication and Representation Standards). Further, students will discover and explore real-life applications of mathematics and social studies and careers in mathematics and social studies (Connections Standard).

Remember to check the appendix for ideas and samples of assessment rubrics.

Matrix of Mathematics and Social Studies Activities

BOOK TITLE	MATHEMATICAL CONCEPTS AND SKILLS	SOCIAL STUDIES CONCEPTS AND SKILLS	SCIENCE CONCEPTS AND SKILLS	VISUAL ARTS CONCEPTS AND SKILLS
Moja Means One: Swahili Counting Book	counting, addition, writing number sentences	African culture, people, language, clothing, animals, and geography	homes and habitats of African animals	colors, shapes, and symmetry in the flags of African countries
Lunch Money and Other Poems about School; 26 Letters and 99 Cents; Money: A Rich History	money, coin value, adding coins, problem solving	historical aspects of coins and paper money; recognition of coins; role, purpose, and value of money	U.S. mints and coin making	artistic design of other countries' currencies
Nine-in-One Grr! Grr!; Teaching with Folk Stories of the Hmong: An Activity Book	skip counting, multiples, numeric and geometric patterns in multiples of numbers, pattern recognition	Hmong culture, traditions, art, and people; folktales; storytelling	tiger homes and habitat	illustrate Hmong proverbs, explore Hmong needlework
F Is for Flag; Red, White, and Blue: The Story of the American Flag	geometric patterns	U.S. flag, flag symbolism, patriotism, loyalty, family	stars	Jasper Johns's painting, *Flag on an Orange Field*; colors, shapes, and symbols in international flags
Me on the Map; Where Do I Live?	perspective; visualization and spatial reasoning; drawing shapes, lines, and angles	civic duties and responsibilities, working for a common good, map creation	animal families, animal homes, and animal habitats	artists' renditions of family and community; create a collage representing images of family, neighborhood, state, or planet
Nine O'Clock Lullaby	telling time, distinction between A.M. and P.M.	timeline of events, geography, world time zones, A.M. vs. P.M.	make and read a sundial, daylight savings time	Salvador Dali's "melting clocks," experience the passage of time while viewing art
Month by Month a Year Goes Round; A Busy Year	ordinal numbers, prediction, data creation and interpretation, bar graphs, more than, less than, the same as	passage of time, timeline of events	weather and the seasons; earth–sun relationship relative to the measurement of time	artists' renditions of seasons and weather

BOOK TITLE	MATHEMATICAL CONCEPTS AND SKILLS	SOCIAL STUDIES CONCEPTS AND SKILLS	SCIENCE CONCEPTS AND SKILLS	VISUAL ARTS CONCEPTS AND SKILLS
If All the Seas Were One Sea	prediction, estimation, data creation and interpretation, bar graphs	distinguishing features on a globe, continents, oceans vs. landmasses, map creation and interpretation	climate and weather in various countries and continents	paint the world on a Styrofoam sphere; use Rebus website to write and illustrate the verse *If All the Seas Were One Sea*
So You Want to Be President?; *First Pets: Presidential Best Friends*	data analysis and interpretation, pie charts	duties and responsibilities of the president, qualities of a leader, U.S. presidents	inventor-presidents	art of Mount Rushmore
Who Uses This?; *ABC of Jobs*	real-life applications of mathematics, careers in mathematics, jobs and careers requiring mathematical skills and knowledge	careers, specialized role of individuals in a community	jobs in the sciences	self-portrait of oneself in a future career

Moja Means One: Swahili Counting Book (1971)

by Muriel Feelings

Puffin Books, ISBN #0140546626

Overview of Book: Learn about the animals, geography, language, culture, and people of Africa in this counting book that counts from one to ten in English and in Swahili.

Mathematical Concepts and Skills: counting, addition, writing number sentences

Social Studies Concepts and Skills: African culture, people, language, clothing, animals, and geography

Overview of Activities: Students learn to count from one to ten in English and in Swahili while learning facts and aspects about the people, culture, and language of those living in Africa. Students write number sentences to express addition problems. Students explore different articles of African clothing and create a colorful and patterned kanga.

National Mathematics Standards (2000):

Students in preK–2 should "count with understanding and recognize 'how many' in sets of objects" and should "connect number words and numerals to the quantities they represent, using various physical models and representations" (Number and Operations Standard) (p. 392). Students in preK–2 should "model situations that involve the addition and subtraction of whole numbers, using objects, pictures, and symbols" (Algebra Standard) (p. 394).

National Social Studies Standards (1994): Social studies programs for early grades should include experiences that provide for the study of *culture and cultural diversity,* so that the learner can "describe ways in which language, stories, folktales, music, and artistic creations serve as expressions of culture and influence behavior of people living in a particular culture," and "give examples and describe the importance of cultural unity and diversity within and across groups" (p. 49).

Materials: map of Africa, decks of cards (one deck for each group of four students), muslin (pre-cut into 1' × 4' swatches), fabric markers

Description of Activities:

1. Engage students in a discussion about Africa (e.g., Where is Africa on a map? What animals live in Africa? What is the climate like in Africa? Do people speak English in Africa? What do you think life is like in Africa?, etc.). The book *Moja Means One: Swahili Counting Book* provides information about Africa in its opening and closing pages.

2. Read *Moja Means One: Swahili Counting Book.* As you read, let students count the number of animals featured on each page and allow them to practice saying the numbers in Swahili. (The phonetic pronunciation of each number name is listed under the numeral.)

3. Place students in groups of four. Give each group a deck of cards containing only the aces, twos, threes, fours, and fives. (Older students might use higher numbered cards.) Let students know that each card is worth its face value and an ace is worth one. Students shuffle the cards and place all twenty cards facedown on a table. (If appropriate, use less cards for younger students.) Students work in pairs and take turns. One pair turns over two cards. Students mentally compute the sum and then record the corresponding number sentence in their journals (e.g., $2 + 3 = 5$). Students also record the sum in Swahili. Continue playing until all of the cards have been summed.

4. Revisit the two pages in *Moja Means One: Swahili Counting Book* on which the number 6 is featured. Engage students in a discussion about how clothing reflects one's culture, and how we choose different clothes to wear to school, work, play, on special occasions, and so forth. Why might people in other countries wear different types of clothing? Ask students how African clothing is similar to and different from Western clothing.

5. Point out the woman (on the page featuring the number 6) who is wearing a kanga. A kanga is a rectangular cotton cloth with a border all around it, printed in bold designs and bright colors, and worn by women. Find out more about and show examples of kangas by viewing the Kanga websites listed below.

6. Distribute muslin swatches and fabric markers to each student. Students design a pattern on their kanga. Encourage them to include shapes and patterns in their designs.

7. Students place their kangas around their necks. Students compare and discuss similarities and differences of the kangas as well as what shapes and patterns they see. Hang the kangas around the perimeter of the classroom for all to view.

Assessment:

- Did students correctly express the number sentence and the sum of the two cards during each turn?

- Did students correctly record the sum in English and in Swahili?

- Did students participate in a discussion about clothing, its purposes, etc.?

- Did students create an African kanga, complete with patterns and shapes?

Activity Extensions:

- Learn about the culture, people, and geography of the people living in the African country of Tanzania by reading *We All Went on Safari: A Counting Journey through Tanzania* (Krebs, 2003).

- Students learn to count to ten in several other languages by reading *Can You Count Ten Toes? Count to 10 in 10 Different Languages* (Evans, 1999).

Cross-Curricular Connections:

Visual Arts

- Explore and reproduce the colors, shapes, and symmetry in the flags of African countries.

Science

- Explore the homes and habitats of animals that live in Africa.

Related Children's Literature

Cave, K. (2002). *One child, on seed: A South African counting book*. New York: Holt.

Evans, L. (1999). *Can you count ten toes? Count to 10 in 10 different languages*. Boston: Houghton Mifflin.

Feelings, M. (1971). *Moja means one: Swahili counting book*. New York: Puffin Books.

Grossman, V. (1991). *Ten little rabbits*. San Francisco: Chronicle Books.

Haskins, J. (1987). *Count your way through China*. Minneapolis: Carolrhoda Books.

Haskins, J. (1989). *Count your way through Africa*. Minneapolis: Carolrhoda Books.

Haskins, J. (1989). *Count your way through Korea*. Minneapolis: Carolrhoda Books.

Haskins, J. (1989). *Count your way through Mexico*. Minneapolis: Carolrhoda Books.

Haskins, J. (1990). *Count your way through Germany*. Minneapolis: Carolrhoda Books.

Haskins, J. (1992). *Count your way through India*. Minneapolis: Carolrhoda Books.

Haskins, J. (1992). *Count your way through Israel*.

Minneapolis: Carolrhoda Books.

Haskins, J. (1996). *Count your way through Brazil*. Minneapolis: Carolrhoda Books.

Haskins, J. (1996). *Count your way through France*. Minneapolis: Carolrhoda Books.

Haskins, J. (1996). *Count your way through Greece*. Minneapolis: Carolrhoda Books.

Haskins, J. (1996). *Count your way through Ireland*. Minneapolis: Carolrhoda Books.

Haskins, J. (1998). *Count your way through Russia*. Minneapolis: Carolrhoda Books.

Knight, M. (2002). *Africa is not a country*. Minneapolis: Lerner.

Krebs, L. (2003). *We all went on safari: A counting journey through Tanzania*. New York: Scholastic.

Mannis, C. (2002). *One leaf rides the wind: Counting in a Japanese garden*. New York: Scholastic.

Medearis, A. (2000). *Seven spools of thread: A Kwanzaa story*. New York: Scholastic.

Pelusey, M. (2005). *Africa*. New York: Chelsea House.

Related Instructional Resources

Croze, H. (2006). *Africa for kids*. Chicago: Chicago Review Press.

Faul, M. (1992). *Africa and her flags*. Santa Barbara, CA: Bellerophon Books.

Green, Y. (1997). *African girl and boy paper dolls*. Mineola, NY: Dover Books.

Green, Y. (1999). *Traditional African costumes paper dolls*. Mineola, NY: Dover Books.

Mazloomi, C. (1998). *Spirits of the cloth: Contemporary African American quilts*. New York: Crown.

Moore, J. (1999). *Africa (Geography units series)*. Monterey, CA: Evan-Moor.

Murray, J. (2003). *Africa*. New York: Facts on File.

Peterson, D. (1998). *Africa*. New York: Scholastic.

Related Websites

African Flags
>   http://www.africaguide.com/flags.htm
>   http://www.enchantedlearning.com/geography/flags/africa.shtml

Ancient Clothing
>   http://www.historyforkids.org/learn/africa/clothing/index.htm

Kanga
>   http://www.glcom.com/hassan/kanga_history.html
>   http://ainamoja.com/catalog/clothes/kanga/

Swahili Language and Culture
>   http://www.glcom.com/hassan/swahili_history.html
>   http://www.yale.edu/swahili/

Virtual Manipulatives Library—Number Line Arithmetic
>   http://nlvm.usu.edu/en/nav/frames_asid_156_g_1_t_1.html?open=activities

Lunch Money and Other Poems about School (1998)

by Carol Shields

Puffin Books, ISBN #014055890X

26 Letters and 99 Cents (1987)

by Tana Hoban

Greenwillow Books, ISBN #068814389X

Money: A Rich History (2003)

by Jon Anderson

Grosset & Dunlap, ISBN #0448432846

Overview of Poem and Books:

Find out where the money is in the poem "Lunch Money," and enjoy over twenty other poems about school in the book, *Lunch Money and Other Poems about School.* In the two-in-one book, *26 Letters and 99 Cents,* count from 1 to 99 using combinations of coins, and then turn the book over and learn the letters of the alphabet. In *Money: A Rich History,* learn a variety of facts about the origins and history of money, explained from the perspective of a child's school report.

Mathematical Concepts and Skills:

money, coin value, adding coins, problem solving

Social Studies Concepts and Skills:

historical aspects of coins and paper money; recognition of coins; role, purpose, and value of money

Overview of Activities:

Students sort coins by value and solve problems involving summing coins. Students explore aspects and features of coins and discuss the purpose of money. Students then create their own unique coin design.

National Mathematics Standards (2000):

Students in preK–2 should "connect number words and numerals to the quantities they represent, using various physical models and representations." Students should "develop and use strategies for whole number computations, with a focus on addition and subtraction" (Number and Operations Standard) (p. 392).

National Social Studies Standards (1994):

Social studies programs for early grades should include experiences that provide for the study of how people organize for the production, distribution, and consumption of goods and services, so that the learner . . . can "explain and demonstrate the role of money in everyday life"; "describe how we depend upon workers with specialized jobs and the ways in which they contribute to the production and exchange of goods and services"; and "describe the influences of incentives, values, traditions, and habits on economic decisions" (p. 65).

Materials:

presorted bags of coins (containing ten pennies, ten nickels, five dimes, and four quarters), white paper plates, crayons or markers

Description of Activities:

1. Read the poem entitled "Lunch Money" in Shields's book to set the stage for the upcoming activities involving money.

2. Students bring to class a bag with presorted coins (ten pennies, ten nickels, five dimes, and four quarters). Students sort the coins into four piles according to their value (pennies, nickels, dimes, and quarters). Review the name and value of each coin.

3. Show students the first page of *26 Letters and 99 Cents*. Students will see the number 1 and a penny (representing 1 cent) and the number 2 and two pennies (representing 2 cents). Before showing the photos on the next page, let students announce what number comes next and then show that amount using their coins. Verify their work by showing them the next page in the book. Continue sharing pages from *26 Letters and 99 Cents*, up to the number 25. If appropriate, ask students to show larger coin amounts.

4. Provide students additional practice with summing the value of coins by playing "What's in My Pocket?" Hide a few coins in your pocket and announce how many are hidden and their sum (e.g., I have two coins in my pocket that add to 6 cents. What coins are in my pocket?). Students use their coins to solve the problems. Older students might try to create their own clue and challenge classmates to determine the answer.

5. Ask students to study each type of coin and to notice its features (e.g., president appearing on the front of the coin, minting date, imprint on back of coin, material from which it is made, etc.). Engage students in a discussion about the information they see on the coins, why money was invented, what people did before money, why it is important, who determines the design appearing on money, the importance of saving money, and so on. Read all or excerpts from Anderson's *Money: A Rich History* to supply the answers to these questions.

6. Inform students that the Treasury Department has placed them in charge of creating a new coin. Using a paper plate and markers or crayons, students create and design a coin, showing its value, and decorating it with icons, symbols, and words representative of our country. Students attach a piece of loose-leaf paper to the plate explaining why money is important in society.

7. Students share and describe their coin designs with their classmates.

Assessment:

- Did students sort coins according to their value?

- Did students correctly guess the solutions to "What's in My Pocket"?

- Did students participate in a discussion about money?

- Did students create a coin?

Activity Extensions:

- Challenge students to think of different ways to sort their coins (by president, by date, by size, by weight, by color, by thickness, etc.).

- Open up a "store" in the classroom (containing simple items such as pencils, stickers, candy, etc.) where students can buy objects. Price each item. Challenge students to determine if they have enough money to buy certain items (e.g., "If you have 22 cents in your pocket can you purchase the blue pencil and an eraser?").

- List several occupations on the board (teacher, professional athlete, artist, doctor, president of the United States, etc.). Students discuss who should earn the highest salaries and why.

- Enjoy poems about money such as "Smart" (Silverstein, 2004) and "Overdues" (Silverstein, 1981).

Cross-Curricular Connections

Visual Arts

- Explore the artistic design of other countries' currencies.

Science

- Visit the U.S. Mint website and discover how coins are made and the various materials from which coins are made.

Related Children's Literature

Amato, W. (2002). *Math in my world: Math at the store.* New York: Children's Press.

Anderson, J. (2003). *Money: a rich history.* New York: Grosset & Dunlap.

Axelrod, A. (1994). *Pigs will be pigs.* New York: Aladdin Paperbacks.

Axelrod, A. (2003). *Pigs at odds: Fun with math and games.* New York: Aladdin Paperbacks.

Berger, M., & Berger, G. (2001). *Round and round the money goes* (Discovery readers series). Nashville: Ideals.

Brisson, P. (1993). *Benny's pennies.* New York: Dell Dragonfly Books.

Hill, M. (2005). *Dimes.* New York: Scholastic.

Hill, M. (2005). *Dollars.* New York: Scholastic.

Hill, M. (2005). *Nickels.* New York: Scholastic.

Hill, M. (2005). *Pennies.* New York: Scholastic.

Hill, M. (2005). *Quarters.* New York: Scholastic.

Hill, M. (2005). *Spending and saving.* New York: Scholastic.

Hoban, T. (1987). *26 letters and 99 cents.* New York: Greenwillow Books.

Mackey, L. (2004). *Money mama and the three little pigs.* Angoura Hills, CA: P4K.

Mollel, T. (1999). *My rows and piles of coins.* New York: Clarion Books.

Murphy, S. (1998). *The penny pot.* New York: Scholastic.

Shields, C. (1998). *Lunch money and other poems about school.* New York: Puffin Books.

Silverstein, S. (1981). *A light in the attic.* New York: HarperCollins.

Silverstein, S. (2004). *Where the sidewalk ends.* New York: HarperCollins.

Williams, R. (2001). *The coin counting book.* Watertown, MA: Charlesbridge.

Related Instructional Resources

Cribb, J. (2005). *Money* (Eyewitness books series). New York: Dorling Kindersley.

Harman, H. (2004). *Money sense for kids.* Hauppauge, NY: Barron's Educational Series.

Related Websites

Money Poems

      http://www.theteacherscorner.net/thematicunits/poem2.htm

      http://www.tooter4kids.com/classroom/math_poems.htm

NOVA—Secrets of Making Money

      http://www.pbs.org/wgbh/nova/moolah/hotsciencemoolah/

Printable Pretend Money

      http://pbskids.org/lions/printables/misc/money.html

The U.S. Mint—Money News and Games

      http://www.usmint.gov/kids/coinnews/index.cfm

      http://www.usmint.gov/kids/index.cfm?fileContents=games

Virtual Manipulatives Library—Count the Money

      http://nlvm.usu.edu/en/nav/frames_asid_325_g_2_t_1.html

Nine-in-One Grr! Grr! (1989)

by Blia Xiong

Children's Book Press, ISBN #0892391103

Teaching with Folk Stories of the Hmong: An Activity Book (2000)

by Dia Cha and Norma Livo

Libraries Unlimited, ISBN #1563086689

Overview of Books: In *Nine-in-One Grr! Grr!,* enjoy an imaginative folktale from the Hmong people of Laos that explains why the earth is not overrun by tigers. Then engage in a variety of hands-on activities while learning about the Hmong people in *Teaching with Folk Stories of the Hmong: An Activity Book.*

Mathematical Concepts and Skills: skip counting, multiples, numeric and geometric patterns in multiples of numbers, pattern recognition

Social Studies Concepts and Skills: Hmong culture, traditions, art, and people; folktales; storytelling

Overview of Activities: Students practice skip counting while noticing numeric and geometric patterns on a hundreds board. Students then enjoy the art of storytelling via a fable and folktale and explore the Hmong culture and people through a variety of activities.

National Mathematics Standards (2000): Students in preK–2 should "recognize, describe, and extend patterns such as sequences of sounds and shapes or simple numeric patterns and translate from one representation to another." They should also "analyze how both repeating and growing patterns are generated" (Algebra Standard) (p. 394). Students in preK–2 should "count with understanding and recognize 'how many' in sets of objects." They should also "connect number words and numerals to the quantities they represent, using various physical models and representations" (Number and Operations Standard) (p. 392).

National Social Studies Standards (1994):

Social studies programs for early grades should include experiences that provide for the study of *culture and cultural diversity,* so that the learner can "describe ways in which language, stories, folktales, music, and artistic creations serve as expressions of culture and influence behavior of people living in a particular culture" (p. 49).

Materials: hundreds boards, clear counters, map of Laos

Description of Activities:

1. Distribute hundreds boards to pairs of students. Demonstrate skip counting by twos, by placing a clear counter on each multiple of two as you count. After counting to twenty, students read aloud the covered numbers, giving them practice skip counting. Ask students what geometric (i.e., visual) pattern was formed on the hundreds board by skip counting by twos. Students should recognize a "checkered" pattern in which every other square is skipped. Challenge students to predict what number comes next if they were to continue skip counting by twos.

2. Repeat the above activity but now skip count with students by fives and then by tens. What geometric patterns do students notice? (The multiples of five and ten appear in column form.) For older students, what numeric pattern do they notice in the multiples of five? (Each multiple ends in a 5 or in a 0.) In the multiples of ten? (Each multiple ends in a 0.)

3. Introduce the fable, *Nine-in-One Grr! Grr!* Ask students if they know what a fable is, and to name any other fables with which they are familiar. Describe how a fable is a story that teaches a lesson and that features animals that speak and act like people. Inform students that at the end of the story, they will explore a number pattern depicted in the book. Tell them to listen carefully for the lesson to be learned.

4. After reading *Nine-in-One Grr! Grr!,* challenge students to use their hundreds board to skip count by nines, covering up each multiple of nine as they count. Explain why they are covering up each multiple of nine, by relating this to the line in the story appearing on page 10 when the great god, Shao, informs the tiger that she will have "Nine each year."

5. After students have skip counted to 27 by nines, ask what geometric (i.e., visual) pattern they see in the multiples of nine and to predict what comes next in the (diagonal) pattern. Students explain their thinking. Skip count by nine to verify that 36 is the next number in the sequence. Using their clear counters, students cover the remaining multiples of nine. Challenge older students to look for a numeric pattern in the multiples of nine (the sum of the digits in each multiple is nine).

6. Remind students that the story *Nine-in-One Grr! Grr!* is a fable. Students explain what lesson was taught in the story. (The tiger has one tiger every nine years as opposed to nine tigers every one year. This explains why the earth is not overpopulated with tigers.)

7. Show students where Laos is located on a map. Revisit the illustrations in *Nine-in-One Grr! Grr!* and ask students to describe the geography of Laos (very mountainous, especially in the north; dense forests cover the northern and eastern areas; the Mekong River, which forms the boundary with Burma and Thailand, flows through the country).

8. Using the information appearing on pages 4–5 in *Teaching with Folk Stories of the Hmong: An Activity Book* as well as the Laos websites listed below, describe the Hmong people, a cultural group who originally lived in modern-day China but who now reside in the highlands of Southeast Asia. Using *Teaching with Folk Stories of the Hmong: An Activity Book,* engage students in activities in which they learn about Hmong culture and traditions. Consider exploring Hmong storytelling and the importance of proverbs, and engage students in activities in which they illustrate stories. Students can also explore Hmong folk arts, music, clothing, and customs.

Assessment:
- Did students correctly skip count by twos, fives, tens, and nines?
- Did students notice the geometric and numeric patterns in the multiples of numbers?
- Did students discern the lesson to be taught in *Nine-in-One Grr! Grr!?*
- Did students create Hmong artifacts?

Activity Extensions:

- Explore numeric and geometric patterns in other multiples or in the Fibonacci sequence.

- Explore the use of fables and folktales as a means of storytelling.

- Read *Jouanah: A Hmong Cinderella* (Coburn & Lee, 1996), a variant of Cinderella.

- Using *Teaching with Folk Stories of the Hmong: An Activity Book,* read other folktales included in the book and search for the hidden lesson.

Cross-Curricular Connections:

Visual Arts

- Read *Many Ideas Open the Way: A Collection of Hmong Proverbs* (Snook, 2003). Students create illustrations that capture the meaning in select proverbs.

- Explore needlework, an art treasured by the Hmong people.

Science

- Explore and discuss the homes and habitat of tigers.

Related Children's Literature

Bryan, N. (2003). *Hmong Americans*. Edina, MN: ABDO.

Coburn, J., & Lee, T. (1996). *Jouanah: A Hmong Cinderella*. Fremont, CA: Shen's Books.

Giraud, H. (2005). *Basha: A Hmong child*. Farmington Hills, MI: Gale.

Tang, G. (2004). *Math fables*. New York: Scholastic.

Xiong, B. (1989). *Nine-in-One Grr! Grr!* San Francisco: Children's Book Press.

 ## Related Instructional Resources

Cha, D., & Livo, N. (2000). *Teaching with folk stories of the Hmong: An activity book*. Westport, CT: Libraries Unlimited.

Livo, N., & Cha, D. (2003). *Folk stories of the Hmong: Peoples of Laos, Thailand, and Vietnam*. Englewood, CO: Libraries Unlimited.

MacDonald, M. (1993). *Storyteller's start-up book: Finding, learning, performing, and using folktales including twelve tellable tales*. Atlanta: August House.

Snook, R. (2003). *Many ideas open the way: A collection of Hmong proverbs*. Fremont, CA: Shen's Books.

 ## Related Websites

Hmong Children's Books
> http://library.uwsuper.edu/hmong/childbooks.html

Laos Facts
> https://www.cia.gov/cia/publications/factbook/geos/la.html
> http://www.infoplease.com/ipa/A0107702.html
> http://www.infoplease.com/country/profiles/laos.html

Tigers
> http://library.advanced.org/11922/cats/tiger.htm
> http://www.enchantedlearning.com/subjects/mammals/tiger/Tigertocolor.shtml
> http://www.indianchild.com/tigers.htm

F Is for Flag (2002)

by Wendy Cheyette Lewison

Grosset & Dunlap, ISBN #0448428385

Red, White, and Blue: The Story of the American Flag (1998)

by John Herman

Grosset & Dunlap, ISBN #0448412705

Overview of Books: Learn all about the origins, evolution, and symbolism of the American flag and why we respect it in *F Is for Flag* and in *Red, White, and Blue: The Story of the American Flag.*

Mathematical Concepts and Skills: geometric patterns

Social Studies Concepts and Skills: U.S. flag, flag symbolism, patriotism, loyalty, family

Overview of Activities: Students discuss the symbolism of and meaning behind the American flag as well as the importance of loyalty to our family and to our country. Then, students experiment with geometric patterns and create a flag using thirteen stars and thirteen stripes.

National Mathematics Standards (2000): Students in preK–2 should "recognize, describe, and extend patterns such as sequences of sounds and shapes or simple numeric patterns and translate from one representation to another" (Algebra Standard) (p. 394).

National Social Studies Standards (1994): Social studies programs for early grades should include experiences that provide for the study of *individual development and identity,* so that the learner can "describe the unique features of one's nuclear and extended families"; "identify and describe ways family, groups, and community influence the individual's daily life and personal choices"; and "work independently and cooperatively to accomplish goals" (p. 57). Social studies programs for early grades should include experiences that provide for the study of *culture and cultural diversity,* so that the learner can "give examples and describe the importance of cultural unity and diversity within and across groups" (p. 49). Social studies programs for early grades should include experiences that provide for the study of *the ideals, principles, and* *practices of citizenship in a democratic republic,* so that the learner can "recognize and interpret how the 'common good' can be strengthened through various forms of citizen action" as well as "identify key ideals of the United States' democratic republican form of government, such as individual human dignity, liberty, justice, equality, and the rule of law, and discuss their application in specific situations" (p. 73).

Materials: precut strips of white and red construction paper, star stickers, glue sticks

Description of Activities:

1. Begin a discussion about the American flag. Why do we pledge to it? What does the flag represent? Why might seeing an American flag or pledging to it invoke emotion? What shapes and symbols are on the flag? What do the symbols on the flag represent (the stars and stripes, the colors)? What patterns do students see (rows of stars, alternating red and white stripes)? Who created the flag? Has it always looked this way? Where do we see flags (on the moon, on battleships, at the Olympic Games, in schools, at parades, in cemeteries, at post offices, etc.)?

2. Read *F Is for Flag,* which will answer many of the discussion questions. Refer to the Symbols on the Flag website for additional information about the American flag.

3. Revisit the pages and text in *F Is for Flag* that read, "We are all kinds of people—different in many ways. But we live and work and play together. We are like one big family. One country, one family, one flag for everybody." Discuss how being a citizen of the United States is like being a member in a family. We are united by commonalities, we work as a team, we live by the same rules, we speak the same language, all members in a family or community should be treated equally, etc.

4. Engage students in a discussion about the importance of loyalty to our family and to our country. In school, we pledge allegiance to the flag as a way to demonstrate our loyalty to the United States. How can we demonstrate loyalty to our family and community?

5. Read *Red, White, and Blue: The Story of the American Flag* and allow students to learn more about the history and creation of the American flag. Allow students to view page 19, which contains illustrations of several of the colonies' flags and which describes the need for all the colonies, since they were uniting, to have one flag.

6. Read pages 22–23 in *Red, White, and Blue: The Story of the American Flag* and allow students to see how people used various patterns and arrangements of stars and stripes in the creation of the first American flag (representing the first thirteen colonies). Using strips of red and white construction paper, gluesticks, and star stickers, challenge students to think of different ways to arrange thirteen stars and thirteen red and white stripes on a piece of white paper. Can they create a more appealing American flag than Betsy Ross did?

7. Hang the flags on a wall for all students to observe and discuss the many patterns that were created and to remind them of our loyalty to our country.

8. Inform students that each state has its own flag. Using the U.S. State Flags website listed below, students view select flags and describe what shapes and patterns they see. How well does the students' state flag represent their state?

Assessment:
- Did students participate in discussions about the American flag and the importance of loyalty?
- Did students create a patterned flag using thirteen stars and thirteen stripes?
- Did students observe and discuss the various patterns and arrangements of stars and stripes on their flags?

Activity Extensions:
- Students create a class flag or school flag using symbols, text, and colors that best represent it.
- Students explore symmetry in state or international flags.
- Sing and discuss lyrics from such songs as "America the Beautiful," "The Star Spangled Banner," "God Bless America," "My Country 'Tis of Thee," etc.
- Read the biography entitled *Betsy Ross* (Wallner, 1994).
- Read all or select pages from *One Nation: America by the Numbers* (Scillian, 2002) or *A Is for America: An American Alphabet* (Scillian, 2001), both of which present facts about the United States, its landmarks, people, and history.
- Read "Flag," a poem in *Where the Sidewalk Ends* (Silverstein, 2004).
- Explore the significance of Flag Day.

Cross-Curricular Connections:

Visual Arts

- Explore and discuss Jasper Johns's painting, *Flag on an Orange Field*.

- Explore the colors, shapes, and symmetry in international flags.

Science

- Begin a unit on stars.

Related Children's Literature

Aigner-Clark, J. (2002). *Baby Einstein: The ABCs of art*. New York: Hyperion Books for Children.

Berlin, I. (2006). *God bless America*. New York: HarperCollins.

Cronin, D. (2004). *Duck for president*. New York: Simon & Schuster Children's Publishing.

Herman, J. (1998). *Red, white, and blue: The story of the American flag*. New York: Grosset & Dunlap.

Lewison, W. (2002). *F Is for flag*. New York: Grosset & Dunlap.

Scillian, D. (2001). *A Is for America: An American alphabet*. Chelsea, MI: Sleeping Bear Press.

Scillian, D. (2002). *One nation: America by the numbers*. Chelsea, MI: Sleeping Bear Press.

Silverstein, S. (2004). *Where the sidewalk ends*. New York: HarperCollins.

Sis, P. (2004). *The train of states*. New York: Greenwillow Books.

Thomson, S. (2003). *Stars and stripes: The story of the American Flag*. New York: HarperCollins.

Wallner, A. (1994). *Betsy Ross*. New York: Scholastic.

Wayman, S. (2002). *God bless America: Children's thoughts on patriotism*. Parker, CO: Thornton.

Related Instructional Resources

Bateman, T. (1989). *Red, white, blue, and Uncle Who? The stories behind some of America's patriotic symbols*. New York: Holiday House.

Buller, J., Schade, S., Cocca-Leffler, M., Holub, J., Kelley, T., & Regan, D. (2003). *Smart about the fifty states: A class report*. New York: Grosset & Dunlap.

Cheney, L. (2002). *America: A patriotic primer*. New York: Simon & Schuster Books for Young Readers.

Cheney, L. (2006). *Our 50 states*. New York: Simon & Schuster Books for Young Readers.

Crouthers, D. (1978). *Flags of American history*. Maplewood, NJ: Hammond.

Davis, K. (2004). *Don't know much about the 50 states (Don't know much about series)*. New York: HarperTrophy.

Devrian Global Industries. (2006). *States activities book*. Union, NJ: Author.

Graham-Barber, L. (1992). *Doodle dandy! The complete book of Independence Day words*. New York: Bradbury Press.

Haban, R. (1989). *How proudly they wave: Flags of the fifty states*. Minneapolis: Lerner.

Hauser, J. (2004). *Celebrate America: Learning about the USA through crafts & activities*. Charlotte, VT: Williamson.

Related Websites

Betsy Ross Homepage
>   http://www.ushistory.org/betsy/

Flag Activities
>   http://www.enchantedlearning.com/crafts/flagday/

Jasper Johns's *Flag on an Orange Field*
>   http://www.artchive.com/artchive/J/johns/flagorng.jpg.html
>   http://www.sanford-artedventures.com/create/try_this_flag.html

Robert G. Heft—Creator of America's Current Flag
>   http://www.usflag.org/flagdesigner.html

Symbols on the Flag
>   http://bensguide.gpo.gov/3-5/symbols/flag.html
>   http://www.usflag.org/history/flagevolution.html
>   http://www.crwflags.com/fotw/flags/us-ststr.html

U.S. State Flags
>   http://www.netstate.com/state_flags.htm
>   http://www.enchantedlearning.com/usa/flags/

Activities Featuring Geometry

Me on the Map (1996)

by Joan Sweeney

Dragonfly Books, ISBN #0517885573

Where Do I Live? (1995)

by Neil Chesanow

Barron's Educational Series, ISBN #0812092414

Overview of Books: *Me on the Map* introduces maps to readers by beginning in a child's room and then taking the reader on a visual journey, placing the bedroom within a home, then on a street, then in a town, then in a state, and all the way out to the universe. Readers take a similar map-like journey in *Where Do I Live?*, but learn facts about each place that is mapped.

Mathematical Concepts and Skills: perspective; visualization and spatial reasoning; drawing shapes, lines, and angles

Social Studies Concepts and Skills: civic duties and responsibilities, working for a common good, map creation

Overview of Activities: Students discuss where they live and then view maps of the places they live (e.g., their room, their house, their neighborhood, their world, etc.). Students then create a map using lines and shapes. Students engage in a discussion and activity focusing on their civic duties and responsibilities as part of a community.

National Mathematics Standards (2000): Students in preK–2 should "recognize and represent shapes from different perspectives" as well as "recognize geometric shapes and structures in the environment and specify their location." Students should also "recognize, name, build, draw, compare, and sort two- and three-dimensional shapes" (Geometry Standard) (p. 396).

National Social Studies Standards (1994):

Social studies programs for early grades should include experiences that provide for the study of *people, places, and environments,* so that the learner can "interpret, use, and distinguish various representations of the earth, such as maps, globes, and photographs" and "use appropriate resources, data sources, and geographic tools such as atlases, databases, grid systems, charts, graphs, and maps to generate, manipulate, and interpret information" (p. 54). Social studies programs for early grades should include experiences that provide for the study of ideals, principles, and practices of citizenship so that the learner can "identify examples of rights and responsibilities of citizens" and "recognize and interpret how the 'common good' can be strengthened through various forms of citizen action" (p. 73).

Materials: 9" × 12" posterboard, pencils, crayons or markers, rulers

Description of Activities:

1. Set the stage for the upcoming activities by asking students, Where do you live? Students might respond by saying they live in a house, by giving their street address, by naming their city, or state, etc. Record their responses on the board.

2. Begin reading *Me on the Map.* After the students recognize the pattern in the story (where the author keeps taking them one step further away from their home to a larger place), let students predict where the author places them next.

3. Distribute 9" × 12" posterboard, rulers, pencils, and crayons or markers to students. Younger students create a map of their bedroom, while older students make a map of their room, their house, or their neighborhood. In designing their sketches, students should focus on drawing to scale and using lines, shapes, and angles in their illustrations.

4. In small groups or as a whole class, students share their maps and describe the shapes and images on their maps.

5. Read *Where Do I Live?,* which mirrors the story line of *Me on the Map,* but provides further details about the map featured on each page. As you read individual pages, emphasize how people interact and support one another in each location (e.g., at home—we interact and support one another as a family; on a street—we interact and support one another as neighbors; on Earth—we work as a community to keep it clean, etc.).

6. Engage students in a discussion about what their duties and responsibilities are at home, in their school, in their community, and as part of the earth. How can we support and create and maintain harmony in the places we live?

7. Give each student one sheet of white paper. Students respond to the prompt, "I live in a community where I . . ." Students sketch themselves partaking in an activity that they view as their civic duty or responsibility or that depicts them working for the common good. Record younger students' responses on one large sheet of butcher paper. Older students record their response to the prompt at the bottom of their sketch (e.g., ". . . throw out my trash, or . . . help someone when they fall, or . . . give money to the poor, etc."). Create a wall collage by hanging their work in a rectangular array on a wall.

Assessment:
- Did students recognize the pattern in *Me on the Map* and make accurate predictions about what is discussed next in the story?

- Did students create an accurate map using lines and shapes?

- Did students make an illustration of and articulately respond to the prompt, "I live in a community where I . . ."?

Activity Extensions:
- Students complete the last page in *Where Do I Live?* (either orally or in writing), which reminds students of their journey from their room and out to the universe in incrementally larger steps.

- Discuss how the classroom is a community.

- Learn what comprises a community by reading and discussing *What Is a Community? From A to Z* (Kalman, 2000).

- Learn about your civic responsibility and the many ways in which you can serve your community in *Serving Your Community* (Ditchfield, 2000). Students then embark on a service project.

Cross-Curricular Connections:

Visual Arts
- Explore *A Child's Book of Art* (Micklethwait, 1993), which displays masterpieces of families and family members (pp. 6–7) and other aspects of a community, including the home (pp. 8–9), transportation (pp. 48–49), places of work (pp. 52–53), and places to play (pp. 54–55).

- Students create a collage of images representing family, a neighborhood, their state, the earth, etc.

Science
- Explore animal families, animal homes, and animal habitats.

Related Children's Literature

Asch, F. (1994). *The earth and I.* New York: Scholastic.

Brocklehurst, R. (2004). *Usborne children's picture atlas.* New York: Scholastic.

Chesanow, N. (1995). *Where do I live?* Hauppauge, NY: Barron's Educational Series.

Ditchfield, K. (2000). *Serving your community.* New York: Scholastic.

Fanelli, S. (1995). *My map book.* New York: HarperCollins.

Garrison, J., & Tubesing, A. (1996). *A million visions of peace: Wisdom from the Friends of Old Turtle.* New York: Scholastic.

Gibbons, G. (1995). *Planet Earth/Inside out.* New York: Morrow.

Hartman, G. (1993). *As the crow flies: A first book of maps.* New York: Aladdin Paperbacks.

Hartman, G. (1994). *As the roadrunner runs: A first book of maps.* New York: Macmillan.

Hoose, P. (2002). *It's our world, too!* New York: Farrar Straus Giroux.

Kalman, B. (1997). *Community helpers from A to Z.* New York: Crabtree.

Kalman, B. (2000). *What is a community?: From A to Z.* New York: Crabtree.

Kincade, S. (1992). *Our time is now (Young people changing the world).* Upper Saddle River, NJ: Pearson Foundation.

Leedy, L. (2003). *Mapping Penny's world.* New York: Holt.

Lewis, J. (2002). *A world of wonders: Geographic travels in verse and rhyme.* New York: Dial Books for Young Readers.

Marzollo, J. (2001). *I am planet Earth.* New York: Scholastic.

Micklethwait, L. (1993). *A child's book of art: Great pictures: First words.* New York: Dorling Kindersley.

Pershing Accelerated School Students. (2002). *We dream of a world.* New York: Scholastic.

Pollak, B. (2004). *Our community garden.* Hillsboro, OR: Beyond Words.

Rabe, T. (2002). *There's a map in my lap!* New York: Random House Children's Books.

Roca, N. (2002). *Boys and girls of the world: From one end to the other.* Hauppauge, NY: Barron's Educational Series.

Rockwell, A. (1998). *Our earth.* New York: Scholastic.

Singer, M. (1991). *Nine o'clock lullaby.* New York: Scholastic.

Spier, P. (1980). *People.* New York: Doubleday.

Sweeney, J. (1996). *Me on the map.* New York: Dragonfly Books.

Sweeney, J. (1998). *Me and my place in space.* New York: Dragonfly Books.

Related Instructional Resources

Knowlton, J. (1985). *Maps and globes.* New York: HarperCollins.

Knowlton, J. (1988). *Geography from A to Z: A picture glossary.* New York: HarperCollins.

Lewis, B. (1992). *Kids with courage: True stories about young people making a difference.* Minneapolis: Free Spirit.

Lewis, B. (1995). *The kid's guide to service projects: Over 500 service ideas for young people who want to make a difference.* Minneapolis: Free Spirit.

Lewis, B. (1998). *The kid's guide to social action: How to solve social problems you choose—and turn creative thinking into positive action.* Minneapolis: Free Spirit.

Wolfman, I. (2003). *My world and globe.* New York: Workman Publishing.

Related Websites

Civic Life in Children's Literature
http://www.udel.edu/dssep/civicslit/chart5_k-2.htm

Community in Children's Literature
http://www.apples4theteacher.com/holidays/labor-day/kids-books/index.html

Maps
http://www.yourchildlearns.com/megamaps.htm
http://county-map.digital-topo-maps.com/united-states-map.gif
http://worldatlas.com/aatlas/newart/imaged.jpg
http://www.kidsolr.com/geography/index.html

Nine O'Clock Lullaby (1991)

by Marilyn Singer

Scholastic, ISBN #0590471856

Overview of Book: In *Nine O'Clock Lullaby,* travel around the world and back again through different time zones and find out what people in different parts of the world are doing.

Mathematical Concepts and Skills: telling time, distinction between A.M. and P.M.

Social Studies Concepts and Skills: timeline of events, geography, world time zones, A.M. vs. P.M.

Overview of Activities: Students discover why day and night occur using a globe and lamp and then learn how a day is evenly divided between A.M. and P.M. hours. Students create and manipulate a handmade clock to model the passage of time by the hour throughout the course of one day while also exploring time zones on a map or globe. Students create and illustrate a timeline of events that occur during their typical day.

National Mathematics Standards (2000):

Students in preK–2 should "recognize the attributes of length, volume, weight, area, and time" and "compare and order objects according to these attributes" (Measurement Standard) (p. 398).

National Social Studies Standards (1994):

Social studies programs for early grades should include experiences that provide for the study of *the ways human beings view themselves in and over time,* so that the learner can "demonstrate an ability to use correctly vocabulary associated with time" as well as "read and construct simple time-lines" (p. 51). Social studies programs for early grades should also include experiences that provide for the study of *people, places, and environments,* so that the learner can "interpret, use, and distinguish various representations of the earth, such as maps, globes, and photographs" and "use appropriate resources, data sources, and geographic tools such as atlases, databases, grid systems, charts, graphs, and maps to generate, manipulate, and interpret information" (p. 54).

Materials: lamp, globe, map, clock with moveable hands, paper plates, pipe cleaners, butcher paper, markers

Description of Activities:
1. Engage students in a discussion about how many hours are in a day, what is day, what is night, why do day and night occur, how many hours of light and dark are there in a day, etc.

2. Using a lamp and a globe, model how, as the earth rotates on its axis, different parts of the earth are lit and other parts are dark. When half of the earth is light, we call this *day*. The other half of the earth that is in darkness is experiencing *night*. The middle part of the day is called *noon*, and this occurs when the sun is at its highest point in the sky. There are twenty-four hours in one day, which is how long it takes the earth to rotate on its axis.

3. Ask students what they normally do at eight o'clock. Some might say that they are on their way to school; others might say they are getting ready for bed. Explain that in a day, twelve hours are considered morning hours and twelve hours are evening hours. Morning hours are called A.M., which is Latin for *ante meridian*. Evening hours are called P.M., which is Latin for *post meridian*. Thus, you might be on your way to school at 8 A.M., but getting ready for bed at 8 P.M.

4. Students create and label a clock using a paper plate and two different colored pipe cleaners pushed through the center of the plate and knotted in the back (for the hands). Identify which color pipe cleaner represents the minute hand and which represents the hour hand. Assist students in placing the numbers, 1 through 12, around the circumference of the paper plate.

5. Begin reading *Nine O'Clock Lullaby*. As you read each page, students adjust the moveable hands on their clocks to match the time. Also, using a globe or large map, point to the location mentioned in the book (or place stickers on a laminated map). Students should notice that you are slowly moving eastward around the world (or across countries and continents) with each page of the book.

6. Using butcher paper students create and label a timeline of their typical (or "ideal") day beginning with the hour when they awake and ending with the hour when they go to bed. Students mark and illustrate four or five more events that occur on the hour on their timeline, indicating whether they occur during the A.M. or P.M.

Assessment:

- Did students engage in a discussion about day and night, hours in a day, the passage of time, etc.?

- Did students create and label their clocks correctly?

- Did students accurately show the time on their clocks as the story was read?

- Did students correctly create, label, and illustrate a timeline that reflected their day?

Activity Extensions:

- Read *All in One Hour* (Crummel, 2003) and let students explore how there are 60 minutes in one hour.

- Print a map showing world time zones. Reread the story and have students label their maps with the time and location mentioned in the book.

- Play "What Time Is It?" The teacher names an activity (e.g., eating dinner), and students move the hands on their clocks to show what time this would occur. Students hold up their clocks to show their answers. Students verbally indicate whether this activity would be in the A.M. or P.M.

Cross-Curricular Connections:

Visual Arts

- Explore the "melting clocks" appearing in many of Salvador Dali's works.

- Students explore masterpieces of art and feel their textures in *Feed Matisse's Fish* (Appel & Guglielmo, 2006) while moving through a day hour by hour.

Science

- Make a sundial or place a sundial outside. Teach students how to read time using a sundial.

- Discuss daylight savings time.

Related Children's Literature

Appel, J., & Guglielmo, A. (2006). *Feed Matisse's fish*. New York: Sterling.

Appelt, K. (2000). *Bats around the clock*. New York: HarperCollins.

Archambault, J. (2004). *Boom chicka rock*. New York: Philomel Books.

Axelrod, A. (2002). *Pigs on the move*. New York: Aladdin.

Branley, F. (1986). *What makes day and night*. New York: Crowell.

Cole, J. (1987). *The magic school bus inside the earth*. New York: Scholastic.

Crummel, S. (2003). *All in one hour*. Tarrytown, NY: Marshall Cavendish.

Dijs, C. (1993). *What do I do at 8 o'clock?* New York: Simon & Schuster.

Fowler, A. (1991). *The sun is always shining somewhere*. Chicago: Children's Press.

Franco, B. (2003). *Something furry in the garage at 6:30 A.M.* Vernon Hills, IL: ETA Cuisenaire.

Gibbons, G. (1983). *Sun up, sun down*. San Diego: Harcourt Brace.

Hutchins, P. (1970). *Clocks and more clocks*. New York: Aladdin Paperbacks.

Kandoian, E. (1987). *Under the sun*. New York: Dodd Mead.

Kandoian, E. (1989). *Is anybody up?* New York: Putnam.

Lionni, L. (1992). *A busy year*. New York: Knopf.

Llewellyn, C. (1992). *My first book of time*. New York: Dorling Kindersley.

Maccarone, G. (1997). *Monster math: School time*. New York: Scholastic.

McIntyre, P. (2006). *It's about time*. Mustang, OK: Tate.

Murphy, S. (2005). *It's about time!* New York: HarperCollins.

Pluckrose, H. (1995). *Time*. New York: Scholastic.

Regier, D. (2006). *What time is it?* New York: Children's Press.

Richards, K. (2000) *It's about time, Max!* New York: Sagebrush Educational Resources.

Schoberle, C. (1994). *Day lights, night lights*. New York: Simon & Schuster.

Schuett, S. (1995). *Somewhere in the world right now*. New York: Dragon Fly Books.

Shields, C. (1998). *Day by day a week goes round*. New York: Dutton Children's Books.

Shields, C. (1998). *Month by month a year goes round*. New York: Dutton Children's Books.

Sierra, J. (2004). *What time is it, Mr. Crocodile?* New York: Harcourt Children's Books.

Simon, S. (1984). *Earth*. New York: Four Winds Press.

Singer, M. (1991). *Nine o'clock lullaby*. New York: Scholastic.

Related Instructional Resources

Maestro, B. (1999). *The story of clocks and calendars*. New York: HarperCollins.

Taylor, B. (1993). *Maps and mapping* (Young discoveries series). New York: Kingfisher.

Wells, R. (2003). *How do you know what time it is?* Morton Grove, IL: Whitman.

Wolfman, I. (2003). *My world and globe*. New York: Workman.

Related Websites

Daylight Savings Time
>   http://webexhibits.org/daylightsaving/b.html

Interactive Telling Time
>   http://www.bbc.co.uk/wales/snapdragon/yesflash/time-1.htm

Time Zones
>   http://geography.about.com/od/geographyglossaryt/g/ggtimezones.htm

Time Zones Map
>   http://www.worldtimezone.com/index.shtml

Virtual Manipulatives Library—Analog and Digital Clocks
>   http://nlvm.usu.edu/en/nav/frames_asid_316_g_1_t_4.html

Virtual Manipulatives Library—Match Clocks
>   http://nlvm.usu.edu/en/nav/frames_asid_317_g_1_t_4.html

Virtual Manipulatives Library—What Time Will It Be?
>   http://nlvm.usu.edu/en/nav/frames_asid_318_g_1_t_4.html

World Clock
>   http://www.timeanddate.com/worldclock/

Month by Month a Year Goes Round (1998)

by Carol Diggory Shields

Dutton Children's Books, ISBN #0525454586

A Busy Year (1992)

by Leo Lionni

Knopf, ISBN #0375827374

Overview of Books:	Learn the months of the year and the seasons associated with each in the rhyming book, *Month by Month a Year Goes Round*. Then, in *A Busy Year*, learn the tale of twin mice who befriend a tree that teaches them about growth, decline, and dormancy as the mice watch the tree grow and change throughout the year and through seasons.
Mathematical Concepts and Skills:	ordinal numbers, prediction, data creation and interpretation, bar graphs, more than, less than, the same as
Social Studies Concepts and Skills:	passage of time, timeline of events
Overview of Activities:	Students learn the names and ordering of the months of the year and create a class bar graph depicting the months in which they were born. Students also discuss the seasons associated with each month and the impact of the passage of time on the growth of living things. Students create a personal timeline illustrating their change in growth, as well as milestones reached or to be reached.
National Mathematics Standards (2000): π	Students in preK–2 should "pose questions and gather data about themselves and their surroundings." Students should also "represent data using concrete objects, pictures, and graphs" and "describe parts of the data and the set of data as a whole to determine what the data show" (Data Analysis and Probability Standard) (p. 400). Students in preK–2 should "develop understanding of the relative position and magnitude of whole numbers and of ordinal and cardinal numbers and their connections" (Number and Operations Standard) (p. 392).

National Social Studies Standards (1994):

Social studies programs for early grades should include experiences that provide for the study of *the ways human beings view themselves in and over time,* so that the learner can "demonstrate an ability to use correctly vocabulary associated with time," "read and construct simple timelines," and "recognize examples of cause-and-effect relationships" (p. 51).

Materials: calendar, sticky notes, butcher paper, markers or crayons

Description of Activities:

1. Ask students to name the months of the year in correct order. One way to recall the months in their correct order is to hum the melody to "Row, Row, Row Your Boat" and, in place of the lyrics, substitute the names of the months of the year beginning with January. Also, see the Months of the Year Poems and Songs websites for more song ideas.

2. Record the name of the months at the top of the board horizontally. How many months are there? While holding a calendar, review the name of each month and its ordinal position (e.g., January is the *first* month of the year. February is the *second* month of the year, etc.).

3. Ask students to guess during what month most of their birthdays occur.

4. Give students sticky notes and ask them to record their names on them. Students create vertical bar graphs by placing their sticky notes underneath the names of their birth months.

5. Analyze the data. During what month(s) were most students born? The least? How do you know this? Were there two months during which the same number of students was born? During what months were no students born? How do you know? How many more students were born in October than in April? Did the data match their predictions?

6. Read *Month by Month a Year Goes Round.* At the end of the book, ask students what the four seasons are and which months are generally associated with each of the four seasons. Use the illustrations in the book to assist students with matching the months to the seasons. Record this information on the board.

7. Students fold a 9" × 12" piece of white construction paper in half vertically and then horizontally. Label the four resulting rectangular regions with the names of each of the four seasons. In each region, students make a sketch of a tree during that season, paying attention to its appearance (e.g., many green leaves in the summer, falling red and orange leaves in the fall, no leaves in the winter, fruit growing on the tree in the spring). Students also sketch an appropriate picture depicting the season (e.g., green grass, rain clouds, flowers blooming, snow falling, etc.).

8. Begin reading *A Busy Year*. Let students announce what month comes next in the book, as it cycles through each of the twelve months beginning with January. Let students make a prediction about what Woody the tree will look like. Then, read the text. Students compare their illustration of each season to the ones in *A Busy Year*.

9. Using butcher paper and markers, each student develops a "Timeline of Me" that uses text and pictures to capture change in appearance during the growth process as well as milestones reached (or soon-to-be reached). The timeline should begin at birth, and each student should label the month, day, and year of his or her birth. Encourage students to sketch themselves as babies, or students can bring in photos of themselves at birth. Students then extend their timelines out to age five or six, make another sketch of themselves (or include a photo), and note on their timelines one major event that occurred between birth and age five to six (e.g., lost a tooth, etc.). Students then extend their timelines out further and note two more events they anticipate will occur and at what ages (e.g., getting a new pet, obtaining a driver's license, traveling out of the country, graduating college, getting married, etc.).

10. Students share their timelines with the class.

Assessment:
- Did students know the names and ordering of the months of the year?
- Did students associate the ordinal number with each month?
- Did students correctly interpret the bar graph?
- Did students correctly associate each season with its corresponding months of the year?
- Did students accurately illustrate a tree's appearance during each of the seasons?
- Did students create accurate timelines?

Activity Extensions:
- Students identify the first, second, third, etc., day of the week by reading *Day by Day a Week Goes Round* (Shields, 1998).
- Share Roca's (2004) books about the seasons so that students can experience and associate more images and ideas with each of the four seasons.
- Create a bar graph or pie chart showing students' favorite season.

Cross-Curricular Connections:

Visual Arts

- View pages 38–41 in *A Child's Book of Art* (Micklethwait, 1993), which display masterpieces illustrating the seasons and weather.

Science

- Begin a unit on weather and the seasons. Use the information appearing in *Sunshine Makes the Seasons* (Branley, 2005) or in *The Reasons for the Seasons* (Gibbons, 1996) to model how the tilt of the earth results in the changing of the seasons.

- Begin a unit on measuring time. Use the information appearing in *What Makes Day and Night* (Branley, 1986) or in *The Reasons for the Seasons* (Gibbons, 1996) to model how the rotation of the earth on its axis results in day and night.

Related Children's Literature

Appel, J., & Guglielmo, A. (2006). *Feed Matisse's fish.* New York: Sterling.

Bader, B. (2003). *All aboard math reader: Graphs.* New York: Grosset & Dunlap.

Branley, F. (2005). *Sunshine makes the seasons.* New York: HarperCollins.

Flood, N. (2006). *The Navajo year, walk through many seasons.* Flagstaff, AZ: Salina Bookshelf.

Fowler, A. (1991). *The sun is always shining somewhere.* Chicago: Children's Press.

Hopkins, L. (1995). *Weather: Poems for all seasons.* New York: HarperCollins.

Leedy, L. (2005). *The great graph contest.* New York: Holiday House.

Lionni, L. (1992). *A busy year.* New York: Knopf.

Llewellyn, C. (1992). *My first book of time.* New York: Dorling Kindersley.

Maher, R. (2003). *Alice Yazzie's year.* Berkeley, CA: Tricycle Press.

Micklethwait, L. (1993). *A child's book of art: Great pictures: First words.* New York: Dorling Kindersley.

Prelutsky, J. (2006). *It's snowing! It's snowing: Winter poems.* New York: HarperCollins.

Roca, N. (2004). *Fall.* Hauppauge, NY: Barron's Educational Series.

Roca, N. (2004). *Spring.* Hauppauge, NY: Barron's Educational Series.

Roca, N. (2004). *Summer.* Hauppauge, NY: Barron's Educational Series.

Roca, N. (2004). *Winter.* Hauppauge, NY: Barron's Educational Series.

Shields, C. (1998). *Day by day a week goes round.* New York: Dutton Children's Books.

Shields, C. (1998). *Month by month a year goes round.* New York: Dutton Children's Books.

Singer, M. (1991). *Nine o'clock lullaby.* New York: Scholastic.

 # Related Instructional Resources

Branley, F. (1986). *What makes day and night.* New York: HarperCollins.

Gibbons, G. (1996). *The reasons for the seasons.* New York: Holiday House.

Mackenzie, F. (1995). *Weather and seasons.* New York: Sterling.

Maestro, B. (1999). *The story of clocks and calendars.* New York: HarperCollins.

Wells, R. (2003). *How do you know what time it is?* Morton Grove, IL: Whitman.

Related Websites

Create a Graph Online
>http://nces.ed.gov/nceskids/createagraph/

Months of the Year Poems and Songs
>http://www.4to40.com/poems/index.asp?article=poems_months
>http://www.4to40.com/poems/print.asp?article=poems_months
>http://gardenofpraise.com/spanish4.htm

Months of the Year Word Search
>http://www.puzzle-club.com/word-searches-kids-months.m.html

Seasons
>http://www.kathimitchell.com/seasons.htm
>http://www.christiananswers.net/kids/edn-seasons.html
>http://www.zoomschool.com/themes/seasons.shtml
>http://edtech.kennesaw.edu/web/seasons.htm

If All the Seas Were One Sea (1996)

by Janina Domanska

Aladdin Paperbacks, ISBN #0689803435

Overview of Book: Enjoy this Mother Goose rhyme, coupled with colored etchings, and speculate what would happen if all the seas were one sea.

Mathematical Concepts and Skills: prediction, estimation, data creation and interpretation, bar graphs

Social Studies Concepts and Skills: features on a globe, oceans, landmasses, map interpretation

Overview of Activities: Students predict how much land and water covers the earth by first observing a globe or map. Students then collect data and create a bar graph depicting the number of times a rolling globe was stopped on water versus land. Students compare their predictions to the results of their experiments and to the actual percentages of water versus land. Students then respond to a writing prompt regarding the oceans.

National Mathematics Standards (2000): Students in preK–2 should "pose questions and gather data about themselves and their surroundings" and "represent data using concrete objects, pictures, and graphs." Students should also "describe parts of the data and the set of data as a whole to determine what the data show" (Data Analysis and Probability Standard) (p. 400).

National Social Studies Standards (1994): Social studies programs for early grades should include experiences that provide for the study of *people, places, and environments,* so that the learner can "interpret, use, and distinguish various representations of the earth, such as maps, globes, and photographs"; "locate and distinguish among varying landforms and geographical features, such as mountains, plateaus, islands, and oceans"; and "construct and use mental maps of locales, regions, and the world that demonstrate understanding of relative location, direction, size, and shape" (p. 54).

Materials: large globe, large map of the world, blue sticky notes, green sticky notes, construction paper, crayons or markers

Description of Activities:

1. Begin a discussion about maps by asking students what a map is, what information is given on a map, what a map is used for, and different maps they have seen. Let students view a large world map to assist them in this discussion.

2. Hold up a globe for students to see. Spin the globe to allow students to see all of the continents and their location on the globe (or students can also view a large map of the world). As you continue to spin the globe slowly, ask students if they think there is more water or land-masses covering the earth. Ask them if we were to spin the globe and stop it without looking, whether it would be more likely that our finger landed on water or on a landmass. Let students explain their reasoning.

3. Move to a space such that students can sit in a large circle. Let one student roll the globe across the circle to another student. As the globe approaches, the second student momentarily shuts his or her eyes, stops the globe with one finger, and then announces whether his or her finger is pointing to water or land. On the board (or on a large piece of butcher paper) record the word WATER and, underneath it, record the word LAND. Place a blue sticky note next to the word WATER, if the student's finger is pointing to water, or a green sticky note next to the word LAND, indicating the student stopped the globe on a landmass.

4. Repeat this activity approximately twenty to thirty times, gathering data with each roll of the globe, and placing a sticky note on the horizontal bar graph.

5. Students examine the data. Which row contains more sticky notes? How many times more? What does the data mean? Inform students that the row labeled WATER ought to have about three times as many sticky notes as the row labeled LAND since three times as much water covers the earth as land (i.e., three-quarters of the earth is covered with water and only one-quarter of the earth is covered with land). Spin the globe slowly so that students can see that much more water than landmasses covers the earth. Now that students know how much water covers the earth, how accurate were their original predictions?

6. Encourage students to use their imaginations and to respond to the prompt, "If All the Seas Were One Sea . . ." What would this look like and mean? Students respond verbally or in writing and create a supporting illustration. Hang their work around the room for all to view.

7. Read *If All the Seas Were One Sea*. Did their illustrations match the poem's finale? Begin a discussion about and identify the different oceans that cover the earth.

Assessment:

- Did students participate in a discussion about maps?

- Did students make reasonable predictions regarding the amount of water versus landmasses covering the earth?

- Did students correctly interpret the data they gathered and the resulting bar graph?

- Did students notice that more water covers the earth than landmasses?

- Did students respond to the prompt, "If All the Seas Were One Sea . . ."?

Activity Extensions:

- Readers enjoy a variety of poems about world geography, travelers, and map terminology in *A World of Wonders: Geographic Travels in Verse and Rhyme* (Lewis, 2002).

- Explore other bodies of water such as the Great Lakes or major rivers (e.g., Nile, Amazon, Yangtze, etc.).

- Using a globe, discuss and locate lines of latitude, longitude, the equator, northern and southern hemispheres, etc.

- Explore, discuss, and illustrate other Mother Goose nursery rhymes using the Mother Goose Nursery Rhymes website listed below.

Cross-Curricular Connections:

Visual Arts

- Students look at a globe (or large map of the world) and paint the shape of the seven continents on a Styrofoam sphere in green and the remaining areas in blue, representing the oceans.

- Students view the If All the Seas Were One Sea in Rebus website and write the verse *If All the Seas Were One Sea* in rebus.

Science

- Using the book *Geography from A to Z* (Knowlton, 1988) or *Usborne Children's Picture Atlas* (Brocklehurst, 2004), students learn about the climate and weather in various countries and continents.

Related Children's Literature

Adler, D. (1991). *A picture book of Christopher Columbus.* New York: Scholastic.

Asch, F. (1994). *The earth and I.* New York: Scholastic.

Bell, N. (1982). *The book of where: Or how to be naturally geographic* (A brown paper schoolbook series). New York: Little, Brown.

Brocklehurst, R. (2004). *Usborne children's picture atlas.* New York: Scholastic.

Chesanow, N. (1995). *Where do I live?* Hauppauge, NY: Barron's Educational Series.

Domanska, J. (1996). *If all the seas were one sea.* New York: Aladdin Paperbacks.

Fanelli, S. (1995). *My map book.* New York: HarperCollins.

Gibbons, G. (1995). *Planet Earth/Inside out.* New York: Morrow.

Hartman, G. (1993). *As the crow flies: A first book of maps.* New York: Aladdin Paperbacks.

Knowlton, J. (1985). *Maps and globes.* New York: HarperCollins.

Knowlton, J. (1988). *Geography from A to Z: A picture glossary.* New York: HarperCollins.

Leedy, L. (2003). *Mapping Penny's world.* New York: Holt.

Lewis, J. (2002). *A world of wonders: Geographic travels in verse and rhyme.* New York: Dial Books for Young Readers.

Marzollo, J. (2001). *I am planet Earth.* New York: Scholastic.

Rabe, T. (2002). *There's a map in my lap!* New York: Random House Children's Books.

Rockwell, A. (1998). *Our earth.* New York: Scholastic.

Singer, M. (1991). *Nine o'clock lullaby.* New York: Scholastic.

Sweeney, J. (1996). *Me on the map.* New York: Dragonfly Books.

Sweeney, J. (1998). *Me and my place in space.* New York: Dragonfly Books.

Related Instructional Resources

Taylor, B. (1993). *Maps and mapping* (Young discoveries series). New York: Kingfisher.

Ward, R. (2006). Paul Revere's mathematical ride: Integrating geography, mathematics, and children's literature. *Arizona Reading Journal, 32*(1), 24–26.

Ward, R. (January, 2006). One if by land; *three* if by sea? *Mathematics Teaching, 194,* 20–21.

Wolfman, I. (2003). *My world and globe.* New York: Workman.

Related Websites

If All the Seas Were One Sea in Rebus

      http://www.enchantedlearning.com/rhymes/ifalltheseas.shtml

Maps for Kids

      http://www.kidsdomain.com/kids/links/Maps.html

      http://www.nationalgeographic.com/homework/

Mother Goose Nursery Rhymes

      http://www.apples4theteacher.com/mother-goose-nursery-rhymes/index.html

National Geographic GeoSpy Interactive Game

      http://www.nationalgeographic.com/geospy/

Ocean Facts

      http://www.mos.org/oceans/planet/index.html

Outline and Printable Maps

      http://www.eduplace.com/ss/maps/

      http://www.nationalgeographic.com/xpeditions/atlas/

So You Want to Be President? (2000)
by Judith St. George
Philomel Books, ISBN #0399234071

First Pets: Presidential Best Friends (2004)
by Nell Fuqua
Scholastic, ISBN #043959846X

Overview of Books:	Enjoy the hilarious anecdotes in *So You Want to Be President?,* which detail the lives of those men who have held the powerful position of president of the United States. In *First Pets: Presidential Best Friends,* learn the names and idiosyncrasies of the more than four hundred animals that have served as pets and faithful friends to U.S. presidents.
Mathematical Concepts and Skills:	data analysis and interpretation, pie charts
Social Studies Concepts and Skills:	duties and responsibilities of the president, qualities of a leader, U.S. presidents
Overview of Activities:	Students discuss the duties and responsibilities of the U.S. president as well as the qualities of a leader. Students interpret pie charts depicting data about the pets owned by U.S. presidents. Students illustrate a presidential poster and record what they would do or change if they were elected president of the United States.
National Mathematics Standards (2000):	Students in preK–2 should "pose questions and gather data about themselves and their surroundings." Students should also "represent data using concrete objects, pictures, and graphs" and "describe parts of the data and the set of data as a whole to determine what the data show" (Data Analysis and Probability Standard) (p. 400). Students in preK–2 should "count with understanding and recognize 'how many' in sets of objects" (Number and Operations Standard) (p. 392).
National Social Studies Standards (1994):	Social studies programs for early grades should include experiences that provide for the study of *how people create and change structures of power, authority, and governance,* so that the learner can "explain the purpose of government"; "distinguish among local, state, and national government, and identify representative leaders at these levels such as mayor, governor, and president" (p. 63).

Materials: map of the United States, 8.5" × 11" white construction paper, 9" × 12" red and blue construction paper, markers or crayons

Description of Activities:

1. Ask students to name the current president of the United States. Ask students what duties and responsibilities they think the job of the president entails. Begin a discussion about whether they would want to serve as president and why. What knowledge and traits make a successful president or leader? Where does the president live? How many presidents have there been? Who was the first president of the United States? Show students where Washington, D.C., is located on a map. Consider sharing images of the White House and portraits of former presidents using the websites below.

2. Begin reading all or select portions of *So You Want to Be President?*

3. At the end of the book, ask students to respond to the following writing prompt: "If I were president of the United States, I would . . ." In responding to this question, encourage students to think about important local or world issues and how they might be able to make the world a better place if they were president. Record students' responses on paper.

4. Using 8.5" × 11" white construction paper, each student creates a portrait of himself or herself as president. Mount their self-portraits onto 9" × 12" red or blue construction paper. Attach students' written responses to "If I were president of the United States, I would . . ." below. Hang the posters, alternating red and blue, around the classroom for all students to view, discuss, and enjoy.

5. Give students practice understanding and interpreting pie charts while learning the names of several U.S. presidents and their pets by sharing information from *First Pets*. Using the Create a Graph Online website, create a pie chart of the pets owned by one of the presidents. Students examine the pie chart and make sense of the data by comparing a table of values (listing the number of pets) to the pie chart. Assist students in graphically interpreting the data by asking such questions as: Why is the red (or color of your choice) pie sector the largest? What would happen to the size of the red sector if we changed the data to include one more dog? Why are the red and green pie sectors the same size? Students should explain their reasoning. Assist students in making connections between the numerical data in the table and the size of each sector in the pie chart.

6. Older students compare two pie charts depicting the number of pets owned by two different presidents (e.g., Jefferson and Tyler, or Wilson and Hayes). Students examine the pie charts and discuss and compare the data. Assist students in graphically interpreting the pie charts by asking such questions as: Who owned more birds? More horses? Did these two presidents own the same total number of pets? Students should explain their reasoning.

7. Share with students select passages that accompany each president's page in *First Pets*, which describe the idiosyncrasies and unusual names and characteristics of many of the presidents' pets.

Assessment:

- Did students participate in the discussion about the president's duties and responsibilities?

- Did students articulate what they would change or do if they were president?

- Did each student create a self-portrait that represented himself or herself as president?

- Did students correctly interpret pie charts?

Activity Extensions:

- Students gain practice learning their ordinal numbers by naming the first, second, third, etc. president of the United States.

- Throughout the book *So You Want to Be President?*, many statistics are provided (name frequency of presidents, their heights, the ages when they became president, number of siblings, number of pets, state in which they were born, instruments played by presidents, presidents who were college graduates, etc.). Students create a bar graph or pictograph depicting a particular set of data. Students share and discuss their graphs with the class.

- Hold a mock election in class.

Cross-Curricular Connections:

Visual Arts

- Visit images of and locate facts about Mount Rushmore, located in South Dakota and created by the sculptor Gutzon Borglum, which features the heads of former presidents Washington, Jefferson, Theodore Roosevelt, and Lincoln.

Science

- Using *What Presidents Are Made Of* (Piven, 2004) or other resources, research and discuss which presidents were inventors and dabbled in science.

Related Children's Literature

Bader, B. (2003). *All aboard math reader: Graphs*. New York: Grosset & Dunlap.

Cronin, D. (2004). *Duck for president*. New York: Simon & Schuster Books for Young Readers.

Davis, G. (2004). *Wackiest White House pets*. New York: Scholastic.

Davis, K. (2002). *Don't know much about the presidents*. New York: HarperCollins.

Fuqua, N. (2004). *First pets: Presidential best friends*. New York: Scholastic.

Goldman, D. (2004). *Presidential losers*. Minneapolis: Lerner.

Gordon, P., & Snow, R. (2004). *Kids learn America! Bringing geography to life with people, places & history*. Charlotte, VT: Williamson.

Grandfield, L. (2003). *America votes: How our president is elected*. Tonawanda, NY: Kids Can Press.

Grodin, E. (2004). *D is for democracy: A citizen's alphabet*. Chelsea, MI: Sleeping Bear Press.

Keenan, S. (2004). *O, say can you see?: America's symbols, landmarks, and important words*. New York: Scholastic.

Keller, L. (2002). *Scrambled states of America*. New York: Holt.

Krull, K. (2004). *A woman for president: The story of Victoria Woodhull*. New York: Walker Books for Young Readers.

Landau, E. (2003). *The president's work: A look at the executive branch* (How government works series). Minneapolis: Lerner.

Lay, K. (2004). *Crown me!* New York: Holiday House.

Leedy, L. (2005). *The great graph contest*. New York: Holiday House.

Piven, H. (2004). *What presidents are made of*. New York: Antheneum Books for Young Readers.

Provensen, A. (1997). *The buck stops here: The president of the United States of America*. New York: Browndeer Press Paperbacks.

Rubel, D. (1994). *Scholastic encyclopedia of the presidents and their times*. New York: Scholastic.

Scillian, D. (2001). *A is for America: An American alphabet*. Chelsea, MI: Sleeping Bear Press.

Scillian, D. (2002). *One nation: America by the numbers*. Chelsea, MI: Sleeping Bear Press.

Sis, P. (2003). *The train of states*. New York: Greenwillow Books.

Smith, R., & Smith, M. (2005). *N is for our nation's capital: A Washington, DC, alphabet* (Discover America state by state alphabet series). Chelsea, MI: Sleeping Bear Press.

Sobel, S. (1999). *How the U.S. government works*. Hauppauge, NY: Barron's Educational Series.

Sobel, S. (2001). *Presidential elections: And other cool facts*. Hauppauge, NY: Barron's Educational Series.

St. George, J. (2000). *So you want to be president?* New York: Philomel Books.

Sullivan, G. (1987). *Facts and fun about the presidents*. New York: Scholastic.

Thimmesh, C. (2004). *Madame President: The extraordinary, true, (and evolving) story of women in politics*. Boston: Houghton Mifflin.

Related Instructional Resources

Bateman, T. (1989). *Red, white, blue, and Uncle Who? The stories behind some of America's patriotic symbols.* New York: Holiday House.

Buller, J., Schade, S., Cocca-Leffler, M., Holub, J., Kelley, T., & Regan, D. (2003). *Smart about the fifty states: A class report.* New York: Grosset & Dunlap.

Cheney, L. (2002). *America: A patriotic primer.* New York: Simon & Schuster Books for Young Readers.

Cheney, L. (2003). *A is for Abigail: An almanac of amazing American women.* New York: Simon & Schuster Books for Young Readers.

Cheney, L. (2005). *A time for freedom: What happened when in America.* New York: Simon & Schuster.

Cheney, L. (2006). *Our 50 states.* New York: Simon & Schuster Books for Young Readers.

Davis, K. (2004). *Don't know much about the 50 states* (Don't know much about series). New York: HarperTrophy.

Devrian Global Industries. (2006). *States activities book.* Union, NJ: Author.

Hauser, J. (2004). *Celebrate America: Learning about the USA through crafts & activities.* Charlotte, VT: Williamson.

Murphy, F. (2002). *Our country.* New York: Scholastic Professional Books.

Related Websites

Create a Graph Online
> http://nces.ed.gov/nceskids/createagraph/

First Ladies
> http://www.whitehouse.gov/history/firstladies/

Mount Rushmore
> http://www.mtrushmore.net/

Presidents of the United States of America
> http://www.worldalmanacforkids.com/explore/presidents.html
> http://www.whitehouse.gov/history/presidents/
> http://www.funbrain.com/who/

White House—For Kids
> http://www.whitehouse.gov/kids/

Who Uses This? (1990)

by Margaret Miller

Greenwillow Books, ISBN #0688082793

ABC of Jobs (2003)

by Roger Priddy

St. Martin's Press, ISBN #0439846315

Overview of Books:	Find out exactly "who uses this" by viewing photographs of tools and objects used by individuals in various trades, professions, and hobbies in *Who Uses This?* Then, in the *ABC of Jobs*, learn about twenty-six careers, one for each letter of the alphabet, and the duties and responsibilities of individuals working in these jobs.
Mathematical Concepts and Skills:	real-life applications of mathematics, careers in mathematics, jobs and careers requiring mathematical skills and knowledge
Social Studies Concepts and Skills:	careers, specialized role of individuals in a community
Overview of Activities:	Students discuss the math skills and knowledge and other qualities individuals in various careers must possess to be successful. Students describe the importance and contributions of certain jobs within a community.
National Mathematics Standards (2000):	Students in preK–2 should "recognize and apply mathematics in contexts outside of mathematics" (Connections Standard) (p. 402).

National Social Studies Standards (1994):

Social studies programs for early grades should include experiences that provide for the study of *how people organize for the production, distribution, and consumption of goods and services,* so that the learner can "describe how we depend upon workers with specialized jobs and the ways in which they contribute to the production and exchange of goods and services" (p. 65). Social studies programs for early grades should also include experiences that provide for the study of *relationships among science, technology, and society,* so that the learner can "identify and describe examples in science and technology that have changed the lives of people, such as home-making, child care, work, transportation, and communication" (p. 67).

Materials:

pages copied out of *ABC of Jobs,* 9" × 12" posterboard, crayons or markers

Description of Activities:

1. Engage students in a discussion about careers. Ask students what they want to be when they grow up and why. What skills, knowledge, talents, and qualities do they need to be successful in this job? What math skills and knowledge might they need to be successful in this job?

2. Begin reading *Who Uses This?* Let students view the photo and then guess who uses this tool or object before revealing the answer on the next page.

3. At the end of the book, revisit select pages and ask students what math skills they might need to be successful in these jobs (e.g., a carpenter and baker both need to be good at measuring; a gardener must know how big his or her garden or land is and how many seeds and trees to plant; a conductor must know how to count beats, etc.).

4. Place students into small groups. Copy several pages out of *ABC of Jobs* and distribute one copy to each group. Students work collaboratively to discuss and record the math skills and other qualities these individuals must have to be successful. Students present their findings to the class.

5. Using 9" × 12" posterboard and crayons or markers, students create an illustration of themselves in their future careers, showing the uniforms they would wear (if any) and the tools they would use. Students record on separate pieces of paper the math skills they will use in their jobs and attach them to the bottom or back of the posterboard. Students also describe why their jobs are important to members in their community.

Assessment:

- Did students clearly articulate their thoughts regarding future careers?

- Did students make accurate guesses as to who uses certain tools or objects appearing in *Who Uses This?*

- Did students create an illustration of themselves in future careers and articulate the math skills needed in their desired careers as well as why their jobs are important to the community?

Activity Extensions:

- Students interview friends or family members about their careers and share their findings with the class.

- Ask local professionals or working parents to visit the classroom to discuss their jobs or careers (e.g., scientist, veterinarian, artist, police officer, coach, etc.), with a focus on the mathematical skills and knowledge they use in their jobs.

- Visit the Bureau of Labor Statistics—Choosing a Career website on which students can read about aspects of various jobs, such as duties and responsibilities, salaries, potential for future jobs, etc.

Cross-Curricular Connections:

Visual Arts

- Students visit the What Do You Want to Be? interactive website and select a career, put on a uniform, and then print and color it.

Science

- Discuss jobs in the sciences (doctor, nurse, zoologist, geologist, marine biologist, astronomer, etc.).

Related Children's Literature

Hayward, L. (2001). *A day in the life of a builder*. New York: Dorling Kindersley.

Hayward, L. (2001). *A day in the life of a dancer*. New York: Dorling Kindersley.

Hayward, L. (2001). *A day in the life of a doctor*. New York: Dorling Kindersley.

Hayward, L. (2001). *A day in the life of a firefighter*. New York: Dorling Kindersley.

Hayward, L. (2001). *A day in the life of a musician*. New York: Dorling Kindersley.

Hayward, L. (2001). *A day in the life of a police officer*. New York: Dorling Kindersley.

Hayward, L. (2001). *A day in the life of a teacher*. New York: Dorling Kindersley.

Kalman, B. (1997). *Community helpers from A to Z*. New York: Crabtree.

Kupchella, R. (2004). *Girls can! Make it happen*. Golden Valley, MN: Tristan.

Miller, M. (1990). *Who uses this?* New York: Greenwillow Books.

Priddy, R. (2003). *ABC of jobs*. New York: St. Martin's Press.

Related Instructional Resources

Marzollo, J. (1994). *My first book of biographies: Great men and women every child should know*. New York: Scholastic.

Saunders, H. (1988). *When are we ever gonna have to use this?* Palo Alto, CA: Seymour.

Related Websites

Bureau of Labor Statistics—Choosing a Career
http://www.bls.gov/k12/

Career Information
http://www.bls.gov/k12/
http://www.kids.gov/k_careers.htm
http://www.kathimitchell.com/careers.htm

What Do You Want to Be?
http://www.econedlink.org/lessons/em207/flash/activity1.html

Literature-Based Mathematics and Visual Arts Activities

The Mathematics—Visual Arts Connection

The arts (visual art, music, movement, and drama) present an ideal and unique forum through which children and students can express their ideas, thoughts, and emotions. In particular, the visual arts, which range from "drawing, painting, sculpture, and design, to architecture, film, video, and folk arts" (MENC, 1994, p. 33), embody mathematics, as students can explore such interrelated concepts as patterns, line, shape, and form. A growing body

123

of evidence documents that learning in the arts involves principles shared with other academic disciplines (Bransford et al., 2004; Deasy, 2002; Fiske, 1999; Scripp, 2002). Thus, integrating the arts with other content areas is mounting (Bickley-Green, 1995; Efland, 2002; McDonald & Fisher, 2006; Muller & Ward, 2007; Phillips & Bickley-Green, 1998; Walling, 2005; Ward & Muller, 2006). Further, while learning the characteristics of and mathematics embedded in the visual arts, students can collaboratively engage in communicating, reasoning, and investigating, activities that both the NCTM (1989, 2000) and MENC (1994) strongly advocate. In his book, *Arts with the Brain in Mind,* Jensen (2001) argues that the "visual arts seem to be strongest when used as a tool for academic learning" (p. 58). Further, Eisner (1998, 2004) cites many studies that report strong links between visual learning and improvement in reading and creativity.

"The visual arts embody interrelated mathematics concepts such as patterns, line, shape, and form."

This chapter articulates a variety of literature-based activities that integrate concepts and skills used and learned in the study of mathematics with those in the visual arts. While engaged in these activities, students will discover and gain practice with such mathematics concepts and skills as counting, numerals, number names, greater than, less than, equal to, grouping, addition (Number and Operations Standard); writing number sentences, creating geometric and repeating patterns (Algebra Standard); points, lines, line segments, angles, curves, two- and three-dimensional shapes, symmetry, line symmetry, reflections, spatial reasoning (Geometry Standard); comparison of size and length (Measurement Standard); and likelihood, probability, random events (Data Analysis and Probability Standard).

Art concepts and skills featured in this chapter include line, shape, color, value, texture, form, space, art history, and using various art mediums. While exploring mathematics, students will simultaneously learn about and mimic the work of such artists as Josef Albers, Salvador Dali, Henri Matisse, Joan Miro, Piet Mondrian, Jackson Pollock, and others.

The integrated literature-based activities also provide students with many opportunities to predict, estimate, problem-solve, and reason (Problem

Solving and Reasoning and Proof Standards) as well as communicate and use various representations to organize, record, model, and interpret mathematical ideas (Communication and Representation Standards). Further, students will discover and explore real-life applications of mathematics and the visual arts and careers in mathematics and the visual arts (Connections Standard).

Remember to check the appendix for ideas and samples of assessment rubrics.

Matrix of Mathematics and Visual Arts Activities

BOOK TITLE	MATHEMATICAL CONCEPTS AND SKILLS	VISUAL ARTS CONCEPTS AND SKILLS	SCIENCE CONCEPTS AND SKILLS	SOCIAL STUDIES CONCEPTS AND SKILLS
I Spy Two Eyes: Numbers in Art; Museum 1 2 3	counting, numerals, number names	creating art (a book of illustrations), art history (various artistic styles)	create an animal number book	exploration of other civilizations' number systems
"How Many, How Much" (a poem in *A Light in the Attic*); *More, Fewer, Less; A Child's Book of Art*	counting, greater than, less than, equal to	creating art (collage), art history (various artistic styles)	compare and contrast quantities in nature	history of money and the minting process
12 Ways to Get to 11; Math-terpieces	grouping, addition, writing number sentences, algebra, problem solving	art history (various artistic styles), creation of a piece of artwork in a particular style of art	stars and constellations	exploration of a biographical piece
Follow the Line; Henri Matisse (Getting to Know the World's Greatest Artists Series)	creating geometric and repeating patterns, lines, line segments, horizontal lines, vertical lines, diagonal lines, curves, shapes	line, shape, color, value, form, space, creating art (lined patterns and a mural), art history (the work of Henri Matisse)	patterns of camouflage in animal skin and fur	lines of latitude and longitude and the equator on a globe, exploration of a biographical piece
When a Line Bends . . . A Shape Begins; Coyote Places the Stars	points, line segments, angles, shapes, attributes of shapes	line, shape, creating art (chalk drawing)	astronomy, animal characteristics and habitats	exploration of a biographical piece of an astronomer
Rectangles (City Shapes Series); *Squares* (City Shapes Series); *Mondrian* (Great Modern Masters Series)	lines, rectangles, squares, attributes of shapes, real-life examples of shapes	line, shape, color, creating art (Mondrian-like work), art history (abstract period and the work of Piet Mondrian)	primary and secondary colors, lines of latitude and longitude	shapes in architecture, exploration of a biographical piece
I Spy Shapes in Art	characteristics and properties of two- and three-dimensional shapes	shape, color, form, space, creating art (abstract art or synthetic cubism), art history (various artistic styles)	examples of shapes in nature	shapes in the architecture, exploration of a biographical piece

BOOK TITLE	MATHEMATICAL CONCEPTS AND SKILLS	VISUAL ARTS CONCEPTS AND SKILLS	SCIENCE CONCEPTS AND SKILLS	SOCIAL STUDIES CONCEPTS AND SKILLS
The Butterfly Counting Book	line symmetry, reflection, shapes, geometric patterns, pattern recognition, counting, odd numbers	line, shape, color, creating art (symmetric art, mobile making), art history (symmetry in Salvador Dali's works containing butterflies)	lifecycle of a butterfly, migration of the monarch butterfly, symmetry in snowflakes and in nature	geography, exploration of a biographical piece, symmetry in flags
The Best Bug Parade; Baby Einstein: The ABCs of Art	comparison of size and length, measurement	line, shape, color, value, creating art (watercolor painting), art history (the work of Josef Albers)	insects, microscopes and magnifying lenses; biggest, strongest, and fastest animals	migration of the monarch butterfly, exploration of a biographical piece
"A Closet Full of Shoes" (a poem in *Falling Up*); Joan Miro (Famous Artists Series)	likelihood, probability, random events, prediction	line, shape, color, form, space, creating art (surrealist art), art history (the work of Joan Miro)	stars and constellations	geography and demographics of the Catalonia region of Spain

Activities Featuring Number and Operations

I Spy Two Eyes: Numbers in Art (1993)

by Lucy Micklethwait

Greenwillow Books, ISBN #0688161588

Museum 1 2 3 (2004)

by The Metropolitan Museum of Art

Little, Brown, ISBN #031616044X

Overview of Books: In both of these books, young readers count objects in a variety of artistic masterpieces while exploring various styles of paintings.

Mathematical Concepts and Skills: counting, numerals, number names

Visual Arts Concepts and Skills: creating art (a book of illustrations), art history (various artistic styles)

Overview of Activities: Students count quantities of objects in famous pieces of artwork while observing the different styles of painting (impressionist, abstract, still life, etc.). Students work in groups to create a collection of their own artwork in the form of a book, created in a particular style, picturing quantities of objects in numerical order.

National Mathematics Standards (2000): Students in preK–2 should "count with understanding and recognize 'how many' in sets of objects." They should also "connect number words and numerals to the quantities they represent, using various physical models and representations" (Number and Operations Standard) (p. 392).

National Visual Arts Standards (1994): Students should understand and apply media, techniques, and processes (Content Standard 1) and "use different media, techniques, and processes to communicate ideas, experiences, and stories" (Achievement Standard c) (p. 34); understand the visual arts in relation to history and cultures (Content Standard 4) and "identify specific works of art as belonging to particular cultures, times, and places" (Achievement Standard b) (p. 34); make connections between visual arts and other disciplines (Content Standard 6) and "identify connections between the visual arts and other disciplines in the curriculum" (Achievement Standard b) (p. 35).

Materials: coloring medium (oil or tempera paints, water colors, pastels, crayons or markers, etc.), 9" × 12" white construction paper, hole punch, yarn or ribbon

Description of Activities:

1. Read *I Spy Two Eyes*. As you read, ask individual students to identify and count aloud the objects featured. Inform students of the title of each painting and its artist. For select paintings, name the style of painting (e.g., impression, abstract, still life, pop art, etc.). Ask students to describe the characteristics of each style of painting that they notice. Ask students what they like and do not like about each style of painting.

2. Next, show select pages (but not in numerical order) from *Museum 1 2 3*. Students observe the collection of paintings and determine what number of objects is featured in all of the paintings on that page and name that number. Again, point out the various styles of paintings. Ask students to continue describing the characteristics of each painting that they notice.

3. Divide the class in half (two groups of approximately ten students) and let each group pick a theme (e.g., flowers, weather, animals, etc.) for their book. Each student is assigned one number to illustrate (in terms of quantity) in his or her group. Consider selecting a particular style of art from the book (e.g., abstract, pop art, etc.) and asking students to create their illustrations as would an abstract artist or pop artist, etc.

4. Give each student a piece of 9" × 12" white construction paper. At the top, students write, "I spy . . ." and fill in the prompt with the number and name of the object (e.g., I spy 3 tulips.). Using an appropriate coloring medium (oil or tempera paints, water colors, pastels, crayons or markers, etc.), students create a picture featuring their assigned number.

5. Once the illustrations are complete, students collate the pages of their group's book in numerical order, creating a book of artwork similar to *I Spy Two Eyes* and *Museum 1 2 3*. Bind each group's book using yarn or ribbon. Both groups share their work and count the objects appearing on the pages of both books.

Assessment:

- Did students accurately count objects?
- Did students create a piece of artwork featuring their assigned number?

Activity Extensions:

- Collate the pages in the groups' books in descending numerical order, creating a counting back in art book.

- Look for shapes in masterpieces appearing in *Museum Shapes* (The Metropolitan Museum of Art, 2005) and *I Spy Shapes in Art* (Micklethwait, 2004).

Cross-Curricular Connections:

Science

- Research, create, and illustrate a number book of animals featuring animals and their body parts (e.g., swordfish have one "sword," a chicken has 2 wings, a sloth has 3 toes, etc.). Refer to *One Is a Snail, Ten Is a Crab* (Sayre & Sayre, 2003) or *Teeth, Tails, & Tentacles: An Animal Counting Book* (Wormell, 2004) as references.

Social Studies

- Explore number systems of other civilizations (e.g., Egyptian, Roman, etc.).

Related Children's Literature

Aigner-Clark, J. (2002). *Baby Einstein: The ABCs of art*. New York: Hyperion Books for Children.

Alda, A. (1998). *Arlene Alda's 1 2 3: What do you see?* Berkeley, CA: Tricycle Press.

Anno, M. (1975). *Anno's counting book*. New York: HarperCollins.

Hoban, T. (1999). *Let's count*. New York: Greenwillow Books.

The Metropolitan Museum of Art. (2004). *Museum 1 2 3*. New York: Little, Brown.

The Metropolitan Museum of Art. (2005). *Museum shapes*. New York: Little, Brown.

Micklethwait, L. (1993). *I spy two eyes: Numbers in art*. New York: Greenwillow Books.

Micklethwait, L. (2004). *I spy shapes in art*. New York: Greenwillow Books.

Rose, D. (2003). *One nighttime sea*. New York: Scholastic.

Sayre, A., & Sayre, J. (2003). *One is a snail, ten is a crab*. Cambridge, MA: Candlewick Press.

Wormell, C. (2004). *Teeth, tails, & tentacles: An animal counting book*. Philadelphia: Running Press.

Related Instructional Resources

Dickins, R. (2005). *The children's book of art: An introduction to famous paintings*. London: Usborne.

Evans, J., & Skelton, T. (2001). *How to teach art to children*. Monterey, CA: Evan-Moor.

Kohl, M., & Gainer, C. (1996). *MathArts: Exploring math through art for 3 to 6 year olds*. Beltsville, MD: Gryphon House.

Kohl, M., & Solga, K. (1996). *Discovering great artists: Hands-on art for children in the styles of the great masters*. Bellingham, WA: Bright Ring.

Krull, K. (1995). *Lives of the artists: Masterpieces, messes*. San Diego: Harcourt Brace.

Press, J. (2001). *Around the world art & activities: Visiting the 7 continents through craft fun*. Charlotte, VT: Williamson.

Renshaw, A., & Ruggi, G. (2005). *The art book for children*. New York: Phaidon Press.

Scieszka, J., & Smith, L. (2005). *Seen art?* New York: Viking Press.

Williams, D. (1995). *Teaching mathematics through children's art*. Portsmouth, NH: Heinemann.

Related Websites

Guggenheim Museum
    http://www.guggenheim.org/new_york_index.shtml

The Metropolitan Museum of Art
    http://www.metmuseum.org/home.asp

"How Many, How Much" (a poem in *A Light in the Attic*) (1981)

by Shel Silverstein

HarperCollins, ISBN #0066236177

More, Fewer, Less (1998)

by Tana Hoban

Greenwillow Books, ISBN #0688156932

A Child's Book of Art (1993)

by Lucy Micklethwait

Dorling Kindersley, ISBN #1564582035

Overview of Poem and Books:	Stretch students' imaginations by trying to answer the title questions in Silverstein's poem, "How Many, How Much." In the wordless book, *More, Fewer, Less,* young readers count what there are more of and fewer of in each colorful photo. Then, explore the world of artistic masterpieces in *A Child's Book of Art.*
Mathematical Concepts and Skills:	counting, greater than, less than, equal to
Visual Arts Concepts and Skills:	creating art (collage), art history (various artistic styles)
Overview of Activities:	Students count and compare quantities of objects in real-life photos as well as in famous pieces of artwork. Students then create a collage featuring objects of varying quantities, challenging their classmates to determine what there is more of, fewer of, and less of.
National Mathematics Standards (2000):	Students in preK–2 should "count with understanding and recognize 'how many' in sets of objects." They should also "connect number words and numerals to the quantities they represent, using various physical models and representations" (Number and Operations Standard) (p. 392).

National Visual Arts Standards (1994):

Students should understand and apply media, techniques, and processes (Content Standard 1) and "use different media, techniques, and processes to communicate ideas, experiences, and stories" (Achievement Standard c) (p. 34); use knowledge of structures and functions (Content Standard 2) and "use visual structures and functions of art to communicate ideas" (Achievement Standard c) (p. 34); choose and evaluate a range of subject matter, symbols, and ideas (Content Standard 3) and "select and use subject matter, symbols, and ideas to communicate meaning" (Achievement Standard b) (p. 34); and make connections between visual arts and other disciplines (Content Standard 6) and "identify connections between the visual arts and other disciplines in the curriculum" (Achievement Standard b) (p. 35).

Materials: 9" × 12" white posterboard, magazines, scissors, gluesticks

Description of Activities:

1. Read Silverstein's "How Many, How Much," to set the stage for the upcoming activity in which students compare quantities of objects.

2. Engage students in a brief activity to encourage counting and comparisons of quantities. For example, ask students to look around the classroom and determine if there are more boys than girls in the class. Are there fewer students with blonde hair than with black hair? In comparing two quantities, what is there less of? The same of?

3. Begin showing all or select photos from *More, Fewer, Less*. Ask students to describe on each page what there is more of, fewer of, and less of. Are there equal quantities of objects in any of the photos?

4. Select particular works of art to show to the class in *A Child's Book of Art*. Ask students to examine the works of art and to determine what there is more of, fewer of, and less of. Ask students how many more of a quantity would be needed to make the same as another quantity. For example, in *Composition* by Bart van der Leck (p. 32), are there more triangles or squares? Fewer red shapes or yellow shapes? In Gonzales Coques's *The Family of Jan-Baptista Anthoine* (p. 6), are there fewer children or adults? Fewer horses or dogs?

5. Give students a piece of 9" × 12" white posterboard, magazines, scissors, and gluesticks. Students create a collage of images and challenge their classmates to determine what there is more of, fewer of, and less of.

Assessment:
- Did students accurately count objects?
- Did students correctly identify what there is more of, fewer of, and less of?
- Did students create a collage and then challenge classmates to compare and contrast quantities of objects?

Activity Extensions:
- Continue exploring counting and comparing quantities by reading *How Many Snails?* and *How Many Blue Birds Flew Away?* (Giganti, 1988, 2005).

- Have students estimate the weight of objects and determine what weighs more or less (e.g., What weighs more: 1 baseball or 3 sponges?).

- Read *Mighty Maddie* (Murphy, 2004), a story about comparing weights.

Cross-Curricular Connections:

Science
- Compare and contrast quantities found in nature: Are there more or fewer colors in the rainbow or planets in the solar system? Are there more or fewer fingers on our hands or the number of our senses?, etc.

Social Studies
- Begin a unit on money, its history, the minting process, etc. Explore the value of coins by comparing various quantities of coins (e.g., What is worth more: 5 pennies or a nickel? Is a quarter more or less than 3 dimes?).

Related Children's Literature

Aigner-Clark, J. (2004). *Baby Einstein: The ABCs of art.* New York: Hyperion Books for Children.

Anno, M. (1975). *Anno's counting book.* New York: HarperCollins.

Giganti, P. (1988). *How many snails?* New York: Greenwillow Books.

Giganti, P. (2005). *How many blue birds flew away?* New York: Greenwillow Books.

Hoban, T. (1998). *More, fewer, less.* New York: Greenwillow Books.

The Metropolitan Museum of Art. (2004). *Museum 1 2 3.* New York: Little, Brown.

The Metropolitan Museum of Art. (2005). *Museum shapes.* New York: Little, Brown.

Micklethwait, L. (1993). *A child's book of art: Great pictures: First words.* New York: Dorling Kindersley.

Micklethwait, L. (1993). *I spy two eyes: Numbers in art.* New York: Greenwillow Books.

Micklethwait, L. (2004). *I spy shapes in art.* New York: Greenwillow Books.

Murphy, S. (1997). *Just enough carrots.* New York: HarperCollins.

Murphy, S. (2004). *Mighty Maddie.* New York: HarperCollins.

Murphy, S. (2005). *More or less.* New York: HarperCollins.

Silverstein, S. (1981). *A light in the attic.* New York: HarperCollins.

Related Instructional Resources

Dickins, R. (2005). *The children's book of art: An introduction to famous paintings.* London: Usborne.

Evans, J., & Skelton, T. (2001). *How to teach art to children.* Monterey, CA: Evan-Moor.

Kohl, M., & Gainer, C. (1996). *MathArts: Exploring math through art for 3 to 6 year olds.* Beltsville, MD: Gryphon House.

Kohl, M., & Solga, K. (1996). *Discovering great artists: Hands-on art for children in the styles of the great masters.* Bellingham, WA: Bright Ring.

Krull, K. (1995). *Lives of the artists: Masterpieces, messes.* San Diego: Harcourt Brace.

Press, J. (2001). *Around the world art & activities: Visiting the 7 continents through craft fun.* Charlotte, VT: Williamson.

Renshaw, A., & Ruggi, G. (2005). *The art book for children.* New York: Phaidon Press.

Scieszka, J., & Smith, L. (2005). *Seen art?* New York: Viking Press.

Williams, D. (1995). *Teaching mathematics through children's art.* Portsmouth, NH: Heinemann.

Related Websites

How Many Buttons—Exploring One More and One Less
http://illuminations.nctm.org/LessonDetail.aspx?ID=L25

Shirts Full of Buttons—Exploring More and Less
http://illuminations.nctm.org/LessonDetail.aspx?ID=L32

Virtual Manipulatives Library—How Much Money
http://nlvm.usu.edu/en/nav/frames_asid_325_g_1_t_1.html

12 Ways to Get to 11 (1996)

by Eve Merriam

Aladdin Paperbacks, ISBN #0689808925

Math-terpieces (2003)

by Greg Tang

Scholastic, ISBN #0439443881

Overview of Books:	In *12 Ways to Get to 11*, discover a variety of ways to obtain 11 by summing different addends. Then, in *Math-terpieces*, view a variety of artistic masterpieces while solving rhyming math problems that involve grouping objects and addition.
Mathematical Concepts and Skills:	grouping, addition, writing number sentences, algebra, problem solving
Visual Arts Concepts and Skills:	art history (various artistic styles), creation of a piece of artwork in a particular style of art
Overview of Activities:	Students work competitively to develop a list of ways to sum to 11, using linking cubes and writing number sentences. Then students view a variety of artistic masterpieces and examine groups of objects, searching for ways to sum to a specified number. Students create a painting of eleven objects, separated into two groups, in the spirit of one of the works appearing in *Math-terpieces*.
National Mathematics Standards (2000):	Students in preK–2 should "model situations that involve the addition and subtraction of whole numbers, using objects, pictures, and symbols" (Algebra Standard) (p. 394). Students in preK–2 should "count with understanding and recognize 'how many' in sets of objects." Students should "develop a sense of whole numbers and represent and use them in flexible ways, including relating, composing, and decomposing numbers." They should also "connect number words and numerals to the quantities they represent, using various physical models and representations" (Number and Operations Standard) (p. 392).

National Visual Arts Standards (1994):

Students should understand and apply media, techniques, and processes (Content Standard 1) and "use different media, techniques, and processes to communicate ideas, experiences, and stories" (Achievement Standard c) (p. 34); understand the visual arts in relation to history and cultures (Content Standard 4) and "identify specific works of art as belonging to particular cultures, times, and places" (Achievement Standard b) (p. 34); and make connections between visual arts and other disciplines (Content Standard 6) and "identify connections between the visual arts and other disciplines in the curriculum" (Achievement Standard b) (p. 35).

Materials:

linking cubes, coloring medium (tempera paints, water colors, pastels, etc.)

Description of Activities:

1. Give pairs of students eleven linking cubes. Challenge students to model and record as many ways as they can to group the cubes to sum to 11. Students should write their solutions as a number sentence (e.g., $5 + 6 = 11$). Encourage older students to use more than two addends in their solutions (e.g., $2 + 3 + 6 = 11$). Students share their solutions.

2. Read *12 Ways to Get to 11*. When quantities of objects are summed to 11 on a page, students model the problem using their linking cubes and then record the corresponding number sentence in their journals.

3. Place students in small groups. Begin reading *Math-terpieces* to students. For each problem posed, students work collaboratively to solve the rhyming word problem and then present their solutions. Students should write their solutions as a number sentence. Is there more than one solution? (Answers are provided at the end of the book.)

4. Revisit select pages from *Math-terpieces*. Printed on the bottom of each right-hand page is the style of art featured in the painting. Share the names of several styles of artwork featured in the book and ask students to describe the characteristics of each style. What do they like about each style of painting? What don't they like?

5. Assign or take a class vote on one particular style of art appearing in *Math-terpieces*. Using appropriate coloring medium (tempera paints, water colors, pastels, etc.), students create a piece of artwork in the spirit of that particular style. In their artwork, students paint eleven objects of their choice. The eleven objects should be separated into two or more groups.

6. Once their paintings have dried, students record on the back of their work the number sentence that models their depiction of eleven objects (e.g., $7 + 4 = 11$).

7. Hang the students' artwork around the classroom for students to observe, enjoy, count, and sum.

Assessment:

- Did students model and record different ways to add two or more addends to sum to 11?

- Did students work collaboratively to solve the word problems?

- Did students express their solutions as a number sentence?

- Did students create a piece of artwork in the spirit of a particular style of art?

Activity Extensions:

- Using coin manipulatives, challenge students to find all the possible ways to sum to a quarter (or some other appropriate amount).

Cross-Curricular Connections:

Science

- Featured on page 12 in *Math-terpieces* is Vincent van Gogh's *The Starry Night*. Begin a unit on stars and constellations

Social Studies

- Read and report on a biography of a painter featured in *Math-terpieces*.

Related Children's Literature

Aigner-Clark, J. (2002). *Baby Einstein: The ABCs of art.* New York: Hyperion Books for Children.

Liatsos, S. (1999). *Poems to count on.* New York: Scholastic.

Long, L. (1996). *Domino addition.* New York: Scholastic.

Merriam, E. (1993). *12 Ways to Get to 11.* New York: Aladdin Paperbacks.

The Metropolitan Museum of Art. (2004). *Museum 1 2 3.* New York: Little, Brown.

Murphy, S. (1998). *Animals on board.* New York: HarperCollins.

Murphy, S. (1998). *The penny pot.* New York: HarperCollins.

Pallotta, J. (2001). *The Hershey's kisses addition book.* New York: Scholastic.

Pallotta, J. (2004). *Hershey's chocolate math: From addition to multiplication.* New York: Scholastic.

Tang, G. (1999). *Math potatoes: Mind stretching brain food.* New York: Scholastic.

Tang, G. (2001). *The grapes of math: Mind stretching math riddles.* New York: Scholastic.

Tang, G. (2002). *The best of times: Math strategies that multiply.* New York: Scholastic.

Tang, G. (2003). *Math appeal: Mind stretching math riddles.* New York: Scholastic.

Tang, G. (2003). *Math-terpieces: The art of problem solving.* New York: Scholastic.

Tang, G. (2004). *Math fables.* New York: Scholastic.

Related Instructional Resources

Dickins, R. (2005). *The children's book of art: An introduction to famous paintings.* London: Usborne.

Evans, J., & Skelton, T. (2001). *How to teach art to children.* Monterey, CA: Evan-Moor.

Kohl, M., & Gainer, C. (1996). *MathArts: Exploring math through art for 3 to 6 year olds.* Beltsville, MD: Gryphon House.

Kohl, M., & Solga, K. (1996). *Discovering great artists: Hands-on art for children in the styles of the great masters.* Bellingham, WA: Bright Ring.

Krull, K. (1995). *Lives of the artists: Masterpieces, messes.* San Diego: Harcourt Brace.

Micklethwait, L. (1993). *A child's book of art: Great pictures first words.* New York: Dorling Kindersley.

Press, J. (2001). *Around the world art & activities: Visiting the 7 continents through craft fun.* Charlotte, VT: Williamson.

Renshaw, A., & Ruggi, G. (2005). *The art book for children.* New York: Phaidon Press.

Scieszka, J., & Smith, L. (2005). *Seen art?* New York: Viking Press.

Williams, D. (1995). *Teaching mathematics through children's art.* Portsmouth, NH: Heinemann.

Related Websites

Guggenheim Museum

http://www.guggenheim.org/new_york_index.shtml

The Metropolitan Museum of Art

http://www.metmuseum.org/home.asp

Follow the Line (2006)

by Laura Ljungkvist

Penguin, ISBN #0670060496

Henri Matisse (Getting to Know the World's Greatest Artists Series) (1997)

by Mike Venezia

Children's Press, ISBN #0516261460

Overview of Books:	In *Follow the Line*, readers can do as the title suggests and follow the unbroken line that stretches across the front cover, through each and every page, and onto the back cover. While following the line extending from page to page, students can count, identify shapes, and make observations, prompted by the questions printed on each page. Then, in *Henri Matisse*, readers learn about the life and artwork of the twentieth-century French artist, Henri Matisse, best known for his artwork exhibiting bold colors, shapes, and many patterns.
Mathematical Concepts and Skills:	creating geometric and repeating patterns, lines, line segments, horizontal lines, vertical lines, diagonal lines, curves, shapes
Visual Arts Concepts and Skills:	line, shape, color, value, form, space, creating art (lined patterns and a mural), art history (the work of Henri Matisse)
Overview of Activities:	Students explore how lines can create all types of forms, shapes, and patterns. Students then gain practice with drawing lines and curves and generating and identifying lined patterns. Students create a mural of index cards in the spirit of Henri Matisse.
National Mathematics Standards (2000):	Students in preK–2 should "recognize, describe, and extend patterns such as sequences of sounds and shapes or simple numeric patterns and translate from one representation to another." They should also "analyze how both repeating and growing patterns are generated" (Algebra Standard) (p. 394).

National Visual Arts Standards (1994):

Students should understand and apply media, techniques, and processes (Content Standard 1) and "use different media, techniques, and processes to communicate ideas, experiences, and stories" (Achievement Standard c) (p. 34); use knowledge of structures and functions (Content Standard 2) and "use visual structures and functions of art to communicate ideas" (Achievement Standard c) (p. 34); make connections between visual arts and other disciplines (Content Standard 6) and "identify connections between the visual arts and other disciplines in the curriculum" (Achievement Standard b) (p. 35).

Materials: 4" × 6" index cards, rulers, markers or crayons, tape

Description of Activities:

1. Begin a discussion by asking students what a line is. What does a line look like? How would you draw a line? Do you see any lines in the classroom? What does a horizontal line look like? A vertical line? A diagonal line? Demonstrate for students how to draw each of these types of lines.

2. Show students the front cover of *Follow the Line* and, using your finger, trace how the line begins at the letter *F* in *Follow* and continues through the rest of the title, and then off of the cover, and onto the inside cover, and then onto the successive pages. Ask students what shapes they see as the line progresses across the pages of the book. Point out how a line can curve, how it forms angles of varying size, and how it can result in the creation of patterns. (If desired, allow students to solve the various math problems posed on pages of *Follow the Line*, which will give them practice with counting and identifying shapes.)

3. Begin reading all or select passages from *Henri Matisse*. Show examples of Matisse's work that feature his colorfully lined patterns (e.g., *Still Life in Seville II* [p. 6], *Woman in Kimono* [p. 7], and *The Family of the Artist* [p. 20]). If desired, show additional images of Matisse's work using the Henri Matisse websites listed below.

4. Give each student two 4" × 6" index cards and rulers. Instruct students to draw a colored pattern of straight lines (horizontal, vertical, or slanted) on one of the cards and a colored pattern of curly or squiggly lines on the other card. For both cards, encourage students to create a repeating pattern of lines (or curves) in terms of alternating thickness and/or color.

5. Explain to students how, later in his life, Matisse had trouble standing for long periods of time; thus he began "drawing with scissors"—that is, he sat and cut shapes out of brightly colored paper and then asked his assistant to place them on a canvas. Clear a spot on a large table or floor. Create a large mural in the spirit of Matisse by encouraging students to determine the placement of the cards in the mural, in an attempt to maximize the aesthetic look of the mural. Tape the cards into place. Hang the mural on a wall for all students to see.

6. Observe and discuss the colorfully lined patterns. How are they different? How are they similar? What repeating patterns do students see? Which patterns do they find the most visually appealing? Why? Which patterns do they find the least visually appealing? Why?

Assessment:
- Did students identify examples of lines in the classroom?
- Did students make a colorful sketch of a straight-line pattern and a squiggly- or curvy-line pattern?
- Did students notice the repeating patterns appearing in other students' designs?

Activity Extensions:
- Students look for and identify real-life examples of lines, shapes, and line patterns in the classroom.
- Students cut shapes from boldly colored paper and make a Matisse-like masterpiece.

Cross-Curricular Connections:

Science
- Explore patterns of camouflage in animal skin and fur.

Social Studies
- Identify and discuss the lines of latitude and longitude on a globe or map.
- Explore a biography of another abstract painter.

Related Children's Literature

Aigner-Clark, J. (2002). *Baby Einstein: The ABCs of art*. New York: Hyperion Books for Children.

Brumbeau, J. (2001). *The quiltmaker's gift*. New York: Scholastic.

Brumbeau, J. (2004). *The quiltmaker's journey*. New York: Orchard Books.

Burns, M. (1994). *The greedy triangle*. New York: Scholastic.

Dodds, D. (1994). *The shape of things*. Cambridge, MA: Candlewick Press.

Dotlich, R. (1999). *What is round?* New York: Scholastic.

Dotlich, R. (1999). *What is a square?* New York: Scholastic.

Dotlich, R. (2000). *What is a triangle?* New York: Scholastic.

Franco, B. (2003). *Shadow shapes*. Vernon Hills, IL: ETA Cuisenaire.

Greene, R. (1997). *When a line bends . . . A shape begins*. New York: Scholastic.

Hoban, T. (1986). *Shapes, shapes, shapes*. New York: Greenwillow Books.

Hoban, T. (1998). *So many circles, so many squares*. New York: Greenwillow Books.

Johnson, K., & O'Connor, J. (2002). *Henri Matisse: Drawing with scissors*. New York: Grosset & Dunlap.

Ljungkvist, L. (2006). *Follow the line*. New York: Penguin.

The Metropolitan Museum of Art. (2005). *Museum shapes*. New York: Little, Brown.

Micklethwait, L. (2004). *I spy shapes in art*. New York: Greenwillow Books.

Reynolds, P. (2003). *The dot*. Cambridge, MA: Candlewick Press.

Reynolds, P. (2004). *Ish*. Cambridge, MA: Candlewick Press.

Scieszka, J., & Smith, L. (2005). *Seen art?* New York: Viking Press.

Tang, G. (2003). *Math-terpieces*. New York: Scholastic.

Thong, R. (2000). *Round is a mooncake*. New York: Scholastic.

Venezia, M. (1997). *Henri Matisse* (Getting to know the world's greatest artists series). New York: Children's Press.

Related Instructional Resources

Dickins, R. (2005). *The children's book of art: An introduction to famous paintings*. London: Usborne.

Evans, J., & Skelton, T. (2001). *How to teach art to children*. Monterey, CA: Evan-Moor.

Kohl, M., & Gainer, C. (1996). *MathArts: Exploring math through art for 3 to 6 year olds*. Beltsville, MD: Gryphon House.

Kohl, M., & Solga, K. (1996). *Discovering great artists: Hands-on art for children in the styles of the great masters*. Bellingham, WA: Bright Ring.

Krull, K. (1995). *Lives of the artists: Masterpieces, messes*. San Diego: Harcourt Brace.

Micklethwait, L. (1993). *A child's book of art: Great pictures: First words*. New York: Dorling Kindersley.

Press, J. (2001). *Around the world art & activities: Visiting the 7 continents through craft fun*. Charlotte, VT: Williamson.

Renshaw, A., & Ruggi, G. (2005). *The art book for children*. New York: Phaidon Press.

Scieszka, J., & Smith, L. (2005). *Seen art?* New York: Viking Press.

Williams, D. (1995). *Teaching mathematics through children's art*. Portsmouth, NH: Heinemann.

Related Websites

Going on a Shape Hunt using *The Greedy Triangle* (Burns, 1994), etc.
     http://www.readwritethink.org/lessons/lesson_view.asp?id=776

Henri Matisse
     http://www.artcyclopedia.com/artists/matisse_henri.html
     http://www.geocities.com/Paris/LeftBank/4208/
     http://www.artchive.com/artchive/m/matisse/snail.jpg
     http://www.ibiblio.org/wm/paint/auth/matisse/

Laura Ljungkvist
     http://www.followtheline.com/home
     http://www.followtheline.com/fun-1.html

Study Art
     http://www.sanford-artedventures.com/study/study.html

Teach Art—Lots of Lines Lesson Plan
     http://www.sanford-artedventures.com/teach/lp_lots_of_lines.html

Activities Featuring Geometry

When a Line Bends . . . A Shape Begins (1997)

by Ronda Gowler Greene

Scholastic, ISBN #0590642057

Coyote Places the Stars (1997)

by Harriett Peck Taylor

Aladdin Books, ISBN #0689815352

Overview of Books:	Enjoy discovering what a line is, where we see lines in everyday life, and how lines form a variety of shapes that we see in our world in the rhyming book, *When a Line Bends . . . A Shape Begins*. In *Coyote Places the Stars*, the author retells a Wasco Indian legend about the origin of the constellations and how a crafty coyote shuffled the stars using his bow and arrow, thus creating pictures of his friends.
Mathematical Concepts and Skills:	points, line segments, angles, shapes, attributes of shapes
Visual Arts Concepts and Skills:	line, shape, creating art (chalk drawing)
Overview of Activities:	Students begin with an exploration of lines and line segments by looking for them in their classroom. Students than create and discuss shapes by experimenting with yarn. Students create a classroom map of the night-time sky by using star stickers for points and drawing line segments to create animal shapes in the night sky.
National Mathematics Standards (2000):	Students in preK–2 should "recognize, name, build, draw, compare, and sort two- and three-dimensional shapes." They should describe "attributes and parts of two- and three-dimensional shapes." Students also "recognize geometric shapes and structures in the environment and specify their location" (Geometry Standard) (p. 396).

National Visual Arts Standards (1994):

Students should understand and apply media, techniques, and processes (Content Standard 1) and "use different media, techniques, and processes to communicate ideas, experiences, and stories" (Achievement Standard c) (p. 34); choose and evaluate a range of subject matter, symbols, and ideas (Content Standard 3) and "select and use subject matter, symbols, and ideas to communicate meaning" (Achievement Standard b); and make connections between visual arts and other disciplines (Content Standard 6) and "identify connections between the visual arts and other disciplines in the curriculum" (Achievement Standard b) (p. 35).

Materials:

precut pieces of yarn for each student measuring 2 feet in length, small star stickers (approximately ten per student), rulers, pencils, colored chalk, black construction paper

Description of Activities:

1. Begin a discussion by asking students what a line is. What does a line look like? How would you draw one? Do you see any lines in the classroom?

2. Read *If a Line Bends . . . A Shape Begins*. After reading the verse on each page, ask students to describe the shape formed by the line. Are the sides of the shape straight? Horizontal? Vertical? Curved? How many sides does each shape have? How is one shape different from another shape?

3. At the end of the book, give each student a piece of yarn measuring about 2 feet in length. Ask students to create a specific shape with the yarn (e.g., a square, rectangle, circle, oval, etc.). After making a shape, students should count how many sides (i.e., line segments) each shape has and to describe its sides as straight or curved. Ask students to articulate the similarities and differences between two shapes (e.g., compare a rectangle to a square), with a focus on each shape's number of sides and their appearance (whether the shape has straight or curved sides, two long sides, two short sides, equal sides, etc.).

4. Begin a discussion by asking students if they have ever gazed at clouds during the day or gazed at the stars at night and have seen patterns, objects, animals, or shapes in the clouds or stars.

5. Read *Coyote Places the Stars*. Let students carefully view the pages in the book where the stars are arranged into the shapes of animals. What geometric shapes do they see? How many sides form each shape? Encourage students to notice that the stars serve as points connecting the sides (i.e., line segments). With older students, describe how angles of different sizes are formed between two sides sharing the same "star" as a common endpoint.

6. Create and hang a night sky in your own classroom. Students decide on an animal to create (or select some other class theme) and, using a pencil and ruler, trace an outline of the animal on a piece of black construction paper. Students place star stickers at the points where sides (i.e., line segments) meet. Students then use colored chalk to re-trace the outline of their shape.

7. Place all of their illustrations in a rectangular array, tape together, and hang on a classroom wall, creating a night sky. Students observe their night sky, count the sides on the shapes they see, and describe the shapes.

Assessment:
- Did students describe and identify examples of lines?
- Did students correctly form the specified shapes using their yarn?
- Did students articulate the attributes of shapes (i.e., number of sides) and how lines form shapes?
- Did students notice similarities and difference between and among various shapes?
- Did students notice the lines and shapes that form the illustrations in *Coyote Places the Stars?*
- Did students create a shape using lines and stars?

Activity Extensions:
- View Vincent van Gogh's *The Starry Night*. If students were to connect the stars in his painting, what shape(s) or patterns would they see?
- Begin a discussion about stars by asking, "What is a star?", "What do stars look like?", "The sun is a star, but the earth is a planet. How is a star different from a planet?" Challenge students to develop a group consensus on what they think a star is. Visit some of the Star websites or resources below for age-appropriate information about stars.
- Enjoy the retelling of a Navajo legend about the stars and constellations in *How the Stars Fell into the Sky* (Oughton, 1992).

- Learn about constellations and animals appearing in the constellations by reading *Zoo in the Sky: A Book of Animal Constellations* (Mitton, 1998).

- Read a poem about stars, "Somebody Has To" in *A Light in the Attic* (Silverstein, 1981).

Cross-Curricular Connections:

Science

- Begin a unit of study on astronomy (e.g., stars and constellations, planets, solar system, Milky Way galaxy, universe).

- Discuss animals and their characteristics, as well as their habitats, especially those included in the book.

Social Studies

- Explore a biographical piece of important astronomers.

Related Children's Literature

Barner, B. (2002). *Stars! Stars! Stars!* San Francisco: Chronicle Books.

Berger, M., & Berger, G. (1999). *Do stars have points? Questions and answers about stars and planets.* New York: Scholastic.

Branley, F. (1981). *The sky is full of stars.* New York: HarperCollins.

Branley, F. (2002). *The sun: Our nearest star.* New York: HarperCollins.

Brown, M. (1998). *I like stars.* New York: Golden Books.

Burns, M. (1994). *The greedy triangle.* New York: Scholastic.

De Paola, T. (1975). *The cloud book.* New York: Holiday House.

Dodds, D. (1994). *The shape of things.* Cambridge, MA: Candlewick Press.

Dotlich, R. (1999). *What is round?* New York: Scholastic.

Dotlich, R. (1999). *What is a square?* New York: Scholastic.

Dotlich, R. (2000). *What is a triangle?* New York: Scholastic.

Driscoll, M. (2004). *A child's introduction to the night sky.* New York: Black Dog & Leventhal.

Franco, B. (2003). *Shadow shapes.* Vernon Hills, IL: ETA Cuisenaire.

Gallant, R. (1991). *The constellations: How they came to be.* New York: Four Winds Press.

Gibbons, G. (1999). *Stargazers.* New York: Holiday House.

Greene, R. (1997). *When a line bends . . . A shape begins.* New York: Scholastic.

Hoban, T. (1986). *Shapes, shapes, shapes.* New York: Greenwillow Books.

Hoban, T. (1998). *So many circles, so many squares.* New York: Greenwillow Books.

Kerrod, R. (2002). *The book of constellations: Discover the secrets in the stars.* Hauppauge, NY: Barron's Educational Series.

Krupp, E. (1991). *Beyond the blue horizon: Myths and legends of the sun, moon, stars, and planets.* New York: HarperCollins.

Krupp, E., & Krupp, R. (1989). *The Big Dipper and you.* New York: Morrow.

Lewis, R. (2002). *All of the earth, all of the sky.* New York: Scholastic.

Ljungkvist, L. (2006). *Follow the line.* New York: Penguin.

Love, A., & Drake, J. (2004). *The kids' book of the night sky.* Tonawanda, NY: Kids Can Press.

The Metropolitan Museum of Art. (2005). *Museum shapes.* New York: Little, Brown.

Micklethwait, L. (2004). *I spy shapes in art.* New York: Greenwillow Books.

Mitton, J. (1998). *Zoo in the sky: A book of animal constellations.* Washington, DC: National Geographic.

Mitton, J. (2004). *Once upon a starry night: A book of constellations.* Washington, DC: National Geographic.

Oughton, J. (1992). *How the stars fell into the sky.* New York: Houghton Mifflin.

Pearce, Q., & Fraser, M. (1991). *The stargazer's guide to the galaxy.* New York: RGA.

Rey, H. (1980). *The stars: A new way to see them.* New York: Houghton Mifflin.

Rey, H. (1982). *Find the constellations.* New York: Houghton Mifflin.

Reynolds, P. (2003). *The dot.* Cambridge, MA: Candlewick Press.

Reynolds, P. (2004). *Ish.* Cambridge, MA: Candlewick Press.

Ridpath, I. (1988). *Star tales.* New York: Universe Books.

Sasaki, C. (2003). *The constellations: Stars and stories.* New York: Sterling.

Silverstein, S. (1981). *A light in the attic*. New York: HarperCollins.

Sipiera, P., & Sipiera, D. (1997). *Constellations*. Danbury, CT: Scholastic.

Stott, C. (2003). *I wonder why stars twinkle (and other questions about space)*. New York: Kingfisher.

Taylor, H. (1997). *Coyote places the stars*. New York: Aladdin Books.

Thompson, C. (1989). *Glow in the dark constellations: A field guide for young stargazers*. New York: Grosset & Dunlap.

Thong, R. (2000). *Round is a mooncake*. New York: Scholastic.

Turnbull, S. (2003). *Sun, moon and stars* (Usborne beginners series). New York: Scholastic.

Venezia, M. (1989). *van Gogh* (Getting to know the world's greatest artists series). Chicago: Children's Press.

Related Instructional Resources

Chartrand, M., Tirion, W., & Mechler, G. (1995). *National Audubon Society pocket guide to constellations of the northern skies*. New York: Knopf.

Heifetz, M., & Tirion, W. (2004). *A walk through the heavens: A guide to stars and constellations and their legends*. New York: Cambridge University Press.

Kohl, M., & Gainer, C. (1996). *MathArts: Exploring math through art for 3 to 6 year olds*. Beltsville, MD: Gryphon House.

Kohl, M., & Solga, K. (1996). *Discovering great artists: Hands-on art for children in the styles of the great masters*. Bellingham, WA: Bright Ring.

Levitt, I., & Marshall, R. (1992). *Star maps for beginners: 50th anniversary edition*. New York: Fireside.

Pasachoff, J., & Percy, J. (Eds.). (2005). *Teaching and learning astronomy: Effective strategies for educators worldwide*. New York: Cambridge University Press.

Press, J. (2001). *Around the world art & activities: Visiting the 7 continents through craft fun*. Charlotte, VT: Williamson.

Scieszka, J., & Smith, L. (2005). *Seen art?* New York: Viking Press.

Williams, D. (1995). *Teaching mathematics through children's art*. Portsmouth, NH: Heinemann.

Related Websites

Astronomy for Kids
> http://www.kidsastronomy.com/

Build the Big Dipper
> http://ology.amnh.org/astronomy/stufftodo/dipper.html?src=schol_space

Connect the Dots Astronomy
> http://www.enchantedlearning.com/subjects/astronomy/activities/dots/index.shtml

Constellations and Their Stars
> http://www.astro.wisc.edu/~dolan/constellations/constellations.html
> http://www.dustbunny.com/afk/index.html
> http://nasaexplores.nasa.gov/extras/constellations/constellation.html
> http://www.cosmobrain.com/cosmobrain/res/constellations.html

Make a Star Finder
> http://spaceplace.nasa.gov/en/kids/st6starfinder/st6starfinder.shtml

Stargazing and Star Maps
> http://www.kidsastronomy.com/astroskymap/constellations.htm
> http://ology.amnh.org/astronomy/stufftodo/stargazing.html?src=schol_space

Vincent van Gogh's *The Starry Night*
> http://www.ibiblio.org/wm/paint/auth/gogh/starry-night/
> http://www.enchantedlearning.com/artists/vangogh/coloring/starrynight.shtml

Rectangles (City Shapes Series) (2000)

by Jennifer S. Burke

Children's Press, ISBN #0516230026

Squares (City Shapes Series) (2000)

by Jennifer S. Burke

Children's Press, ISBN #0516230034

Mondrian (Great Modern Masters Series) (1997)

by Jose Maria Faerna

Abrams, ISBN #0810946874

Overview of Books: Learn about rectangles and squares and enjoy photos of rectangles and squares appearing in a city in the two books, *Rectangles* and *Squares*. In Faerna's *Mondrian*, readers explore the artwork of the twentieth-century Dutch abstract painter, Piet Mondrian.

Mathematical Concepts and Skills: lines, rectangles, squares, attributes of shapes, real-life examples of shapes

Visual Arts Concepts and Skills: line, shape, color, creating art (Mondrian-like work), art history (abstract period and the work of Piet Mondrian)

Overview of Activities: Students explore, discuss, and identify real-life examples of rectangles and sqaures. Students then explore how the Dutch artist, Piet Mondrian, used a series of horizontal and vertical lines and primary colors to create his abstract work comprised of rectangles and squares. Students create a Mondrian-like painting.

National Mathematics Standards (2000): Students in preK–2 should "name, build, draw, compare, and sort two- and three-dimensional shapes." They should "describe attributes and parts of two- and three-dimensional shapes." Students also "recognize geometric shapes and structures in the environment and specify their location" (Geometry Standard) (p. 396).

National Visual Arts Standards (1994):

Students should understand and apply media, techniques, and processes (Content Standard 1) and "describe how different materials, techniques, and processes cause different responses" (Achievement Standard b) (p. 33); use knowledge of structures and functions (Content Standard 2) and "know the differences among visual characteristics and purposes of art in order to convey ideas" (Achievement Standard a) (p. 34); choose and evaluate a range of subject matter, symbols, and ideas (Content Standard 3) and "select and use subject matter, symbols, and ideas to communicate meaning" (Achievement Standard b) (p. 34); and make connections between visual arts and other disciplines (Content Standard 6) and "identify connections between the visual arts and other disciplines in the curriculum" (Achievement Standard b) (p. 35).

Materials:

9" × 12" white construction paper, black construction paper precut into ¼" thick strips, red, yellow, and blue crayons or markers, glue sticks

Description of Activities:

1. Begin a discussion about rectangles and squares. Ask students such questions as, What is a rectangle? How would you describe its shape? What is a square? How would you describe its shape? How are a rectangle and square similar? Different? Ask students to look around the classroom and to identify examples of rectangles and squares.

2. Read *Rectangles* followed by *Squares*. As you read both books, challenge students to identify the rectangles (or squares) as well as other shapes they see in the photos.

3. Show samples of the "Composition" paintings created by the twentieth-century Dutch abstract artist, Piet Mondrian, in *Mondrian* (pp. 42–51). Do students see rectangles or squares in his works? Describe how Mondrian used intersecting horizontal and vertical lines in his works, creating squares and rectangles, which he then colored red, yellow, and blue.

4. Students place pieces of 9" × 12" white construction paper, landscape style, on their desks. Students glue two or three horizontal and two or three vertical black strips onto their paper, creating a series of perpendicular lines (intersecting at right angles). What shapes result?

5. Students now create Mondrian-style paintings by coloring in the resulting squares and rectangular regions using red, yellow, and blue crayons or markers.

6. Hang the students' artwork and let students compare and contrast their works. Do they all contain the same number of square regions? Rectangular regions? Red, yellow, or blue regions? Which pieces of artwork are most visually appealing? The least?

Assessment:

- Did students identify examples of rectangles and squares in the classroom?

- Did students correctly describe, compare, and contrast attributes of rectangles and squares?

- Did students create a piece of art in the spirit of Mondrian's "Composition" paintings?

Activity Extensions:

- Students visually estimate what portions of their Mondrian-like masterpieces are red, blue, yellow, or white using comparative terms (e.g., There are more red regions than blue; there are fewer yellow regions than white, etc.).

- Older students estimate what fractional parts of their Mondrian-like artwork is red, blue, etc.

- Visit the Mondrimat website and let students experiment with color and shape by creating their own online artwork in the spirit of Mondrian.

Cross-Curricular Connections:

Science

- Explore the primary colors and how they can be combined to create the secondary colors.

- Discuss and locate lines of latitude and longitude on a globe.

Social Studies

- Explore other books in Burke's (2000) City Shapes Series and see how cities, skyscrapers, and other forms of architecture are comprised of shapes. Students design and sketch buildings or skylines using lines and shapes.

- Explore biographies of other abstract painters.

Related Children's Literature

Aigner-Clark, J. (2002). *Baby Einstein: The ABCs of art*. New York: Hyperion Books for Children.

Burke, J. (2000). *Circles* (City shapes series). New York: Children's Press.

Burke, J. (2000). *Ovals* (City shapes series). New York: Children's Press.

Burke, J. (2000). *Rectangles* (City shapes series). New York: Children's Press.

Burke, J. (2000). *Squares* (City shapes series). New York: Children's Press.

Burke, J. (2000). *Triangles* (City shapes series). New York: Children's Press.

Burns, M. (1994). *The greedy triangle*. New York: Scholastic.

Dodds, D. (1994). *The shape of things*. Cambridge, MA: Candlewick Press.

Dotlich, R. (1999). *What is round?* New York: Scholastic.

Dotlich, R. (1999). *What is a square?* New York: Scholastic.

Dotlich, R. (2000). *What is a triangle?* New York: Scholastic.

Franco, B. (2003). *Shadow shapes*. Vernon Hills, IL: ETA Cuisenaire.

Greene, R. (1997). *When a line bends . . . A shape begins*. New York: Scholastic.

Hoban, T. (1986). *Shapes, shapes, shapes*. New York: Greenwillow Books.

Hoban, T. (1998). *So many circles, so many squares*. New York: Greenwillow Books.

Jones, C. (2006). *Two short, two long: A book about rectangles*. Mankato, MN: Capstone Press.

Ljungkvist, L. (2006). *Follow the line*. New York: Penguin.

The Metropolitan Museum of Art. (2005). *Museum shapes*. New York: Little, Brown.

Micklethwait, L. (2004). *I spy shapes in art*. New York: Greenwillow Books.

Olson, N. (2006). *Rectangles around town*. Mankato, MN: Capstone Press.

Rau, D. (2006). *The shape of the world: Rectangles*. New York: Benchmark Books.

Rau, D. (2006). *The shape of the world: Squares*. New York: Benchmark Books.

Reynolds, P. (2003). *The dot*. Cambridge, MA: Candlewick Press.

Reynolds, P. (2004). *Ish*. Cambridge, MA: Candlewick Press.

Scieszka J., & Smith, L. (2005). *Seen art?* New York: Viking Press.

Silverstein, S. (1981). *A light in the attic*. New York: HarperCollins.

Tang, G. (2003). *Math-terpieces*. New York: Scholastic.

Thong, R. (2000). *Round is a mooncake*. New York: Scholastic.

Related Instructional Resources

Dickins, R. (2005). *The children's book of art: An introduction to famous paintings.* London: Usborne.

Evans, J., & Skelton, T. (2001). *How to teach art to children.* Monterey, CA: Evan-Moor.

Faerna, J. (1997). *Mondrian* (Great modern masters series). New York: Abrams.

Kohl, M., & Gainer, C. (1996). *MathArts: Exploring math through art for 3 to 6 year olds.* Beltsville, MD: Gryphon House.

Kohl, M., & Solga, K. (1996). *Discovering great artists: Hands-on art for children in the styles of the great masters.* Bellingham, WA: Bright Ring.

Krull, K. (1995). *Lives of the artists: Masterpieces, messes.* San Diego: Harcourt Brace.

Micklethwait, L. (1993). *A child's book of art: Great pictures: First words.* New York: Dorling Kindersley.

Press, J. (2001). *Around the world art & activities: Visiting the 7 continents through craft fun.* Charlotte, VT: Williamson.

Renshaw, A., & Ruggi, G. (2005). *The art book for children.* New York: Phaidon Press.

Scieszka, J., & Smith, L. (2005). *Seen art?* New York: Viking Press.

Williams, D. (1995). *Teaching mathematics through children's art.* Portsmouth, NH: Heinemann.

Related Websites

Mondrimat
> http://www.stephen.com/mondrimat/

Piet Mondrian
> http://www.artcyclopedia.com/artists/mondrian_piet.html
> http://www.storyboardtoys.com/gallery/Piet-Mondrian.htm
> http://www.fiu.edu/~andiaa/cg2/chronos.html
> http://www.mossfoundation.org/page.php?id=81
> http://www.ibiblio.org/wm/paint/auth/mondrian/

Piet Mondrian Coloring Page
> http://www.enchantedlearning.com/paint/artists/mondrian/coloring/matrix.shtml
> http://www.enchantedlearning.com/artists/mondrian/coloring/matrix.shtml

Rectangle Songs and Ideas
> http://stepbystepcc.com/shapes/rectangle.html

Study Art
> http://www.sanford-artedventures.com/study/study.html

Teach Art—Lots of Lines Lesson Plan
> http://www.sanford-artedventures.com/teach/lp_lots_of_lines.html

I Spy Shapes in Art (2004)

by Lucy Micklethwait

Greenwillow Books, ISBN #0060731931

Overview of Book:	Explore two- and three-dimensional shapes featured in a variety of artistic masterpieces.
Mathematical Concepts and Skills:	characteristics and properties of two- and three-dimensional shapes
Visual Arts Concepts and Skills:	shape, color, form, space, creating art (abstract art or synthetic cubism), art history (various artistic styles)
Overview of Activities:	Students identify the names and attributes of a variety of two- and three-dimensional shapes and then create their own piece of abstract or synthetic cubism artwork featuring various shapes.
National Mathematics Standards (2000):	Students in preK–2 should "recognize, name, build, draw, compare, and sort two- and three-dimensional shapes." Students also "recognize geometric shapes and structures in the environment and specify their location" (Geometry Standard) (p. 396).
National Visual Arts Standards (1994):	Students should understand and apply media, techniques, and processes (Content Standard 1) and "use different media, techniques, and processes to communicate ideas, experiences, and stories" (Achievement Standard c) (p. 34); choose and evaluate a range of subject matter, symbols, and ideas (Content Standard 3) and "select and use subject matter, symbols, and ideas to communicate meaning" (Achievement Standard b) (p. 34); and make connections between visual arts and other disciplines (Content Standard 6) and "identify connections between the visual arts and other disciplines in the curriculum" (Achievement Standard b) (p. 35).
Materials:	real-life examples of two- and three-dimensional objects, 9" × 12" poster-board, construction paper, shape stencils, scissors, glue

Description of Activities:

1. Place real-life examples of several two-dimensional shapes (e.g., a lid for a circle, a picture of a yield sign for a triangle, a cracker for a square, an envelope for a rectangle, etc.) and three-dimensional solids (e.g., a can for a cylinder, a party hat for a cone, a ball for a sphere, a die for a cube, etc.) on a table for students to hold and view. Hold up the shapes one by one and ask students to identify each shape by name (if they know it) and to describe its characteristics and properties. Let students compare and articulate the differences between squares and rectangles and circles and ovals. Ask students to compare and explain how a triangle differs from a cone, a square from a cube, a circle from a sphere, etc. Describe how two-dimensional shapes (e.g., triangles, squares, circles, etc.) are comprised of sides, whereas three-dimensional solids (e.g., cones, cubes, spheres, etc.) are comprised of faces.

2. Begin showing the works of art included in *I Spy Shapes in Art*. Ask students to spy; that is, identify each shape featured on the pages and to also describe its characteristics.

3. Create one of the following:

   - The last page featured in Micklethwait's book (and on the front cover) is a painting created by the twentieth-century French abstract painter, August Herbin, entitled *Composition on the Word "Vie," 2*. Students create pieces of artwork in the spirit of Herbin by using shape stencils (or shapes cut out of colored construction paper) and gluing them onto pieces of 9" × 12" posterboard. Spend time explaining the color wheel and encourage students to choose complementary colors when coloring and pasting their shapes onto their posterboards. Students should include several as well as different types of shapes in their work and in various colors. Students should list on the reverse side of their work the number of each of the various shapes they "spy" in their work. Students should title their artwork. Students share their work with the class and count and identify which shapes they spy.

   - Students create pieces of artwork in the spirit of synthetic cubism, a artistic period begun in 1912 by Pablo Picasso and Georges Braque in which the artists adhered pieces of materials and objects onto their work. Students work collaboratively and glue various two- and three-dimensional shapes onto large pieces of posterboard. Students share and discuss their shape collages with the class.

Assessment:
- Did students correctly identify each shape and describe the characteristics and properties of each shape?
- Did students correctly discern the similarities and difference between two- and three-dimensional shapes?
- Did students create a piece of artwork that contains shapes?

Activity Extensions:
- Students take a geometry walk and look for and identify shapes on their school's campus.
- Each student brings 3 pictures (magazine clippings, photos, etc.) of various two- and three-dimensional objects to class. Create a class collage of shapes.

Cross-Curricular Connections:

Science
- Find examples of shapes in nature (hexagonal shape of a honeycomb or snowflake, the circular shape of a bird's nest, etc.).

Social Studies
- Explore and identify shapes in architecture (pyramids, skyscrapers, gothic cathedrals, etc.).
- Explore biographical pieces of artists who experimented with shapes (Henri Matisse, Wassily Kandinsky, Paul Klee, Josef Albers, etc.).

Related Children's Literature

Aigner-Clark, J. (2002). *Baby Einstein: The ABCs of art.* New York: Hyperion Books for Children.

Dodds, D. (1994). *The shape of things.* Cambridge, MA: Candlewick Press.

Dotlich, R. (1999). *What is round?* New York: Scholastic.

Dotlich, R. (1999). *What is a square?* New York: Scholastic.

Dotlich, R. (2000). *What is a triangle?* New York: Scholastic.

Ehlert, L. (1990). *Color farm.* New York: HarperCollins.

Ehlert, L. (1997). *Color zoo.* New York: HarperCollins.

Franco, B. (2003). *Shadow shapes.* Vernon Hills, IL: ETA Cuisenaire.

Greene, R. (1997). *When a line bends . . . A shape begins.* New York: Scholastic.

Hoban, T. (1986). *Shapes, shapes, shapes.* New York: Greenwillow Books.

Hoban, T. (1998). *So many circles, so many squares.* New York: Greenwillow Books.

Hoban, T. (2000). *Cubes, cones, cylinders, & spheres.* New York: Greenwillow Books.

The Metropolitan Museum of Art. (2004). *Museum 1 2 3.* New York: Little, Brown.

The Metropolitan Museum of Art. (2005). *Museum shapes.* New York: Little, Brown.

Micklethwait, L. (1993). *A child's book of art: Great pictures: First words.* New York: Dorling Kindersley.

Micklethwait, L. (1993). *I spy two eyes: Numbers in art.* New York: Greenwillow Books.

Micklethwait, L. (2004). *I spy shapes in art.* New York: Greenwillow Books.

Neuschwander, C. (2005). *Mummy math: An adventure in geometry.* New York: Holt.

Thong, R. (2000). *Round is a mooncake.* New York: Scholastic.

Related Instructional Resources

Dickins, R. (2005). *The children's book of art: An introduction to famous paintings.* London: Usborne.

Evans, J., & Skelton, T. (2001). *How to teach art to children.* Monterey, CA: Evan-Moor.

Kohl, M., & Gainer, C. (1996). *MathArts: Exploring math through art for 3 to 6 year olds.* Beltsville, MD: Gryphon House.

Kohl, M., & Solga, K. (1996). *Discovering great artists: Hands-on art for children in the styles of the great masters.* Bellingham, WA: Bright Ring.

Krull, K. (1995). *Lives of the artists: Masterpieces, messes.* San Diego: Harcourt Brace.

Press, J. (2001). *Around the world art & activities: Visiting the 7 continents through craft fun.* Charlotte, VT: Williamson.

Renshaw, A., & Ruggi, G. (2005). *The art book for children.* New York: Phaidon Press.

Scieszka, J., & Smith, L. (2005). *Seen art?* New York: Viking Press.

Williams, D. (1995). *Teaching mathematics through children's art.* Portsmouth, NH: Heinemann.

Related Websites

Artcyclopedia—Henri Matisse
>   http://www.artcyclopedia.com/artists/matisse_henri.html

Artcyclopedia—Josef Albers
>   http://www.artcyclopedia.com/artists/albers_josef.html

Artcyclopedia—Paul Klee
>   http://www.artcyclopedia.com/artists/klee_paul.html

Artcyclopedia—Wassily Kandinsky
>   http://www.artcyclopedia.com/artists/kandinsky_wassily.html

Guggenheim Museum
>   http://www.guggenheim.org/new_york_index.shtml

The Metropolitan Museum of Art
>   http://www.metmuseum.org/home.asp

Pablo Picasso and Synthetic Cubism
>   http://www.artchive.com/artchive/P/picasso.html
>   http://picasso.csdl.tamu.edu/picasso/
>   http://www.picasso.fr/anglais/

Shapes
>   http://www.kidport.com/gradeK/Math/MeasureGeo/MathK_Shapes.htm
>   http://www.mathcats.com/explore/polygons.html
>   http://www.enchantedlearning.com/themes/shapes.shtml
>   http://www.first-school.ws/theme/shapes_preschool_printables.htm

The Butterfly Counting Book (1998)

by Jerry Pallotta

Scholastic, ISBN #0590049380

Overview of Book: In *The Butterfly Counting Book*, readers will enjoy the beautiful illustrations of butterflies while learning about symmetry, the odd numbers 1 to 21, the names of various species of butterflies, and the word for *butterfly* in several languages.

Mathematical Concepts and Skills: line symmetry, reflection, shapes, geometric patterns, pattern recognition, counting, odd numbers

Visual Arts Concepts and Skills: line, shape, color, creating art (symmetric art, mobile making), art history (symmetry in Salvador Dali's works containing butterflies)

Overview of Activities: Students explore patterns, symmetry, and reflections by creating colorful butterflies and turning them into a mobile. Students also describe the patterns and symmetry they see in a variety of Salvador Dali's works of painted butterflies.

National Mathematics Standards (2000):

Students in preK–2 should "recognize and create shapes that have symmetry" (Geometry Standard) (p. 396). Students should also "recognize, describe, and extend patterns such as sequences of sounds and shapes" and "analyze how both repeating and growing patterns are generated" (Algebra Standard) (p. 394).

National Visual Arts Standards (1994):

Students should understand and apply media, techniques, and processes (Content Standard 1) and "use different media, techniques, and processes to communicate ideas, experiences, and stories" (Achievement Standard c) (p. 34); use knowledge of structures and functions (Content Standard 2) and "use visual structures and functions to communicate ideas" (Achievement Standard c) (p. 34); make connections between visual arts and other disciplines (Content Standard 6) and "identify connections between the visual arts and other disciplines in the curriculum" (Achievement Standard b) (p. 35).

Materials: hand mirrors, watercolors (or finger paints), outline of a butterfly, scissors, string or colored yarn, dowel rods or hangers

Description of Activities:

1. Show the front cover and the inside page of *The Butterfly Counting Book*. Begin a discussion about symmetry by asking students what they notice about the butterflies. How are the butterflies the same? Different? After students have shared their observations, describe how butterflies are symmetric (i.e., they have symmetry) because the color and patterns on their left wings are identical to the colors and patterns on their right wings.

2. Read all or select pages from *The Butterfly Counting Book*. As you read, ask students to describe the symmetric patterns they see on the butterflies' wings. Do they see patterns of spots? Stripes? What color patterns do they see? Allow students to sound out and say the word for *butterfly* in the various languages. Print the word for *butterfly* in each of the various languages on the board.

3. Provide students an outline of a butterfly. Students fold the paper in half vertically, down the center of the butterfly's body. Students paint one side of the butterfly using watercolors (or finger paints). Encourage students to use shapes, colors, and patterns (dots, stripes, etc.) as they paint. While the paint is still wet, students fold along the crease, creating a mirror image of the insect on the other side of the paper. Students describe the symmetry they see.

4. Once the watercolored butterflies have dried, create a butterfly mobile using string (or colored yarn) and dowel rods (or hangers). Students should observe and describe the various symmetric patterns they see in the butterflies.

5. Using the Salvador Dali and His Butterfly Paintings websites below, show images of the paintings of Salvador Dali's that feature butterflies (e.g., *Butterflies, Landscape with Butterflies, Allegorie de Soie, Queen of the Butterflies,* etc.). Encourage students to identify the symmetric patterns they see.

Assessment:

- Did students describe the symmetric patterns they noticed in the wings of butterflies?

- Did students create a symmetric butterfly?

- Did students see and identify symmetric patterns in Salvador Dali's butterfly works?

Activity Extensions:

- Students locate several pictures in a magazine of objects with reflective symmetry (e.g., facial photo, corporate logo, etc.) and create a collage. Students draw the line of reflection(s) on each photo.

- Explore the symmetry in Navajo rugs and quilts or in ancient or modern architecture.

- Take a picture of a student's face. Using image manipulation software, highlight the left-hand side of the face, reflect it, and then take this mirror image (which is now the right-hand side of the student's face) and place it next to the original left-hand side of the student's face. How symmetric is this student's face?

- Enjoy poetry about reflections including "Reflection" (Silverstein, 1981), "Mirror" (Lewis, 1998), or "egamI rorriM ruoY mA I" (Prelutsky, 1996).

- Explore and discuss patterns in odd and even numbers using a hundreds board.

Cross-Curricular Connections:

Science

- Explore the lifecycle of a butterfly.

- Explore the migration of the monarch butterfly.

- Undertake a unit on weather and seasons, beginning with snow and winter. Explore and discuss the symmetry in and uniqueness of snowflakes.

- Explore symmetry in other things in nature (e.g., flowers, animals, human body, etc.).

Social Studies

- Locate on a map each of the countries mentioned in *The Butterfly Counting Book.*

- Read *Snowflake Bentley*, a biography of Wilson Bentley who, as a boy, was fascinated with ice crystals and recorded their unique characteristics and symmetry over the course of his lifetime.

- Visit one of the Flag websites listed below and search for flags that are symmetric. Learn facts about each country.

Related Children's Literature

Birmingham, D. (1988). *M is for mirror*. Norfolk, UK: Tarquin.

Boring, M. (1999). *Caterpillars, bugs, and butterflies*. Minnetonka, MN: T&N Children's.

Chorao, K. (2001). *Shadow night*. New York: Dutton Children's Books.

Franco, B. (2003). *Shadow shapes*. Vernon Hills, IL: ETA Cuisenaire.

Gibbons, G. (1989). *Monarch butterfly*. New York: Scholastic.

Heiligman, D. (1996). *From caterpillar to butterfly*. New York: HarperCollins.

Jonas, A. (1987). *Reflections*. New York: Greenwillow Books.

Lewis, J. (1998). *Doodle dandies: Poems that take shape*. New York: Aladdin.

Martin, J. (1998). *Snowflake Bentley*. Boston: Houghton Mifflin.

Murphy, S. (2000). *Let's fly a kite*. New York: Scholastic.

Pallotta, J. (1992). *The icky bug counting book*. Watertown, MA: Charlesbridge.

Pallotta, J. (1998). *The butterfly counting book*. New York: Scholastic.

Prelutsky, J. (1996). *A pizza the size of the sun*. New York: Scholastic.

Ryder, J. (1996). *Where butterflies grow*. New York: Penguin Young Readers Group.

Siddals, M. (1998). *Millions of snowflakes*. New York: Scholastic.

Silverstein, S. (1981). *A light in the attic*. New York: HarperCollins.

Silverstein, S. (2004). *Where the sidewalk ends*. New York: HarperCollins.

Sitomer, M., & Sitomer, H. (1970). *What is symmetry?* New York: Crowell.

Venezia, M. (1993). *Salvador Dali* (Getting to know the world's greatest artists series). Chicago: Children's Press.

Related Instructional Resources

Bentley, W. (2000). *Snowflakes in photographs*. Mineola, NY: Dover Books.

Kohl, M., & Gainer, C. (1996). *MathArts: Exploring math through art for 3 to 6 year olds*. Beltsville, MD: Gryphon House.

Kohl, M., & Solga, K. (1996). *Discovering great artists: Hands-on art for children in the styles of the great masters*. Bellingham, WA: Bright Ring.

Press, J. (2001). *Around the world art & activities: Visiting the 7 continents through craft fun*. Charlotte, VT: Williamson.

Reed, B. L. (1987). *Easy-to-make decorative paper snow-flakes*. Mineola, NY: Dover Books.

Scieszka, J., & Smith, L. (2005). *Seen art?* New York: Viking Press.

Whalley, P. (1988). *Butterfly & moth*. New York: Dorling Kindersley.

Williams, D. (1995). *Teaching mathematics through children's art*. Portsmouth, NH: Heinemann.

Related Websites

Butterfly Facts and Pictures

http://members.enchantedlearning.com/subjects/butterfly/index.shtml
http://members.enchantedlearning.com/painting/butterflies.shtml

Butterfly Outline

http://www.eduplace.com/hac/arts/butterfly.html
http://www.everythingesl.net/lessons/camouflage_game.php
http://etc.usf.edu/clipart/26200/26287/butterfly_26287.htm

Flags

http://www.usflags.com/browsestore.asp?CategoryID=6
http://www.50states.com/flag/
http://www.flags.net/
http://www.anbg.gov.au/flags/flags.html

Kaleidoscope

http://www.pbs.org/parents/creativity/sensory/kaleidoscope.html

Monarch Butterfly Migration

http://www.surfnetkids.com/monarch_butterfly.htm
http://www.pbs.org/wnet/nature/alienempire/voyagers.html
http://www.learner.org/jnorth/monarch/

Salvador Dali and His Butterfly Paintings

http://www.artland.co.uk/page125a.html
http://www.artcyclopedia.com/artists/dali_salvador.html

Symmetry

http://www.adrianbruce.com/Symmetry/
http://www.adrianbruce.com/Symmetry/whiteboard-activity.htm
http://regentsprep.org/Regents/math/symmetry/Photos.htm
http://ksnn.larc.nasa.gov/k2/m_whatPatterns_a.html

Virtual Manipulatives Library—Reflections

http://nlvm.usu.edu/en/nav/frames_asid_206_g_1_t_3.html?open=activities

The Best Bug Parade (1996)

by Stuart Murphy

HarperCollins, ISBN #0064467007

Baby Einstein: The ABCs of Art (2002)

by Julie Aigner-Clark

Hyperion Books for Children, ISBN #0786808829

Overview of Books:	In *The Best Bug Parade,* readers enjoy comparing and contrasting bugs of varying size as they form a parade. Then, explore a variety of artistic masterpieces in *Baby Einstein: The ABCs of Art.*
Mathematical Concepts and Skills:	comparison of size and length, measurement
Visual Arts Concepts and Skills:	line, shape, color, value, creating art (watercolor painting), art history (the work of Josef Albers)
Overview of Activities:	Students gain practice with comparing and ordering objects in terms of their size and create pictures of objects of varying size and length. Students then explore how the German abstract artist, Josef Albers, painted squares of varying size, resulting in optical illusions. Students create a painting in the spirit of Albers's style.
National Mathematics Standards (2000): π	Students in preK–2 should "recognize the attributes of length, volume, weight, area, and time" and be able to "compare and order objects according to these attributes." Students should "develop common referents for measures to make comparisons and estimates" (Measurement Standard) (p. 398).

National Visual Arts Standards (1994):

Students should understand and apply media, techniques, and processes (Content Standard 1) and "use different media, techniques, and processes to communicate ideas, experiences, and stories" (Achievement Standard c) (p. 34); use knowledge of structures and functions (Content Standard 2) and "know the differences among visual characteristics and purposes of art in order to convey ideas" (Achievement Standard a) (p. 34); choose and evaluate a range of subject matter, symbols, and ideas (Content Standard 3) and "select and use subject matter, symbols, and ideas to communicate meaning" (Achievement Standard b) (p. 34); and make connections between visual arts and other disciplines (Content Standard 6) and "identify connections between the visual arts and other disciplines in the curriculum" (Achievement Standard b) (p. 35).

Materials:

9" × 12" white construction paper, 9" × 12" watercolor paper precut into a 9" × 9" squares, rulers, pencils, square stencils, watercolor paints, markers, or crayons

Description of Activities:

1. Give students practice estimating size by asking them to stand up and to look around the room. Who do they think is tallest? Shortest? Of medium height? Challenge students to arrange themselves from shortest to tallest. Were their guesses correct? Who has the longest hair? Who has the shortest hair? Ask students to name an object that is big in the classroom. Can they name an object that is even bigger?

2. Read *The Best Bug Parade*. Before reading the text on select pages, ask students to articulate how the bugs look different, prompting them to use such vocabulary as *bigger than, smaller than, longer than,* etc.

3. Using markers or crayons and 9" × 12" white construction paper, students create illustrations of their own bug parades. The illustrations should show three bugs appearing in ascending or descending order according to size (e.g., big, bigger, biggest; or small, smaller, smallest) or length (e.g., short, shorter, shortest; or long, longer, longest). To assist students with their sketches, show images of actual bugs using the Insect Images websites listed below. After students finish their sketches, students should write the words underneath each bug that describes its size or length (e.g., short, shorter, shortest; or big, bigger, biggest, etc.).

4. Create a bug parade in your classroom by hanging each student's illustration side by side around the perimeter of the room. Let students view the class's bug parade and compare and contrast the bugs in terms of size and length. Ask students to identify which bugs are the biggest of all, shortest of all, etc.

5. Share with students Josef Albers's *Study for Homage to the Square* appearing in *Baby Einstein: The ABCs of Art.* Ask students to describe what they see. How many squares do they see in this painting? Which square is smallest? Biggest? Do the squares appear as though they are coming toward you or moving away from you? Explain how this work of Albers is an example of op art (or optical art), as the painting gives the impression of movement, although still. Show other examples of Albers's work using the Josef and Anni Albers Gallery—*Homage to the Square* series website.

6. Give students 9" × 9" square pieces of watercolor paper. Students create Albers-like masterpieces by using square stencils (younger students) or rulers (older students) and sketching in pencil three squares of varying size, one inside the other. Students should select varying hues of color (e.g., light pink, medium pink, and dark pink) and create watercolor paintings similar to *Study for Homage to the Square.* Or, students might select contrasting or complementary colors to shade their squares, as did Albers in his *Homage to the Square* series.

7. Create a square mural by hanging each student's Albers-like masterpiece on a wall. Students compare and discuss the sizes of the squares (e.g., The light pink square is the smallest and the dark pink square is biggest.). Students also articulate whether the squares in the artwork appear to be coming toward them or moving away from them.

Assessment:
- Did students arrange themselves from shortest to tallest?
- Did students correctly describe the bugs in terms of their size and length?
- Did students sketch and label three bugs in order of ascending or descending size or length?
- Did students notice the number of and the size difference in squares in Albers's various paintings?
- Did students create pieces of artwork in the spirit of Albers?

Activity Extensions:
- Students use rulers and measure and record their bugs' lengths.
- Challenge students to think of other things in the classroom they can order (e.g., the weight of different books in the room from lightest to heaviest; the lengths of pieces of chalk from longest to shortest; the age of a group of students from youngest to oldest, etc.).

- Read *Is It Larger? Is It Smaller?* (Hoban, 1997) and allow students to visually experience size comparisons of everyday objects.

- Explore other paintings in Aigner-Clark's book (e.g., Paul Klee's *Balloon Rouge* or William H. Johnson's *Children at the Ice Cream Stand*). Ask students to compare the sizes of the objects appearing in these paintings.

- Explore the artwork of other op art artists including Bridget Riley and Victor Vasarely.

Cross-Curricular Connections:

Science

- Begin a unit on insects.

- Students experiment with microscopes and magnifying lenses and see how size changes using these tools.

- Explore which animals are biggest, strongest, and fastest by reading *Biggest, Strongest, Fastest* (Jenkins, 1995).

Social Studies

- Using a map, explore the migration of the monarch butterfly.

- Explore biographies of other abstract painters and op art artists.

Related Children's Literature

Adler, D. (1999). *How tall how short how far away.* New York: Holiday House.

Aigner-Clark, J. (2002). *Baby Einstein: The ABCs of art.* New York: Hyperion Books for Children.

Beaton, C. (2000). *How big is a pig?* Cambridge, MA: Barefoot Books.

Hoban, T. (1997). *Is it larger? Is it smaller?* New York: Greenwillow Books.

Jenkins, S. (1995). *Biggest, strongest, fastest.* Boston: Houghton Mifflin.

Leedy, L. (1997). *Measuring Penny.* New York: Holt.

Lionni, L. (1960). *Inch by inch.* New York: HarperCollins.

The Metropolitan Museum of Art. (2005). *Museum shapes.* New York: Little, Brown.

Micklethwait, L. (2004). *I spy shapes in art.* New York: Greenwillow Books.

Murphy, S. (1996). *The best bug parade.* New York: HarperCollins.

Murphy, S. (1999). *Room for Ripley.* New York: HarperCollins.

Murphy, S. (2002). *Bigger, better, best!* New York: HarperCollins.

Murphy, S. (2003). *Three little firefighters.* New York: HarperCollins.

Murphy, S. (2004). *A house for birdie.* New York: HarperCollins.

Murphy, S. (2004). *Mighty Maddie.* New York: HarperCollins.

Myller, R. (1990). *How big is a foot?* New York: Random House.

Pinczes, E. (2001). *Inch worm and a half.* New York: Houghton Mifflin.

Pluckrose, H. (1995). *Capacity.* New York: Scholastic.

Pluckrose, H. (1995). *Length.* New York: Scholastic.

Pluckrose, H. (1995). *Size.* New York: Scholastic.

Tang, G. (2003). *Math-terpieces.* New York: Scholastic.

Related Instructional Resources

Albers, J., & Rosenthal, T. (2006). *Josef Albers: Formulation: Articulation.* London: Thames & Hudson.

Dickins, R. (2005). *The children's book of art: An introduction to famous paintings.* London: Usborne.

Evans, J., & Skelton, T. (2001). *How to teach art to children.* Monterey, CA: Evan-Moor.

Kohl, M., & Gainer, C. (1996). *MathArts: Exploring math through art for 3 to 6 year olds.* Beltsville, MD: Gryphon House.

Kohl, M., & Solga, K. (1996). *Discovering great artists: Hands-on art for children in the styles of the great masters.* Bellingham, WA: Bright Ring.

Krull, K. (1995). *Lives of the artists: Masterpieces, messes.* San Diego: Harcourt Brace.

Micklethwait, L. (1993). *A child's book of art: Great pictures: First words.* New York: Dorling Kindersley.

Press, J. (2001). *Around the world art & activities: Visiting the 7 continents through craft fun.* Charlotte, VT: Williamson.

Renshaw, A., & Ruggi, G. (2005). *The art book for children.* New York: Phaidon Press.

Scieszka, J., & Smith, L. (2005). *Seen art?* New York: Viking Press.

Seckel, A. (2005). *Ambiguous optical illusions (SuperVision series).* New York: Sterling.

Seckel, A. (2005). *Impossible optical illusions (SuperVision series).* New York: Sterling.

Williams, D. (1995). *Teaching mathematics through children's art.* Portsmouth, NH: Heinemann.

Related Websites

Bridget Riley
>http://www.artcyclopedia.com/artists/riley_bridget.html

Insect Coloring Pages
>http://www.first-school.ws/theme/animals/cp_insects.htm
>http://www.dltk-kids.com/animals/minsectposter.html
>http://www.west-ext.com/fun_stuff.html
>http://www.coloringbookfun.com/

Insect Images
>http://www.earthlife.net/insects/imagedir.html
>http://www.ivyhall.district96.k12.il.us/4TH/KKHP/
>   1insects/bugmenu.html
>http://www.insectimages.org/

Josef Albers
>http://www.artcyclopedia.com/artists/albers_josef.html

Josef and Anni Albers Gallery—*Homage to the Square* series
>http://www.albersfoundation.org/Albers.php?inc=Galleries&i=J_2

Op Art
>http://www.sanford-artedventures.com/study/g_op_art.html

Victor Vasarely
>http://www.artcyclopedia.com/artists/vasarely_victor.html

"A Closet Full of Shoes" (a poem in Falling Up) (1996)

by Shel Silverstein

HarperCollins, ISBN #0060248025

Joan Miro (Famous Artists Series) (1994)

by Nicholas Ross

Barron's Educational Series, ISBN #0812094271

Overview of Poem and Book:	In the poem "A Closet Full of Shoes," you won't believe how many different types of shoes can fit into one closet! In *Joan Miro,* explore the life and works of Joan Miro, the Spanish surrealist painter and sculptor, considered to be one of the most versatile masters of twentieth-century art.
Mathematical Concepts and Skills:	likelihood, probability, random events, prediction
Visual Arts Concepts and Skills:	line, shape, color, form, space, creating art (surrealist art), art history (the work of Joan Miro)
Overview of Activities:	Students use probability vocabulary (likely, unlikely, equal chance, etc.) to predict the outcome of drawing shoes randomly from a large bag. Students then learn about the technique of random, imaginative drawing used by the Spanish surrealist artist, Joan Miro, to create his artwork. Students create Miro-like works of art, using his random drawing technique.
National Mathematics Standards (2000):	Students in preK–2 should "discuss events related to students' experiences as likely or unlikely" (Data Analysis and Probability Standard) (p. 400).
National Visual Arts Standards (1994):	Students should understand and apply media, techniques, and processes (Content Standard 1) and "use different media, techniques, and processes to communicate ideas, experiences, and stories" (Achievement Standard c) (p. 34); choose and evaluate a range of subject matter, symbols, and ideas (Content Standard 3) and "select and use subject matter, symbols, and ideas to communicate meaning" (Achievement Standard b) (p. 34); make connections between visual arts and other disciplines (Content Standard 6) and "identify connections between the visual arts and other disciplines in the curriculum" (Achievement Standard b) (p. 35).

175

Materials: large shopping bag full of various pairs of different types of shoes (ballet slippers, sneakers, sandals, cleats, etc.), images of Miro's *Constellations* works (e.g., *Harlequin's Carnival, Woman Encircled by the Flight of a Bird*, etc.), Internet, thick black markers, oil paints (or another coloring medium), large white paper

Description of Activities:

1. Begin a discussion with students, posing questions as to whether something is likely or not likely, has more or less of a chance, or has an equal chance of occurring. For example, if it is sunny, ask students, is it likely or unlikely it will rain today? In this case, help students to see the difference and meaning of *likely* and *unlikely*. Or, ask students, if you flip a coin, is there more or less of a chance that the coin will land on heads? (Students should respond that there is an equal chance of getting heads or tails.) Challenge students to describe events as likely, unlikely, even chance, etc., by thinking of examples of probabilistic events (e.g., "Since tomorrow is Friday, it is likely I will go to school."). Students explain their thinking.

2. Read the poem "A Closet Full of Shoes" to set the stage for the next activity.

3. Prior to class, fill a large shopping bag with a variety of shoes. (For younger students, place up to five shoes; for older students place up to ten.) Pull the shoes out of the bag for the students to see. Count the shoes, name them (e.g., sneaker, ballet shoe, etc.), and then place the shoes back in the bag.

4. Reach into the bag and, before showing students the shoe in your hand, ask students to predict what shoe it is and to explain their reasoning. The goal is for students to use terminology such as *likely, unlikely,* etc. If there are two sandals and one sneaker in the bag, ask students if there is more or less of a chance of drawing a sneaker from the bag. Or, ask students, will I likely draw a sneaker from the bag? Repeat this line of questioning using different types and numbers of shoes in the bag.

5. Share with students the front cover appearing on *Joan Miro*. Read short excerpts describing how Miro was a twentieth-century Spanish surrealist painter and sculptor whose work has a whimsical and humorous quality, containing images of playfully distorted animal forms, twisted shapes, and odd geometric constructions. Miro has been described as drawing by chance, a technique of random, imaginative draw, evident in his *Constellations* series. Share with students some of Miro's works appearing in *Joan Miro* and by referring to the Joan Miro websites listed below. Ask students what they like or dislike about his works.

6. Implement the activity described on page 19 in Ross's book where students create a Miro work by using his technique called drawing by chance. Provide students with a thick black marker, oil paints (or another coloring medium), and large white paper. Using their black markers, students close their eyes and make bold, random marks on their papers. Students open their eyes and, using their imaginations, look for and complete figures and shapes. Fill in the shapes using colored oil paints. Students then think of creative titles for their paintings, as did Miro.

7. Students share their artwork with the class. Students discuss whose artwork is most visually appealing and why and whose artwork is most appropriately or cleverly titled.

Assessment:
- Did students make reasonable predictions about what might be drawn from the bag of shoes?

- Did students use probability terms correctly when describing events and outcomes?

- Did students create pieces of artwork in the spirit of Miro?

Activity Extensions:
- Read *Probably Pistachio* (Murphy, 2001) in which students discover and hear other probability terms used in context (e.g., *probably, probably not, never, always, for sure*, etc.).

- Visit the Virtual Manipulatives—Spinners website and explore probability using spinners with colored regions.

- Visit the Marble Mania! website where an interactive tool allows the user to explore randomness and probability by drawing larger numbers of marbles from a bag.

- Using the Jackson Pollock Emulator websites, create a piece of artwork in the spirit of Jackson Pollock, the twentieth-century American artist known for his random "drip and splash" style of abstract painting.

- Explore the artwork of Hans (Jean) Arp, a twentieth-century dadaist who made "chance collages," a technique in which he tore colored paper into squares and dropped them onto a large sheet of paper. Wherever the squares of paper landed, he glued them into place.

**Cross-Curricular
Connections:**

Science

- Miro's most famous series of paintings was his *Constellations* series. Begin a unit on stars and constellations.

Social Studies

- Explore the geography and other demographics of the Catalonia region of Spain, where Joan Miro was born and lived most of his life.

Related Children's Literature

Axelrod, A. (2001). *Pigs at odds: Fun with math and games*. New York: Aladdin.

Blanquet, C. (1993). *Miro: Earth and sky* (Art for children series). New York: Chelsea House.

Linn, C. (1972). *Probability*. New York: Crowell.

Murphy, S. (2001). *Probably pistachio*. New York: HarperCollins.

Ross, N. (1994). *Joan Miro* (Famous artists series). Hauppauge, NY: Barron's Educational Series.

Silverstein, S. (1996). *Falling up*. New York: HarperCollins.

Srivastava, J. (1975). *Averages*. New York: Crowell.

Related Instructional Resources

Aigner-Clark, J. (2004). *Baby Einstein: The ABCs of art*. New York: Hyperion Books for Children.

Cushman, J. (1991). *Do you wanna bet? Your chance to find out about probability*. New York: Clarion Books.

Dickins, R. (2005). *The children's book of art: An introduction to famous paintings*. London: Usborne.

Evans, J., & Skelton, T. (2001). *How to teach art to children*. Monterey, CA: Evan-Moor.

Kohl, M., & Solga, K. (1996). *Discovering great artists: Hands-on art for children in the styles of the great masters*. Bellingham, WA: Bright Ring.

Krull, K. (1995). *Lives of the artists: Masterpieces, messes*. San Diego: Harcourt Brace.

Malet, R. (2003). *Joan Miro*. New York: Rizzoli.

Mink, J. (2000). *Miro*. Hohenzollernring, Germany: Taschen.

Renshaw, A., & Ruggi, G. (2005). *The art book for children*. New York: Phaidon Press.

Scieszka, J., & Smith, L. (2005). *Seen art?* New York: Viking Press.

Related Websites

Hans (Jean) Arp

    http://www.moma.org/collection/browse_results.php?object_id=37013

    http://www.artchive.com/artchive/A/arp.html

Jackson Pollock

    http://www.artcyclopedia.com/artists/pollock_jackson.html

    http://www.ibiblio.org/wm/paint/auth/pollock/

    http://www.nga.gov/feature/pollock/

Jackson Pollock Emulator

    http://jayisgames.com/archives/2006/09/the_jackson_pollock_emulator.php

    http://www.jacksonpollock.org/

Joan Miro

    http://www.artnet.com/artist/675008/joan-miro.html

    http://www.artcyclopedia.com/artists/miro_joan.html

    http://www.artelino.com/articles/joan_miro.asp

    http://www.enchantedlearning.com/artists/miro/

    http://www.halter.net/gallery/miro.html

Marble Mania!

    http://www.sciencenetlinks.com/interactives/marble/marblemania.html

Virtual Manipulatives—Spinners

    http://nlvm.usu.edu/en/nav/frames_asid_186_g_1_t_1.html?open=activities

Assessment Resources References

Bright, G., & Joyner, J. (1998). *Classroom assessment in mathematics*. Lanham, MD: University Press of America.

British Columbia Ministry of Education. (n.d.). *Handbook of assessment tools for process evaluation in mathematics*. Victoria, BC: The Ministry.

Bryant, D., & Driscoll, M. (1998). *Exploring classroom assessment in mathematics: A guide for professional development*. Reston, VA: NCTM.

Bush, W. (2001). *Mathematics assessment: Cases and discussion questions for grades K–5*. Reston, VA: NCTM.

Charles, R., Lester, F., & O'Daffer, P. (1987). *How to evaluate progress in problem solving*. Reston, VA: NCTM.

Clarke, D. (1997). *Constructive assessment in mathematics: Practical steps for classroom teachers*. Emeryville, CA: Key Curriculum Press.

Glanfield, F., Bush, W., & Stenmark, J. (2003). *Mathematics assessment: A practical handbook for grades K–2*. Reston, VA: NCTM.

Kulm, G. (1994). *Mathematics assessment: What works in the classroom*. San Francisco: Jossey-Bass.

Madfes, T. (1999). *Learning from assessment: Tools for examining assessment through standards*. Reston, VA: NCTM.

Mathematical Sciences Education Board. (1994). *Measuring up: Prototypes for mathematics assessment*. Washington, DC: National Academy Press.

Montgomery, K. (2001). *Authentic assessment: A guide for elementary teachers*. New York: Addison Wesley Longman.

National Council of Teachers of Mathematics (NCTM). (1995). *Assessment standards for school mathematics*. Reston, VA: NCTM.

Ott, J. (1994). *Alternate assessment in the mathematics classroom*. Columbus, OH: Glencoe/McGraw-Hill.

Pandey, T. (1991). *A sampler of mathematics assessment*. Sacramento: California Department of Education.

Schoenfeld, A. (1999). *Elementary grades assessment*. White Plains, NY: Dale Seymour.

Stenmark, J. (1989). *Assessment alternatives in mathematics: An overview of assessment techniques that promote learning*. Berkeley: University of California.

Stenmark, J. (Ed.). (1991). *Mathematics assessment: Myths, models, good questions, and practical suggestions*. Reston, VA: NCTM.

Stenmark, J., & Bush, W. (2001). *Mathematics assessment: A practical handbook for grades 3–5*. Reston, VA: NCTM.

Walch, J. (2003). *Assessment: Strategies for math*. Portland, ME: Walch.

Webb, N., & Coxford, A. (1993). *Assessment in the mathematics classroom*. Reston, VA: NCTM.

Children's Literature References

Adler, D. (1991). *A picture book of Christopher Columbus*. New York: Scholastic.

Adler, D. (1992). *A picture book of Helen Keller*. New York: Holiday House.

Adler, D. (1999). *How tall how short how far away*. New York: Holiday House.

Aigner-Clark, J. (2002). *Baby Einstein: The ABCs of art*. New York: Hyperion Books for Children.

Aker, S. (1990). *What comes in 2's, 3's, & 4's?* New York: Simon & Schuster.

Alda, A. (1998). *Arlene Alda's 1 2 3: What do you see?* Berkeley, CA: Tricycle Press.

Amato, W. (2002). *Math in my world: Math at the store*. New York: Children's Press.

Anderson, J. (2003). *Money: A rich history*. New York: Grosset & Dunlap.

Anno, M. (1975). *Anno's counting book*. New York: HarperCollins.

Appel, J., & Guglielmo, A. (2006). *Feed Matisse's fish*. New York: Sterling.

Appelt, K. (2000). *Bats around the clock*. New York: HarperCollins.

Archambault, J. (2004). *Boom chicka rock*. New York: Philomel Books.

Arnold, T. (2000). *Parts*. New York: Puffin Books.

Arnold, T. (2005). *More parts*. New York: Puffin Books.

Arnold, T. (2007). *Even more parts*. New York: Puffin Books.

Asch, F. (1994). *The earth and I*. New York: Scholastic.

Axelrod, A. (1994). *Pigs will be pigs*. New York: Aladdin Paperbacks.

Axelrod, A. (2002). *Pigs on the move*. New York: Aladdin.

Axelrod, A. (2003). *Pigs at odds: Fun with math and games*. New York: Aladdin Paperbacks.

Bader, B. (2003). *All aboard math reader: Graphs*. New York: Grosset & Dunlap.

Balestrino, P. (1989). *The skeleton inside you*. New York: HarperCollins.

Barner, B. (1996). *Dem bones*. San Francisco: Chronicle Books.

Barner, B. (2002). *Stars! Stars! Stars!* San Francisco: Chronicle Books.

Barton, B. (1988). *I want to be an astronaut*. New York: HarperCollins.

Bell, N. (1982). *The book of where: Or how to be naturally geographic* (A brown paper schoolbook series). New York: Little, Brown.

Berger, M., & Berger, G. (1999). *Do stars have points? Questions and answers about stars and planets*. New York: Scholastic.

Berger, M., & Berger, G. (2001). *Round and round the money goes* (Discovery readers series). Nashville: Ideals.

Berlin, I. (2006). *God bless America*. New York: HarperCollins.

Birmingham, D. (1988). *M is for mirror*. Norfolk, UK: Tarquin.

Blackstone, S. (2006). *How big is a pig?* Cambridge, MA: Barefoot Books.

Blanquet, C. (1993). *Miro: Earth and sky* (Art for children series). New York: Chelsea House.

Boring, M. (1999). *Caterpillars, bugs, and butterflies.* Minnetonka, MN: T&N Children's.

Brandenburg, A. (1963). *The story of Johnny Appleseed.* New York: Aladdin Paperbacks.

Brandenburg, A. (1989). *My five senses.* New York: HarperCollins.

Branley, F. (1981). *The sky is full of stars.* New York: HarperCollins.

Branley, F. (1986). *What makes day and night.* New York: Crowell.

Branley, F. (1997). *Down comes the rain.* New York: HarperCollins.

Branley, F. (2002). *The sun: Our nearest star.* New York: HarperCollins.

Branley, F. (2005). *Sunshine makes the seasons.* New York: HarperCollins.

Bredeson, C. (2003). *Astronauts.* New York: Children's Press.

Brisson, P. (1993). *Benny's pennies.* New York: Dell Dragonfly Books.

Brocklehurst, R. (2004). *Usborne children's picture atlas.* New York: Scholastic.

Brown, C. (1998). *Animal at homes.* Lanham, MD: Rinehart.

Brown, M. (1998). *I like stars.* New York: Golden Books.

Brown, S. (2003). *Professor Aesop's the crow and the pitcher.* Berkeley, CA: Tricycle Press.

Brumbeau, J. (2001). *The quiltmaker's gift.* New York: Scholastic.

Brumbeau, J. (2004). *The quiltmaker's journey.* New York: Orchard Books.

Bryan, N. (2003). *Hmong Americans.* Edina, MN: ABDO.

Bunting, E. (2000). *Flower garden.* San Diego: Harcourt Children's Books.

Burke, J. (2000). *Circles* (City shapes series). New York: Children's Press.

Burke, J. (2000). *Ovals* (City shapes series). New York: Children's Press.

Burke, J. (2000). *Rectangles* (City shapes series). New York: Children's Press.

Burke, J. (2000). *Squares* (City shapes series). New York: Children's Press.

Burke, J. (2000). *Triangles* (City shapes series). New York: Children's Press.

Burns, M. (1994). *The greedy triangle.* New York: Scholastic.

Carle, E. (1999). *The tiny seed.* New York: Simon & Schuster Books for Young Readers.

Cave, K. (2002). *One child, one seed: A South African counting book.* New York: Holt.

Charman, A. (2003). *I wonder why trees have leaves and other questions about plants.* Boston: Houghton Mifflin.

Chesanow, N. (1995). *Where do I live?* Hauppauge, NY: Barron's Educational Series.

Chorao, K. (2001). *Shadow night.* New York: Dutton Children's Books.

Coburn, J., & Lee, T. (1996). *Jouanah: A Hmong Cinderella.* Fremont, CA: Shen's Books.

Cohen, J. (2000). *You can be a woman engineer.* Culver City, CA: Cascade Pass.

Cole, H. (1997). *Jack's garden.* New York: HarperTrophy.

Cole, J. (1987). *The magic school bus inside the earth* (Magic school bus series). New York: Scholastic.

Cole, J. (1995). *The magic school bus hops home: A book about animal habitats* (Magic school bus series). New York: HarperCollins.

Cole, J. (1999). *The magic school bus explores the senses* (Magic school bus series). New York: Scholastic.

Cole, J. (2000). *The magic school bus explores the world of animals* (Magic school bus series). New York: Scholastic.

Cole, J. (2001). *The magic school bus plants seeds: A book about how living things grow* (Magic school bus series). New York: Scholastic.

Crews, L. (2000). *This is the sunflower.* New York: Scholastic.

Cristaldi, K. (1996). *Even Steven and odd Todd.* New York: Scholastic.

Cronin, D. (2004). *Duck for president.* New York: Simon & Schuster Books for Young Readers.

Crummel, S. (2003). *All in one hour.* Tarrytown, NY: Marshall Cavendish.

Cumbaa, S. (2006). *The bones book and skeleton.* New York: Workman.

Davis, G. (2004). *Wackiest White House pets.* New York: Scholastic.

Davis, K. (2002). *Don't know much about the presidents.* New York: HarperCollins.

De Paola, T. (1975). *The cloud book.* New York: Holiday House.

DeWitt, L. (1991). *What will the weather be?* New York: HarperCollins.

Dijs, C. (1993). *What do I do at 8 o'clock?* New York: Simon & Schuster.

Ditchfield, K. (2000). *Serving your community.* New York: Scholastic.

Dodds, D. (1994). *The shape of things.* Cambridge, MA: Candlewick Press.

Domanska, J. (1996). *If all the seas were one sea.* New York: Aladdin Paperbacks.

Dotlich, R. (1999). *What is round?* New York: Scholastic.

Dotlich, R. (1999). *What is a square?* New York: Scholastic.

Dotlich, R. (2000). *What is a triangle?* New York: Scholastic.

Driscoll, M. (2004). *A child's introduction to the night sky.* New York: Black Dog & Leventhal.

Ehlert, L. (1990). *Color farm.* New York: HarperCollins.

Ehlert, L. (1990). *Growing vegetable soup.* San Diego: Harcourt Children's Books.

Ehlert, L. (1993). *Eating the alphabet.* San Diego: Harcourt Children's Books.

Ehlert, L. (1997). *Color zoo.* New York: HarperCollins.

Ehlert, L. (2001). *Planting a rainbow.* San Diego: Harcourt Children's Books.

Evans, L. (1999). *Can you count ten toes?: Count to 10 in 10 different languages.* Boston: Houghton Mifflin.

Fanelli, S. (1995). *My map book.* New York: HarperCollins.

Feelings, M. (1971). *Moja means one: Swahili counting book*. New York: Puffin Books.

Flood, N. (2006). *The Navajo year, walk through many seasons*. Flagstaff, AZ: Salina Bookshelf.

Florian, D. (2001). *Lizards, frogs, and polliwogs*. Orlando, FL: Voyager Books.

Fowler, A. (1991). *The sun is always shining somewhere*. Chicago: Children's Press.

Fowler, A. (2001). *From seed to plant*. New York: Scholastic.

Franco, B. (2003). *Shadow shapes*. Vernon Hills, IL: ETA Cuisenaire.

Franco, B. (2003). *Something furry in the garage at 6:30 A.M.* Vernon Hills, IL: ETA Cuisenaire.

Fuqua, N. (2004). *First pets: Presidential best friends*. New York: Scholastic.

Gallant, R. (1991). *The constellations: How they came to be*. New York: Four Winds Press.

Garrison, J., & Tubesing, A. (1996). *A million visions of peace: Wisdom from the Friends of Old Turtle*. New York: Scholastic.

Ghez, A., & Cohen, J. (2006). *You can be a woman astronomer*. Culver City, CA: Cascade Pass.

Gibbons, G. (1983). *Sun up, sun down*. San Diego: Harcourt Brace.

Gibbons, G. (1989). *Monarch butterfly*. New York: Scholastic.

Gibbons, G. (1990). *Weather words and what they mean*. New York: Holiday House.

Gibbons, G. (1992). *Recycle! A handbook for kids*. Boston: Little, Brown.

Gibbons, G. (1993). *From seed to plant*. New York: Holiday House.

Gibbons, G. (1995). *Planet Earth/inside out*. New York: Morrow Books.

Gibbons, G. (1999). *Stargazers*. New York: Holiday House.

Giganti, P. (1988). *How many snails?* New York: Greenwillow Books.

Giganti, P. (1992). *Each orange had 8 slices: A counting book*. New York: Scholastic.

Giganti, P. (2005). *How many blue birds flew away?* New York: Greenwillow Books.

Giraud, H. (2005). *Basha: A Hmong child*. Farmington Hills, MI: Thomas Gale.

Glaser, O. (1997). *Round the garden*. New York: Scholastic.

Goldie, S. (2006). *Animals in their homes*. New York: Lark Books.

Goldman, D. (2004). *Presidential losers*. Minneapolis: Lerner.

Gordon, P., & Snow, R. (2004). *Kids learn America! Bringing geography to life with people, places & history*. Charlotte, VT: Williamson.

Grandfield, L. (2003). *America votes: How our president is elected*. Tonawanda, NY: Kids Can Press.

Green, J. (1992). *Why should I recycle?* Hauppauge, NY: Barron's Educational Series.

Greene, R. (1997). *When a line bends . . . A shape begins*. New York: Scholastic.

Grodin, E. (2004). *D is for democracy: A citizen's alphabet*. Chelsea, MI: Sleeping Bear Press.

Grossman, V. (1991). *Ten little rabbits*. San Francisco: Chronicle Books.

Hartman, G. (1993). *As the crow flies: A first book of maps*. New York: Aladdin Paperbacks.

Hartman, G. (1994). *As the roadrunner runs: A first book of maps.* New York: Macmillan.

Haskins, J. (1987). *Count your way through China.* Minneapolis: Carolrhoda Books.

Haskins, J. (1989). *Count your way through Africa.* Minneapolis: Carolrhoda Books.

Haskins, J. (1989). *Count your way through Korea.* Minneapolis: Carolrhoda Books.

Haskins, J. (1989). *Count your way through Mexico.* Minneapolis: Carolrhoda Books.

Haskins, J. (1990). *Count your way through Germany.* Minneapolis: Carolrhoda Books.

Haskins, J. (1992). *Count your way through India.* Minneapolis: Carolrhoda Books.

Haskins, J. (1992). *Count your way through Israel.* Minneapolis: Carolrhoda Books.

Haskins, J. (1996). *Count your way through Brazil.* Minneapolis: Carolrhoda Books.

Haskins, J. (1996). *Count your way through France.* Minneapolis: Carolrhoda Books.

Haskins, J. (1996). *Count your way through Greece.* Minneapolis: Carolrhoda Books.

Haskins, J. (1996). *Count your way through Ireland.* Minneapolis: Carolrhoda Books.

Haskins, J. (1998). *Count your way through Russia.* Minneapolis: Carolrhoda Books.

Hayward, L. (2001). *A day in the life of a builder.* New York: Dorling Kindersley.

Hayward, L. (2001). *A day in the life of a dancer.* New York: Dorling Kindersley.

Hayward, L. (2001). *A day in the life of a doctor.* New York: Dorling Kindersley.

Hayward, L. (2001). *A day in the life of a firefighter.* New York: Dorling Kindersley.

Hayward, L. (2001). *A day in the life of a musician.* New York: Dorling Kindersley.

Hayward, L. (2001). *A day in the life of a police officer.* New York: Dorling Kindersley.

Hayward, L. (2001). *A day in the life of a teacher.* New York: Dorling Kindersley.

Heiligman, D. (1996). *From caterpillar to butterfly.* New York: HarperCollins.

Heller, R. (1999). *Plants that never ever bloom.* New York: Penguin Young Readers.

Heller, R. (1999). *The reason for a flower.* New York: Penguin Young Readers.

Herman, J. (1998). *Red, white, and blue: The story of the American flag.* New York: Grosset & Dunlap.

Hill, M. (2005). *Dimes.* New York: Scholastic.

Hill, M. (2005). *Dollars.* New York: Scholastic.

Hill, M. (2005). *Nickels.* New York: Scholastic.

Hill, M. (2005). *Pennies.* New York: Scholastic.

Hill, M. (2005). *Quarters.* New York: Scholastic.

Hill, M. (2005). *Spending and saving.* New York: Scholastic.

Hoban, T. (1986). *Shapes, shapes, shapes.* New York: Greenwillow Books.

Hoban, T. (1987). *26 letters and 99 cents.* New York: Greenwillow Books.

Hoban, T. (1997). *Is it larger? Is it smaller?* New York: Greenwillow Books.

Hoban, T. (1998). *More, fewer, less.* New York: Greenwillow Books.

Hoban, T. (1998). *So many circles, so many squares*. New York: Greenwillow Books.

Hoban, T. (1999). *Let's count*. New York: Greenwillow Books.

Hoban, T. (2000). *Cubes, cones, cylinders, & spheres*. New York: Greenwillow Books.

Holub, J. (2001). *Vincent van Gogh: Sunflowers and swirly stars*. New York: Grosset & Dunlap.

Hoose, P. (2002). *It's our world, too!* New York: Farrar Straus Giroux.

Hopkins, L. (1995). *Weather: Poems for all seasons*. New York: HarperCollins.

Hutchins, P. (1970). *Clocks and more clocks*. New York: Aladdin Paperbacks.

Hutchins, P. (1993). *The wind blew*. New York: Simon & Schuster Children's.

Jenkins, S. (1995). *Biggest, strongest, fastest*. Boston: Houghton Mifflin.

Jenkins, S. (2004). *Actual size*. Boston: Houghton Mifflin.

Jenkins, S. (2006). *Almost gone: The world's rarest animals*. New York: Scholastic.

Jenkins, S., & Page, R. (1995). *I see a kookaburra!* Boston: Houghton Mifflin.

Jenkins, S., & Page, R. (2003). *What do you do with a tail like this?* Boston: Houghton Mifflin.

Johnson, K., & O'Connor, J. (2002). *Henri Matisse: Drawing with scissors*. New York: Grosset & Dunlap.

Jolivet, J. (2002). *Zoo-ology*. New Milford, CT: Roaring Brook Press.

Jolivet, J. (2005). *Almost everything*. New Milford, CT: Roaring Brook Press.

Jonas, A. (1987). *Reflections*. New York: Greenwillow Books.

Jordan, H. (1992). *How a seed grows*. New York: HarperCollins.

Kalman, B. (1994). *Animal homes*. New York: Crabtree.

Kalman, B. (1997). *Community helpers from A to Z*. New York: Crabtree.

Kalman, B. (2000). *What is a community? From A to Z*. New York: Crabtree.

Kandoian, E. (1987). *Under the sun*. New York: Dodd Mead.

Kandoian, E. (1989). *Is anybody up?* New York: Putnam.

Keenan, S. (2004). *O, say can you see? America's symbols, landmarks, and important words*. New York: Scholastic.

Keller, H. (2001). *Growing like me*. San Diego: Harcourt.

Keller, L. (2002). *Scrambled states of America*. New York: Holt.

Kerrod, R. (2002). *The book of constellations: Discover the secrets in the stars*. Hauppauge, NY: Barron's Educational Series.

Kincade, S. (1992). *Our time is now (Young people changing the world)*. Upper Saddle River, NJ: Pearson Foundation.

Knight, M. (2002). *Africa is not a country*. Minneapolis: Lerner.

Knowlton, J. (1985). *Maps and globes*. New York: HarperCollins.

Knowlton, J. (1988). *Geography from A to Z: A picture glossary*. New York: HarperCollins.

Krauss, R. (1989). *The carrot seed*. New York: HarperCollins.

Krebs, L. (2003). *We all went on safari: A counting journey through Tanzania*. New York: Scholastic.

Krull, K. (2004). *A woman for president: The story of Victoria Woodhull*. New York: Walker Books for Young Readers.

Krupp, E. (1991). *Beyond the blue horizon: Myths and legends of the sun, moon, stars, and planets*. New York: HarperCollins.

Krupp, E., & Krupp, R. (1989). *The Big Dipper and you*. New York: Morrow.

Kupchella, R. (2004). *Girls can! Make it happen*. Golden Valley, MN: Tristan.

Landau, E. (2003). *The president's work: A look at the executive branch* (How government works series). Minneapolis: Lerner.

Lay, K. (2004). *Crown me!* New York: Holiday House.

Leedy, L. (1997). *Measuring Penny*. New York: Holt.

Leedy, L. (2000). *The great trash bash*. New York: Holiday House.

Leedy, L. (2003). *Mapping Penny's world*. New York: Holt.

Leedy, L. (2005). *The great graph contest*. New York: Holiday House.

Lehn, B. (1988). *What is a scientist?* New York: HarperCollins.

Lesser, C. (1999). *Spots: Counting creatures from sea to sky*. San Diego: Harcourt Brace.

Lewin, B. (1980). *Animal snackers*. New York: Scholastic.

Lewis, J. (1998). *Doodle dandies: Poems that take shape*. New York: Aladdin.

Lewis, J. (1999). *A hippopotamusn't and other animal poems*. New York: Dial Books for Young Readers.

Lewis, J. (2002). *A world of wonders: Geographic travels in verse and rhyme*. New York: Dial Books for Young Readers.

Lewis, R. (2002). *All of the earth, all of the sky*. New York: Scholastic.

Lewison, W. (2002). *F is for flag*. New York: Grosset & Dunlap.

Liatsos, S. (1999). *Poems to count on*. New York: Scholastic.

Linn, C. (1972). *Probability*. New York: Crowell.

Lionni, L. (1960). *Inch by inch*. New York: HarperCollins.

Lionni, L. (1992). *A busy year*. New York: Knopf.

Ljungkvist, L. (2006). *Follow the line*. New York: Penguin.

Llewellyn, C. (1992). *My first book of time*. New York: Dorling Kindersley.

Long, L. (1996). *Domino addition*. New York: Scholastic.

Love, A., & Drake, J. (2004). *The kid's book of the night sky*. Tonawanda, NY: Kids Can Press.

Lundell, M. (1995). *A girl named Helen Keller*. New York: Scholastic.

Maccarone, G. (1997). *Monster math: School time*. New York: Scholastic.

Mackey, L. (2004). *Money mama and the three little pigs*. Angoura Hills, CA: P4K.

Maher, R. (2003). *Alice Yazzie's year*. Berkeley, CA: Tricycle Press.

Mannis, C. (2002). *One leaf rides the wind: Counting in a Japanese garden*. New York: Scholastic.

Martin, J. (1998). *Snowflake Bentley*. Boston: Houghton Mifflin.

Marzollo, J. (1996). *I'm a seed*. New York: Scholastic.

Marzollo, J. (2001). *I am planet Earth*. New York: Scholastic.

Maze, S. (2006). *Peaceful moments in the wild: Animals and their homes*. Potomac, MD: Moonstone Press.

McAlary, F., & Cohen, J. (2001). *You can be a woman marine biologist*. Culver City, CA: Cascade Pass.

McCallum, A. (2005). *Beanstalk: The measure of a giant*. Watertown, MA: Charlesbridge.

McIntyre, P. (2006). *It's about time*. Mustang, OK: Tate.

Medearis, A. (2000). *Seven spools of thread: A Kwanzaa story*. New York: Scholastic.

Merriam, E. (1993). *12 Ways to Get to 11*. New York: Aladdin Paperbacks.

The Metropolitan Museum of Art. (2004). *Museum 1 2 3*. New York: Little, Brown.

The Metropolitan Museum of Art. (2005). *Museum shapes*. New York: Little, Brown.

Metzger, S. (2003). *The little snowflake*. New York: Scholastic.

Micklethwait, L. (1993). *A child's book of art: Great pictures: First words*. New York: Dorling Kindersley.

Micklethwait, L. (1993). *I spy two eyes: Numbers in art*. New York: Greenwillow Books.

Micklethwait, L. (2004). *I spy shapes in art*. New York: Greenwillow Books.

Miller, M. (1990). *Who uses this?* New York: Greenwillow Books.

Miller, M. (1998). *My five senses*. New York: Simon & Schuster's Children's.

Mitton, J. (1998). *Zoo in the sky: A book of animal constellations*. Washington, DC: National Geographic.

Mitton, J. (2004). *Once upon a starry night: A book of constellations*. Washington, DC: National Geographic.

Mollel, T. (1999). *My rows and piles of coins*. New York: Clarion Books.

Murphy, S. (1996). *The best bug parade*. New York: HarperCollins.

Murphy, S. (1997). *Just enough carrots*. New York: HarperCollins.

Murphy, S. (1998). *Animals on board*. New York: HarperCollins.

Murphy, S. (1998). *The penny pot*. New York: Scholastic.

Murphy, S. (1999). *Room for Ripley*. New York: HarperCollins.

Murphy, S. (2000). *Let's fly a kite*. New York: Scholastic.

Murphy, S. (2001). *Missing mittens*. New York: HarperCollins.

Murphy, S. (2001). *Probably pistachio*. New York: HarperCollins.

Murphy, S. (2002). *Bigger, better, best!* New York: HarperCollins.

Murphy, S. (2003). *Double the ducks.* New York: HarperCollins.

Murphy, S. (2003). *Three little firefighters.* New York: HarperCollins.

Murphy, S. (2004). *A house for birdie.* New York: HarperCollins.

Murphy, S. (2004). *Mighty Maddie.* New York: HarperCollins.

Murphy, S. (2005). *It's about time!* New York: HarperCollins.

Murphy, S. (2005). *More of less.* New York: HarperCollins.

Myller, R. (1990). *How big is a foot?* New York: Random House.

Neuschwander, C. (2005). *Mummy math: An adventure in geometry.* New York: Holt.

Nicolson, J. (2006). *Animal architects.* Crows Nest, NSW: Allen & Unwin.

Numeroff, L. (1985). *If you give a mouse a cookie.* New York: HarperCollins.

Numeroff, L. (1991). *If you give moose a muffin.* New York: HarperCollins.

Numeroff, L. (1998). *If you give a pig a pancake.* New York: HarperCollins.

Numeroff, L. (2005). *If you give a pig a party.* New York: HarperCollins.

Olson, N. (2006). *Rectangles around town.* Mankato, MN: Capstone Press.

Otto, C. (1996). *What color is camouflage?* New York: HarperCollins.

Oughton, J. (1992). *How the stars fell into the sky.* Boston: Houghton Mifflin.

Pallotta, J. (1992). *The icky bug counting book.* Watertown, MA: Charlesbridge.

Pallotta, J. (1998). *The butterfly counting book.* New York: Scholastic.

Pallotta, J. (2001). *The Hershey's kisses addition book.* New York: Scholastic.

Pallotta, J. (2001). *Underwater counting: Even numbers.* Watertown, MA: Charlesbridge.

Pallotta, J. (2004). *Hershey's chocolate math: From addition to multiplication.* New York: Scholastic.

Pallotta, J. (2005). *Ocean counting: Odd numbers.* Watertown, MA: Charlesbridge.

Pallotta, J. (2006). *Snakes: Long, longer, longest.* New York: Scholastic.

Parker, K. (2005). *Counting in the garden.* New York: Orchard Books.

Parker, S. (2004). *The human body* (100 things you should know about series). New York: Barnes & Noble Books.

Pearce, Q., & Fraser, M. (1991). *The stargazer's guide to the galaxy.* New York: RGA.

Pelusey, M. (2005). *Africa.* New York: Chelsea House.

Pershing Accelerated School Students. (2002). *We dream of a world.* New York: Scholastic.

Pfeffer, W. (2004). *From seed to pumpkin.* New York: HarperCollins.

Pinczes, E. (2001). *Inch worm and a half.* Boston: Houghton Mifflin.

Piven, H. (2004). *What presidents are made of.* New York: Antheneum Books for Young Readers.

Pluckrose, H. (1995). *Capacity*. New York: Scholastic.

Pluckrose, H. (1995). *Length*. New York: Scholastic.

Pluckrose, H. (1995). *Size*. New York: Scholastic.

Pluckrose, H. (1995). *Sorting*. New York: Children's Press.

Pluckrose, H. (1995). *Time*. New York: Scholastic.

Pollak, B. (2004). *Our community garden*. Hillsboro, OR: Beyond Words.

Pomeroy, D. (1996). *One potato: A counting book of potato prints*. San Diego: Harcourt Brace.

Prelutsky, J. (1984). *The new kid on the block*. New York: Scholastic.

Prelutsky, J. (1996). *A pizza the size of the sun*. New York: Scholastic.

Prelutsky, J. (2006). *It's snowing! It's snowing: Winter poems*. New York: HarperCollins.

Priddy, G. (2003). *ABC of jobs*. New York: Scholastic.

Provensen, A. (1997). *The buck stops here: The President of the United States of America*. New York: Browndeer Press Paperbacks.

Rabe, T. (2002). *There's a map in my lap!* New York: Random House Children's Books.

Rachlin, A. (1994). *Beethoven* (Famous children series). Hauppauge, NY: Barron's Educational Series.

Rau, D. (2006). *The shape of the world: Rectangles*. New York: Benchmark Books.

Rau, D. (2006). *The shape of the world: Squares*. New York: Benchmark Books.

Regier, D. (2006). *What time is it?* New York: Children's Press.

Rey, H. (1980). *The stars: A new way to see them*. Boston: Houghton Mifflin.

Rey, H. (1982). *Find the constellations*. Boston: Houghton Mifflin.

Reynolds, P. (2003). *The dot*. Cambridge, MA: Candlewick Press.

Reynolds, P. (2004). *Ish*. Cambridge, MA: Candlewick Press.

Richards, K. (2000) *It's about time, Max!* New York: Sagebrush Educational Resources.

Ridpath, I. (1988). *Star tales*. New York: Universe Books.

Rius, M., Parramon, J., & Puig, J. (1985). *Hearing* (The five senses series). Hauppauge, NY: Barron's Educational Series.

Rius, M., Parramon, J., & Puig, J. (1985). *Sight* (The five senses series). Hauppauge, NY: Barron's Educational Series.

Rius, M., Parramon, J., & Puig, J. (1985). *Smell* (The five senses series). Hauppauge, NY: Barron's Educational Series.

Rius, M., Parramon, J., & Puig, J. (1986). *Taste* (The five senses series). Hauppauge, NY: Barron's Educational Series.

Rius, M., Parramon, J., & Puig, J. (1986). *Touch* (The five senses series). Hauppauge, NY: Barron's Educational Series.

Robinson, F. (1995). *Recycle that!* New York: Scholastic.

Roca, N. (2002). *Boys and girls of the world: From one end to the other*. Hauppauge, NY: Barron's Educational Series, Inc.

Roca, N. (2004). *Fall*. Hauppauge, NY: Barron's Educational Series.

Roca, N. (2004). *Spring*. Hauppauge, NY: Barron's Educational Series.

Roca, N. (2004). *Summer*. Hauppauge, NY: Barron's Educational Series.

Roca, N. (2004). *Winter*. Hauppauge, NY: Barron's Educational Series.

Rockwell, A. (1998). *Our earth*. New York: Scholastic.

Rose, D. (2003). *One nighttime sea*. New York: Scholastic.

Ross, N. (1994). *Miro* (Famous artists series). Hauppauge, NY: Barron's Educational Series.

Royston, A. (1998). *How plants grow*. Chicago: Heinemann Library.

Rubel, D. (1994). *Scholastic encyclopedia of the presidents and their times*. New York: Scholastic.

Russo, M. (2000). *The big brown box*. New York: Greenwillow Books.

Ryder, J. (1996). *Where butterflies grow*. New York: Penguin Young Readers Group.

Sacks, J. (2004). *Magic skeleton: Human body*. New York: Sterling.

Sasaki, C. (2003). *The constellations: Stars and stories*. New York: Sterling.

Sayre, A. & Sayre, J. (2003). *One is a snail, ten is a crab*. Cambridge, MA: Candlewick Press.

Schaefer, L. (2000). *This is the sunflower*. New York: Scholastic.

Schnetzler, P. (2004). *Earth day birthday*. Nevada City, CA: Dawn.

Schoberle, C. (1994). *Day lights, night lights*. New York: Simon & Schuster.

Schuett, S. (1995). *Somewhere in the world right now*. New York: Dragon Fly Books.

Schwartz, D. (1999*). If you hopped like a frog*. New York: Scholastic.

Scieszka, J., & Smith, L. (2005). *Seen art?* New York: Viking Press.

Scillian, D. (2001). *A is for America: An American alphabet*. Chelsea, MI: Sleeping Bear Press.

Scillian, D. (2002). *One nation: America by the numbers*. Chelsea, MI: Sleeping Bear Press.

Sendak, M. (1988). *Where the wild things are*. New York: HarperCollins.

Shields, C. (1998). *Day by day a week goes round*. New York: Dutton Children's Books.

Shields, C. (1998). *Lunch money and other poems about school*. New York: Puffin Books.

Shields, C. (1998). *Month by month a year goes round*. New York: Dutton Children's Books.

Shipman, W. (1994). *Animal architects: How animals weave, tunnel, and build their remarkable homes*. Mechanicsburg, PA: Stackpole Books.

Shipton, J. (1999). *What if?* New York: Dial Books for Young Readers.

Showers, P. (1994). *Where does the garbage go?* New York: HarperCollins.

Siddals, M. (1998). *Millions of snowflakes*. New York: Scholastic.

Sierra, J. (2004). *What time is it, Mr. Crocodile?* New York: Harcourt Children's Books.

Silverstein, S. (1981). *A light in the attic*. New York: HarperCollins.

Silverstein, S. (1996). *Falling up*. New York: HarperCollins.

Silverstein, S. (2004). *Where the sidewalk ends*. New York: HarperCollins.

Simon, S. (1984). *Earth*. New York: Four Winds Press.

Simon, S. (2000). *Bones: Our skeletal system*. New York: HarperCollins.

Singer, M. (1991). *Nine o'clock lullaby*. New York: Scholastic.

Sipiera, P. (1999). *Seasons* (True book series). New York: Scholastic.

Sipiera, P., & Sipiera, D. (1997). *Constellations*. Danbury, CT: Scholastic.

Sis, P. (1996). *Starry messenger*. New York: Farrar Strauss Giroux.

Sis, P. (2003). *The train of states*. New York: Greenwillow Books.

Sitomer, M., & Sitomer, H. (1970). *What is symmetry?* New York: Crowell.

Smith, R., & Smith, M. (2005). *N is for our nation's capital: A Washington, DC, alphabet* (Discover America state by state alphabet series). Chelsea, MI: Sleeping Bear Press.

Sobel, S. (1999). *How the U.S. government works*. Hauppauge, NY: Barron's Educational Series.

Sobel, S. (2001). *Presidential elections: And other cool facts*. Hauppauge, NY: Barron's Educational Series.

Spier, P. (1980). *People*. New York: Doubleday.

Squire, A. (2001). *Animal babies*. New York: Children's Press.

Squire, A. (2002). *Animal homes*. New York: Scholastic.

Srivastava, J. (1975). *Averages*. New York: Crowell.

St. George, J. (2000). *So you want to be president?* New York: Philomel Books.

Stewart, D. (2002). *Animal builder*. New York: Scholastic.

Stott, C. (2003). *I wonder why stars twinkle (and other questions about space)*. New York: Kingfisher.

Sullivan, G. (1987). *Facts and fun about the presidents*. New York: Scholastic.

Sweeney, J. (1996). *Me on the map*. New York: Dragonfly Books.

Sweeney, J. (1998). *Me and my place in space*. New York: Dragonfly Books.

Tang, G. (1999). *Math potatoes: Mind stretching brain food*. New York: Scholastic.

Tang, G. (2001). *The grapes of math: Mind stretching math riddles*. New York: Scholastic.

Tang, G. (2002). *The best of times: Math strategies that multiply*. New York: Scholastic.

Tang, G. (2003). *Math appeal: Mind stretching math riddles*. New York: Scholastic.

Tang, G. (2003). *Math-terpieces: The art of problem solving*. New York: Scholastic.

Tang, G. (2004). *Math fables*. New York: Scholastic.

Taylor, H. (1997). *Coyote places the stars*. New York: Aladdin.

Thimmesh, C. (2004). *Madame President: The extraordinary, true, (and evolving) story of women in politics*. Boston: Houghton Mifflin.

Thompson, C. (1989). *Glow in the dark constellations: A field guide for young stargazers*. New York: Grosset & Dunlap.

Thompson, V., & Cohen, J. (2001). *You can be a woman marine biologist*. Marina del Ray, CA: Cascade Pass.

Thompson, V., & Cohen, J. (2001). *You can be a woman zoologist*. Marina del Ray, CA: Cascade Pass.

Thomson, S. (2003). *Stars and stripes: The story of the American Flag*. New York: HarperCollins.

Thong, R. (2000). *Round is a mooncake*. New York: Scholastic.

Trapanzi, I. (1992). *What am I? An animal guessing game*. New York: Whispering Coyote.

Turnbull, S. (2003). *Usborne beginners: Sun, moon, and stars*. New York: Scholastic.

Turnbull, S. (2005). *Your body* (Usborne beginners series). New York: Scholastic.

Venezia, M. (1989). *Van Gogh* (Getting to know the world's greatest artists series). Chicago: Children's Press.

Venezia, M. (1993). *Georgia O'Keeffe* (Getting to know the world's greatest artists series). Chicago: Children's Press.

Venezia, M. (1993). *Salvador Dali* (Getting to know the world's greatest artists series). Chicago: Children's Press.

Venezia, M. (1996). *Ludwig van Beethoven* (Getting to know the world's greatest composers series). New York: Children's Press.

Venezia, M. (1997). *Henri Matisse* (Getting to know the world's greatest artists series). New York: Children's Press.

Wallner, A. (1994). *Betsy Ross*. New York: Scholastic.

Wayman, S. (2002). *God bless America: Children's thoughts on patriotism*. Parker, CO: Thornton.

Wells, R. (1995). *What's smaller than a pygmy shrew?* Morton Grove, IL: Whitman.

Williams, J. (2005). *How does the sun make weather?* Berkeley Heights, NJ: Enslow.

Williams, R. (2001). *The coin counting book*. Watertown, MA: Charlesbridge.

Wormell, C. (2004). *Teeth, tails, & tentacles: An animal counting book*. Philadelphia: Running Press.

Worth, B. (2001). *Oh say can you seed?* New York: Random House.

Wyatt, V. (2000). *Wacky plant cycles*. New York: Mondo.

Xiong, B. (1989). *Nine-in-one Grr! Grr!* San Francisco: Children's Book Press.

Instructional Resources References

Recommended Book Series

100 Things You Should Know About Series (Barnes & Noble Books)

Artists in Their Times Series (Scholastic)

Barron's Famous Artist Series (Aladdin)

Childhood of Famous Americans Series (Aladdin)

Discover America State by State Alphabet Series (Sleeping Bear Press)

Discoveries Series (Barnes & Noble Books)

Don't Know Much About Series (HarperTrophy)

Eyewitness Books Series (Dorling Kindersley)

Getting to Know the World's Greatest Artists Series (Children's Press)

Giants of Science Series (Penguin Young Readers)

History Maker Bio Series (Lerner)

How Government Works Series (Lerner)

Inventions that Shaped the World Series (Scholastic)

Inventor and Inventions Series (Benchmark Books)

Once Upon America Series (Puffin Books)

Scientists Who Made History Series (Raintree Steck-Vaughn)

Smart About Series (Grosset & Dunlap)

Smart About Art Series (Grosset & Dunlap)

Spend the Day In Series (Jossey-Bass)

Time for Kids Series (HarperCollins)

Timelines Series (Franklin Watts)

True Books: American Indian Series (Children's Press)

Who Was . . . ? Series (Penguin Young Readers)

Books

Aigner-Clark, J. (2002). *Baby Einstein: The ABCs of art.* New York: Hyperion Books for Children.

Albers, J., & Rosenthal, T. (2006). *Josef Albers: Formulation: Articulation.* London: Thames & Hudson.

Bateman, T. (1989). *Red, white, blue, and Uncle Who? The stories behind some of America's patriotic symbols.* New York: Holiday House.

Bentley, W. (2000). *Snowflakes in photographs.* Mineola, NY: Dover Books.

Berger, M., & Berger, G. (1998). *Why don't haircuts hurt? Questions and answers about the human body.* New York: Scholastic.

Book Studio. (2004). *Big book of the human body.* Kettering, UK: DK Children.

Branley, F. (1986). *What makes day and night.* New York: HarperCollins.

Buller, J., Schade, S., Cocca-Leffler, M., Holub, J., Kelley, T., & Regan, D. (2003). *Smart about the fifty states: A class report.* New York: Grosset & Dunlap.

Burnie, D. (2004). *Plant (Eyewitness books series).* London: Dorling Kindersley.

Burnie, D. (2005). *Animal. The definitive visual guide to the world's wildlife.* New York: Scholastic.

Cha, D., & Livo, N. (2000). *Teaching with folk stories of the Hmong: An activity book.* Westport, CT: Libraries Unlimited.

Chartrand, M., Tirion, W., & Mechler, G. (1995). *National Audubon Society pocket guide to constellations of the northern skies.* New York: Knopf.

Cheney, L. (2002). *America: A patriotic primer.* New York: Simon & Schuster Books for Young Readers.

Cheney, L. (2003). *A is for Abigail: An almanac of amazing American women.* New York: Simon & Schuster Books for Young Readers.

Cheney, L. (2005). *A time for freedom: What happened when in America.* New York: Simon & Schuster.

Cheney, L. (2006). *Our 50 states.* New York: Simon & Schuster Books for Young Readers.

Chipman, D., Florence, M., & Wax, N. (1998). *Cool women.* Chicago: Girl Press.

Cribb, J. (2005). *Money* (Eyewitness books series). New York: Dorling Kindersley.

Crouthers, D. (1978). *Flags of American history.* Maplewood, NJ: Hammond.

Croze, H. (2006). *Africa for kids.* Chicago: Chicago Review Press.

Cushman, J. (1991). *Do you wanna bet? Your chance to find out about probability.* New York: Clarion Books.

Davis, K. (2004). *Don't know much about the 50 states* (Don't know much about series). New York: HarperTrophy.

Devrian Global Industries. (2006). *States activities book.* Union, NJ: Author.

Dickins, R. (2005). *The children's book of art: An introduction to famous paintings.* London: Usborne.

DK Publishing. (1998). *The DK nature encyclopedia.* New York: Dorling Kindersley.

Donald, R. (2001). *Recycling.* New York: Children's Press.

Dorros, A. (1990). *Feel the wind.* New York: HarperCollins.

Evans, J., & Skelton, T. (2001). *How to teach art to children.* Monterey, CA: Evan-Moor.

Faerna, J. (1997). *Mondrian.* New York: Abrams.

Farndon, J. (2002). *1000 facts on human body.* New York: Barnes & Noble Books.

Faul, M. (1992). *Africa and her flags.* Santa Barbara, CA: Bellerophon Books.

Gibbons, G. (1996). *The reasons for the seasons.* New York: Holiday House.

Graham-Barber, L. (1992). *Doodle dandy! The complete book of Independence Day words.* New York: Bradbury Press.

Green, Y. (1997). *African girl and boy paper dolls.* Mineola, NY: Dover Books.

Green, Y. (1999). *Traditional African costumes paper dolls.* Mineola, NY: Dover Books.

Greenaway, T. (2004). *Jungle* (Eyewitness book series). New York: Dorling Kindersley.

Guerra, R. (2004). *The kite-making handbook.* Devon, UK: David & Charles.

Haban, R. (1989). *How proudly they wave: Flags of the fifty states.* Minneapolis: Lerner.

Hall, E. (2005). *Recycling.* Farmington Hills, MI: Kidhaven Press.

Harman, H. (2004). *Money sense for kids.* Hauppauge, NY: Barron's Educational Series.

Hare, T. (2005). *Animal fact file: Head-to-tail profiles of more than 90 mammals.* New York: Checkmark Books.

Hauser, J. (2004). *Celebrate America: Learning about the USA through crafts & activities.* Charlotte, VT: Williamson.

Heifetz, M., & Tirion, W. (2004). *A walk through the heavens: A guide to stars and constellations and their legends.* New York: Cambridge University Press.

Hall, E. (2005). *Recycling.* Farmington Hills, MI: Kidhaven Press.

Hunt, L. (1971). *25 kites that fly.* Mineola, NY: Dover.

Hunter, R. (2001). *Pollution and conservation.* Austin, TX: Raintree Steck-Vaughn.

Kalman, B. (2000). *What is a plant?* New York: Crabtree.

Knowlton, J. (1985). *Maps and globes.* New York: HarperCollins.

Knowlton, J. (1988). *Geography from A to Z: A picture glossary.* New York: HarperCollins.

Kohl, M., & Gainer, C. (1996). *MathArts: Exploring math through art for 3 to 6 year olds.* Beltsville, MD: Gryphon House.

Kohl, M., & Solga, K. (1996). *Discovering great artists: Hands-on art for children in the styles of the great masters.* Bellingham, WA: Bright Ring.

Krull, K. (1995). *Lives of the artists: Masterpieces, messes.* San Diego: Harcourt Brace.

Kudlinski, K. (1991). *Animal tracks and traces.* New York: Franklin Watts.

Levine, S., & Johnstone, L. (2003). *First science experiments: Super senses.* New York: Sterling.

Levine, S., & Johnstone, L. (2005). *First science experiments: Nature, senses, weather, & machines.* New York: Sterling.

Levitt, I., & Marshall, R. (1992). *Star maps for beginners: 50th anniversary edition.* New York: Fireside.

Lewis, B. (1992). *Kids with courage: True stories about young people making a difference.* Minneapolis: Free Spirit.

Lewis, B. (1995). *The kid's guide to service projects: Over 500 service ideas for young people who want to make a difference.* Minneapolis: Free Spirit.

Lewis, B. (1998). *The kid's guide to social action: How to solve social problems you choose—and turn creative thinking into positive action.* Minneapolis: Free Spirit.

Livo, N., & Cha, D. (2003). *Folk stories of the Hmong: Peoples of Laos, Thailand, and Vietnam.* Englewood, CO: Libraries Unlimited.

Maass, R. (2000). *Garbage.* New York: Holt.

MacDonald, M. (1993). *Storyteller's start up book: Finding, learning, performing, and using folktales including twelve tellable tales.* Atlanta: August House.

Mack, L. (2004). *Weather* (Eye wonder series). New York: Dorling Kindersley.

Mackenzie, F. (1995). *Weather and seasons.* New York: Sterling.

Macquitty, M. (2004). *Desert* (Eyewitness book series). New York: Dorling Kindersley.

Macquitty, M. (2004). *Ocean* (Eyewitness book series). New York: Dorling Kindersley.

Maestro, B. (1999). *The story of clocks and calendars.* New York: HarperCollins.

Malet, R. (2003). *Joan Miro.* New York: Rizzoli.

Martin, J. (1998). *Snowflake Bentley*. Boston: Houghton Mifflin.

Marzollo, J. (1994). *My first book of biographies: Great men and women every child should know.* New York: Scholastic.

Mazloomi, C. (1998). *Spirits of the cloth: Contemporary African American quilts.* New York: Crown.

Micklethwait, L. (1993). *A child's book of art: Great pictures: First words.* New York: Dorling Kindersley.

Mink, J. (2000). *Miro.* Hohenzollernring, Germany: Taschen.

Moore, J. (1999). *Africa* (Geography units series). Monterey, CA: Evan-Moor.

Murphy, F. (2002). *Our country.* New York: Scholastic Professional Books.

Murray, J. (2003). *Africa.* New York: Facts on File.

National Geographic Society. (2000). *National Geographic animal encyclopedia.* Hanover, PA: National Geographic Children's Books.

Oliver, C. (2004). *The weather* (100 things you should know about series). New York: Barnes & Noble Books.

Parker, S. (2004). *Mammals* (Eyewitness book series). New York: Dorling Kindersley.

Parker, S. (2004). *Seashore* (Eyewitness book series). New York: Dorling Kindersley.

Parsons, J. (2000). *Children's illustrated encyclopedia.* London: DK Children.

Pasachoff, J., & Percy, J. (Eds.). (2005). *Teaching and learning astronomy: Effective strategies for educators worldwide.* New York: Cambridge University Press.

Pelham, D. (2000). *Kites.* New York: Overlook TP.

Peterson, D. (1998). *Africa.* New York: Scholastic.

Press, J. (2001). *Around the world art & activities: Visiting the 7 continents through craft fun.* Charlotte, VT: Williamson.

Read, R. (1965). *Tangrams: 330 puzzles.* Mineola, NY: Dover.

Reed, B. L. (1987). *Easy-to-make decorative paper snowflakes.* Mineola, NY: Dover.

Renshaw, A., & Ruggi, G. (2005*). The art book for children.* New York: Phaidon Press.

Robinson, W. (1999). *Animal architects: How birds build their amazing homes.* Farmington Hills, MI: Blackbirch Press.

Robinson, W. (1999). *Animal architects: How insects build their amazing homes.* Farmington Hills, MI: Blackbirch Press.

Robinson, W. (1999). *Animal architects: How mammals build their amazing homes.* Farmington Hills, MI: Blackbirch Press.

Robinson, W. (1999). *Animal architects: How shell-makers build their amazing homes.* Farmington Hills, MI: Blackbirch Press.

Robinson, W. (1999). *Animal architects: How spiders and other silkmakers build their amazing homes.* Farmington Hills, MI: Blackbirch Press.

Ross, K. (1995). *Every day is Earth Day.* Brookfield, CT: Millbrook Press.

Royston, A. (1999). *Recycling.* Austin, TX: Raintree Steck-Vaughn.

Saunders, H. (1988). *When are we ever gonna have to use this?* Palo Alto, CA: Dale Seymour.

Scieszka, J., & Smith, L. (2005). *Seen art?* New York: Viking Press.

Seckel, A. (2005). *Ambiguous optical illusions* (SuperVision series). New York: Sterling.

Seckel, A. (2005). *Impossible optical illusions* (SuperVision series). New York: Sterling.

Simon, S. (193). *Weather*. New York: HarperCollins.

Sitomer, M., & Sitomer, H. (1970). *What is symmetry?* New York: Crowell.

Slocum, J., Botermans, J., Gebhardt, D., Ma, M., Ma, X., Raizer, H., Sonnevald, D., van Splunteren, C. (2003). *The tangram book*. New York: Sterling.

Snook, R. (2003). *Many ideas open the way: A collection of Hmong proverbs*. Fremont, CA: Shen's Books.

Spilsbury, L. (2002). *Plant parts* (Life of plants series). Portsmouth, NH: Heinemann.

Taylor, B. (1993). *Maps and mapping* (Young discoveries series). New York: Kingfisher.

Tocci, S. (2001). *Experiments with plants*. New York: Children's Press.

Twist, C. (2005). *Reptiles and amphibians dictionary: An A to Z of cold-blooded creatures*. New York: Scholastic.

Unwin, M. (1993). *Science with plants* (Science activities series). Tulsa, OK: EDC.

VanCleave, J. (2004). *Scientists through the ages*. Hoboken, NJ: Wiley.

Ward, R. (2006). Paul Revere's mathematical ride: Integrating geography, mathematics, and children's literature. *Arizona Reading Journal,32*(1), 24–26.

Ward, R. (2006, January). One if by land; *three* if by sea? *Mathematics Teaching, 194,* 20–21.

Weldon, A. (1998). *Girls who rocked the world: Heroines from Sacagawea to Sheryl Swoopes*. Hillsboro, OR: Beyond Words.

Wells, R. (2003). *How do you know what time it is?* Morton Grove, IL: Whitman.

Whalley, P. (1988) *Butterfly & moth*. New York: Dorling Kindersley.

Wilkes, A. (2003). *Animal homes* (Kingfisher young knowledge series). Boston: Kingfisher.

Williams, D. (1995). *Teaching mathematics through children's art*. Portsmouth, NH: Heinemann.

Wolfman, I. (2003). *My world and globe*. New York: Workman.

Research References

Arhar, J. (1997). The effects of interdisciplinary teaming on students and teachers. In J. L. Irvin (Ed.), *What current research says to the middle level practitioner* (pp. 49–56). Columbus, OH: National Middle School Association.

Avery, C., & Avery, K. (2001). Kids teaching kids. *Journal of Adolescent & Adult Literacy, 44*(5), 434–435.

Bailey, L. (2000). Integrated curriculum: What parents tell us about their children's experience. *The Educational Forum, 64*(3), 236–242.

Basista, B., & Mathews, S. (2002). Integrated science and mathematics professional development programs. *School Science and Mathematics, 102*(7), 359–370.

Beane, J. (1993). *The middle school curriculum: From rhetoric to reality* (2nd ed.). Columbus, OH: National Middle School Association.

Beane, J. (1995). Curriculum integration and the disciplines of knowledge. *Phi Delta Kappan, 76*(8), 616–622.

Beane, J. (1997). *Curriculum integration: Designing the core of democratic education*. New York: Teachers College Press.

Bickley-Green, C. (1995). Math and art curriculum integration: A post-modern foundation. *Studies in Art Education, 37*(1), 6–18.

Bransford, J., Catterall, J., Deasy, R., Goren, P., Harman, A., Herbert, D., Levine, F., Seidel, S., & Sroufe, G. (2004). *The arts and education: New opportunities for research*. Washington, DC: Arts Education Partnership.

Bruner, J. (1977). *The process of education*. Cambridge, MA: Harvard University Press.

Burns, M. (1995). *Math and literature (K–3), vol. 1*. Sausalito, CA: Math Solutions.

Burns, M., & Sheffield, S. (2004). *Math and literature*. Sausalito, CA: Math Solutions.

Butzow, C., & Butzow, J. (2006). *The world of work through children's literature: An integrated approach*. Greenwood Village, CO: Teacher Ideas Press.

Capraro, R. M., & Capraro, M. M. (2006). Are you really going to read us a story? Learning geometry through children's mathematics literature. *Reading Psychology, 27*(1), 21–36.

Carr, K., Buchanan, D., Wentz, J., Weiss, M., & Brant, K. (2001). Not just for the primary grades: A bibliography of picture books for secondary content teachers. *Journal of Adolescent & Adult Literacy, 45*(2), 146–153.

Caskey, M. (2001). A lingering question for middle school: What is the fate of integrated curriculum? *Childhood Education 78*(2), 97–99.

Caskey, M. M., & Johnston, J. H. (1996). Hard work ahead: Authentic curriculum under construction. *Schools in the Middle, 6*(2), 11–18.

Cobb, P. (2000). The importance of a situated view of learning to the design of research and instruction. In J. Boaler (Ed.), *Multiple perspectives on mathematics teaching and learning*. Westport, CT: Greenwood.

Cornett, C. (2003). *Creating meaning through literature and the arts*. Upper Saddle River, NJ: Merrill/Prentice-Hall

Davies, M. A. (1992). Are interdisciplinary units worthwhile? Ask students. In J. Lounsbury (Ed.), *Connecting the curriculum through interdisciplinary instruction*. Columbus, OH: National Middle School Association.

Deasy, R. J. (Ed.). (2002). *Critical links: Learning in the arts and student academic and social development.* Washington, DC: Arts Education Partnership.

Dewey, J. (1924). *Democracy and education: An introduction to the philosophy of education.* New York: Macmillan.

Dewey, J. (1933). *How we think.* Chicago: Regnery.

Donoghue, M. (2001). *Using literature activities to teach content areas to emergent readers.* Needham Heights, MA: Allyn & Bacon.

Drake, S. (1998). *Creating integrated curriculum: Proven ways to increase student learning.* Thousand Oaks, CA: Corwin Press.

Drake, S., & Burns, R. (2004). *Meeting standards through integrated curriculum.* Alexandria, VA: Association for Supervision and Curriculum Development.

Draper, R. (2002). School mathematics reform, constructivism, and literacy: A case for literacy instruction in the reform-oriented math classroom. *Journal of Adolescent & Adult Literacy, 45*(6), 520–529.

Efland, A. (2002). *Art and cognition: Integrating the visual arts in the curriculum.* New York: Teachers College Press.

Eisner, E. (1998). Does experience in the arts boost academic achievement? *Arts Education, 51*(1), 5–15.

Eisner, E. (2004). *The arts and the creation of mind.* New Haven, CT: Yale University Press.

Fiske, E. B. (Ed.). (1999). *Champions of change: The impact of the arts on learning.* Washington, DC: Arts Education Partnership

Fredericks, A. (1991). *Social studies through children's literature: An integrated approach.* Greenwood Village, CO: Teacher Ideas Press.

Fredericks, A. (2000). *More social studies through children's literature: An integrated approach.* Greenwood Village, CO: Teacher Ideas Press.

Gallavan, N. (2001). Four lessons that integrate math and social studies. *Social Studies and the Young Learner, 13*(3), 25–28.

Gardner, H. (1997). A primer of multiple intelligences. *NEA Today, 15*(7), 17.

Gelineau, R. (2003). *Integrating arts across the elementary school curriculum.* Belmont, CA: Thomson Wadsworth.

Hellwig, S., Monroe, E. E., & Jacobs, J. S. (2000). Making informed choices: Selecting children's trade books for mathematics instruction. *Teaching Children Mathematics, 7,* 138–143.

Howey, K. (1996). Designing coherent and effective teacher education programs. In J. Sikula, T. J. Buttery, & E. Guyton (Eds.), *Handbook of research on teacher education* (2nd ed., pp. 143–170). New York: Simon & Schuster.

Hunsader, P. (2004). Mathematics trade books: Establishing their value and assessing their quality. *The Reading Teacher, 7*(57), 618–629.

International Reading Association (IRA) (2006). Excellent reading teachers: A position statement of the International Reading Association. In R. D. Robinson (Ed.), *Issues and innovations in literacy education* (pp. 19–24). Newark, DE: Author.

Jacobs, H. (1989). The interdisciplinary concept model: A step-by-step approach for developing integrated units of study. In H. H. Jacobs (Ed.), *Interdisciplinary curriculum: Design and implementation* (pp. 53–65). Alexandria, VA: Association for Supervision and Curriculum Development.

Jensen, E. (2001). *Arts with the brain in mind.* Alexandria, VA: Association for Supervision and Curriculum Development.

Johnson, N., & Giorgis, C. (2001). Interacting with the curriculum. *The Reading Teacher, 55*(2), 204–213.

Kaser, S. (2001). Searching the heavens with children's literature: A design for teaching science. *Language Arts, 78*(4), 348–356.

Kim, M., Andrews, R., & Carr, D. (2004). Traditional versus integrated preservice teacher education curriculum. *Journal of Teacher Education, 55*(4), 341–356.

Kleiman, G. (1991). Mathematics across the curriculum. *Educational Leadership, 49*(2), 48–51.

Leitze, A. R. (1997). Connecting process problem solving to children's literature. *Teaching Children Mathematics, 3*, 398–405.

Leu, D. J., Castek, J., Henry, L. A., Coiro, J., & McMullan, M. (2004). The lessons that children teach us: Integrating children's literature and the new literacies of the Internet. *The Reading Teacher, 57*(5), 496–503.

MacGregor, M., & Price, E. (1999). An exploration of aspects of language proficiency and algebra learning. *Journal for Research in Mathematics Education, 30*, 449–467.

Martinez, M., & McGee, L. (2000). Children's literature and reading instruction: Past, present, and future. *Reading Research Quarterly, 35*(1), 54–169.

McCoy, M. (2003, Spring/Summer). Language, math, social studies, and . . . worms? *Integrating the Early Childhood Curriculum, 2*, 3–8.

McDonald, N., & Fisher, D. (2006). *Teaching literacy through the arts*. New York: Guilford Press.

Meinbach, A., Fredericks, A., & Rothlein, L. (2000). *The complete guide to thematic units: Creating the integrated curriculum*. Norwood, MA: Christopher Gordon.

Monroe, E., & Livingston, N. (2002). It figures: Language and mathematics add up through children's literature. *The Dragon Lode, 20*(2), 37–41.

Moss, B. (2003). *Exploring the literature of fact: Children's nonfiction trade books in the elementary classroom*. New York: Guilford Press.

Moyer, P. (2000). Communicating mathematically: Children's literature as a natural connection. *The Reading Teacher, 54*, 246–255.

Muller, D., & Ward, R. (2007). Art and algebra? Middle school students discover algebra in Calder mobiles. *Mathematics in Schools, 36*(3), 15–21.

Music Educators National Conference (MENC). (1994). *National standards for arts education*. Reston, VA: Author.

National Association for Core Curriculum. (2000). *A bibliography of research on the effectiveness of block-time, core, and interdisciplinary team teaching programs*. Kent, OH: Author.

National Council for the Social Studies (NCSS). (1994). *Curriculum standards for the social studies*. Silver Spring, MD: Author.

National Council of Teachers of English (NCTE) and International Reading Association (IRA). (1996). *Standards for the English language arts*. Urbana, IL: NCTE.

National Council of Teachers of Mathematics (NCTM). (1989). *Curriculum and evaluation standards for school mathematics*. Reston, VA: Author.

National Council of Teachers of Mathematics (NCTM). (2000). *Principles and standards for school mathematics*. Reston, VA: Author.

National Middle School Association (NMSA). (1995). *This we believe: Developmentally responsive middle level schools*. Columbus, OH: Author.

National Research Council (NRC). (1996). *National science education standards*. Washington, DC: National Academy Press.

Perkins, D. (1989). Selecting fertile themes for integrated learning. In H. H. Jacobs (Ed.), *Interdisciplinary curriculum: Design and implementation* (pp. 67–76). Alexandria, VA: Association for Supervision and Curriculum Development.

Phillips, P., & Bickley-Green, C. (1998). Integrating art and mathematics. *Principal, 77*(4), 46–49.

Putnam, R., & Borko, H. (2000). What do new views of knowledge and thinking have to say about research on teacher learning? *Educational Researcher, 29*(1), 4–15.

Rose, M. (2000). Lessons: Social Studies/Math Millennium mastery. *Instructor, 109*(5), 14.

Roth, W., & McGinn, M. (1998). Knowing, researching, and reporting science education: Lessons from science and technology studies. *Journal of Research in Science Teaching, 35*(2), 213–235.

Schiro, M. (1997). *Integrating children's literature and mathematics in the classroom: Children as meaning makers, problem solvers, and literary critics*. New York: Teachers College Press.

Schwartz, S., & Pollishuke, M. (2005). Planning an integrated curriculum. In K. Revington (Ed.), *Creating the dynamic classroom: A handbook for teachers* (pp. 44–69). Toronto: Pearson Education Canada.

Scripp, L. (2002). An overview of research on music and learning. In R. J. Deasy (Ed.), *Critical links: Learning in the arts and student academic and social development*. Washington, DC: Arts Education Partnership.

Thompson, D., & Holyoke, K. (2000, Summer). Using children's literature to link mathematics and social studies: A multicultural exploration with bread. *Trends & Issues: The Publication of the Florida Council for the Social Studies, 12*, 22–24.

Vars, G. (1996). Effects of interdisciplinary curriculum and instruction. In P. S. Hlebowitsh & W. G. Wraga (Eds.), *Annual review of research for school leaders* (pp. 147–164). Reston, VA: National Association of Secondary School Principals and Scholastic Publishing.

Vars, G. (1997). Effects of integrative curriculum and instruction. In J. E. Irvin (Ed.), *What current research says to the middle level practitioner* (pp. 179–186). Columbus, OH: National Middle School Association.

Vars, G., & Beane. J. (2000). Integrative curriculum in a standards-based world. ERIC Digest. (ERIC Document Reproduction Service No. ED 441618) [Online]. Available: www.ed.gov/ databases/ERIC_Digests/ ed441618.html

Walling, D. (2005). *Visual knowing: Connecting art and ideas across the curriculum*. Thousand Oaks, CA: Corwin Press.

Ward, R. (2003). How much is a billion? A lot more than you think! *Arizona Reading Journal, 30*(1), 27–29.

Ward, R. (2004a). K–8 preservice teachers author a mathematical piece of children's literature. *The California Reader, 38*(1), 24–30.

Ward, R. (2004b). K–8 preservice teachers' journey into the global village: exploring real-world data using children's literature and technology. *Arizona Reading Journal, 31*(1), 43–47.

Ward, R (2004c). Looking for math in all the right places. *The California Reader, 38*(2), 58–65.

Ward, R. (2005). Using children's literature to inspire K–8 preservice teachers' future mathematics pedagogy. *The Reading Teacher, 59*(2), 132–143.

Ward, R. (2006a, Spring). Modeling effective pedagogical strategies for teaching mathematics. *The Charter Schools Resource Journal,* 1–9.

Ward, R. (2006b, January). One if by land; *three* if by sea? *Mathematics Teaching, 194,* 20–21.

Ward, R. & Muller, D. (2006, September). Algebra and art. *Mathematics Teaching, 198,* 22–26.

Watts, S. (2004, Summer). Arts-infused summer school. *New Horizons for Learning Online Journal, 10*(3). Retrieved March 12, 2007, from http://www.newhorizons.org/strategies/arts/watts2.htm

Whitin, D., & Whitin, P. (1996). Fostering metaphorical thinking through children's literature. In P. C. Elliott (Ed.), *Communication in mathematics K–12 and beyond, 1996 yearbook of the National Council of Teachers of Mathematics* (pp. 60–65). Reston, VA: National Council of Teachers of Mathematics.

Whitin, D., & Whitin, P. (2004). *New visions for linking literature and mathematics.* Urbana, IL: National Council of Teachers of English.

Whitin, D., & Wilde, S. (1992). *Read any good math lately?* Portsmouth, NH: Heinemann.

Whitin, D., & Wilde, S. (1995). *It's the story that counts.* Portsmouth, NH: Heinemann.

Wortham, S. (1996). Bringing it all together. In S. C. Wortham (Ed.), *The integrated classroom: The assessment-curriculum link in early childhood education* (pp. 326–346). Englewood Cliffs, NJ: Prentice-Hall.

Young, J. (2001). Why are we reading a book during math time? How mathematics and literature relate. *The Dragon Lode, 19*(2), 13–18.

Appendix
Assessment Tools and Rubrics

As described in the introduction to this book, this appendix includes several assessment tools and rubrics (see below) that a teacher might employ as a means to better assess students as they engage in the literature-based activities. Other helpful assessment resources are included in the "Assessment Resources References" section.

Observation Log

Name: _____

Date	Activity	Observed Behavior

Comments:

Observation Log

Name: _____

Activity: _____

Date: _____

Objectives or Goals	Observed Behavior	Comments

Observation Log

Name: _____

Date	Activity	Participation in Tasks 0: Little or none 1: Engaged 2: Fully engaged	Participation in Discussions 0: Little or none 1: Engaged 2: Fully engaged	Collaboration with Team 0: Little or none 1: Average 2: Above Average	Comments

Analytic Scoring Scale

Understanding the problem   0: Complete misunderstanding of the problem

    1: Part of the problem misunderstood or misinterpreted

    2: Complete understanding of the problem

Planning a solution   0: No attempt, or totally inappropriate plan

    1: Partially correct plan based on part of the problem being interpreted correctly

    2: Plan could have led to a correct solution if implemented properly

Getting an answer   0: No answer, or wrong answer based on an inappropriate plan

    1: Copying error; computational error; partial answer for a problem with multiple answers

    2: Correct answer and correct label for the answer

(Source: Charles, Lester, & O'Daffer, 1987)

Inventory of Student's Mathematical Disposition

Name: _____

	Date	Comments
Confident in using mathematics		
Flexible in doing mathematics		
Perseveres at mathematical tasks		
Shows curiosity in doing mathematics		
Reflects on own thinking		
Values applications of mathematics		
Appreciates role of mathematics		

(Derived from Stenmark, 1991, p. 34)

Mathematical Disposition Checklist

	Student 1	Student 2	Student 3	Student 4
Confidence • Initiates questions • Is sure answers will be found • Helps others with problems • Other:				
Flexibility • Solves problems in more than one way • Changes opinion when given a convincing argument • Other:				
Perseverance				
Curiosity				
Reflective				
Appreciation for mathematics				

(Derived from Stenmark, 1991, p. 34)

Observation Log

Group members: _____

Activity title: _____

Name	Assigned Task	Task Completed? (Y or N)	Comments

Group Assessment

Group members: _____

Activity title: _____

Did your group . . .	🙂	😐	🙁
Listen			
Talk about the task			
Cooperate			
Finish the task			

What went well? _____

_____

_____

What would you do differently? _____

_____

_____

(Derived from Stenmark, 1991, p. 34)

Collaborative Report

Student Name: _____   Date: _____

Teacher Name: _____   Date: _____

Scale: 2 – Mastered fully   1 – Partial mastery   0 – Did not master

Criterion or Task	Student Rating	Teacher Rating

Student's comments: _____

_____

Teacher's comments: _____

_____

Sample Writing Prompts

- In your own words, explain the meaning of . . .

- The most important thing I learned in math class today (or this week) is . . .

- The most important thing to understand about *polygons* is . . .
  (*Note:* change *polygons* to the concept explored)

- I discovered that . . .

- Explain your reasoning about . . .

- I know my solution is correct because . . .

- I feel confident about my solution because . . .

- I am still uncertain about . . .

- Describe any instances during which you became stuck and how you became "unstuck" while solving the problem.

- Describe a real-world experience/connection to the mathematical concept you learned about today.

- Write a letter to a classmate who did not attend class today so that he or she will understand what you learned about.

- Draw a picture or diagram showing how the concepts you learned about today are connected.

(Derived from Stenmark, 1991, p. 34)

Index

A

ABC of Jobs (Priddy), 119–121

Abstract ideas, 2

Addition
  in algebra activities, 137–139
  in number and operations activities, 72–74, 77–79

African culture, number and operations activities and, 72–74

Aigner-Clark, Julie, *Baby Einstein: The ABCs of Art*, 169–172

Aker, Susan, *What Comes in 2's, 3's, & 4's?*, 19–22

Algebra activities
  with science connection, 25–36
  with social studies connection, 82–92
  with visual arts connection, 137–146

A.M./P.M. distinction, measuring activities and, 98–100

Anderson, Jon, *Money: A Rich History*, 77–79

Angles, in geometry activities
  with social studies connection, 93–97
  with visual arts connection, 147–150

Animals
  algebra activities and, 31–34
  measurement activities and, 49–51
  number and operations activities and, 72–74

Animals in Their Homes (Goldie), 49–51

ante meridian. See A.M./P.M. distinction

Art, algebra activities and, 82–85

Art creation
  algebra activities and, 137–139, 142–144
  data analysis and probability activities and, 175–178
  geometry activities and, 147–150, 154–156, 159–161, 164–166
  measurement activity and, 169–172
  number and operations activities and, 128–130, 132–134

Art history
  algebra activities and, 137–139, 142–144
  data analysis and probability activities and, 175–178
  geometry activities and, 154–156, 159–161, 164–166
  measurement activity and, 169–172
  number and operations activities and, 128–130, 132–134

Asch, Frank, *The Earth and I*, 54–57

B

Baby Einstein: The ABCs of Art (Aigner-Clark), 169–172

Balestrino, Philip, *The Skeleton Inside You*, 44–47

Bar graphs, in data analysis and probability activities
  with science connection, 54–57, 59–62
  with social studies connection, 103–106, 109–111

Barner, Bob, *Dem Bones*, 44–47

The Best Bug Parade (Murphy), 169–172

Biographical works, 142–144, 154–156, 175–178

Bones, measurement activities and, 44–47

Book pairs/trios, described, 5

Branley, Franklyn, *Sunshine Makes the Seasons*, 59–62

Burke, Jennifer S.
  Rectangles (City Shapes Series), 154–156
  Squares (City Shapes Series), 154–156

A Busy Year (Lionni), 103–106

C

Capacity measurements, with science connection, 49–51

Cartography, algebra activities and, 87–90

Cause-and-effect relationships, in algebra activities, 25–28

Cha, Dia, and Norma Livo, *Teaching with Folk Stories of the Hmong: An Activity Book*, 82–85

Change of seasons, data analysis and probability activities and, 59–62

Chesanow, Neil, *Where Do I Live?*, 93–95

A Child's Book of Art (Micklethwait), 132–134

Civic duties and responsibilities, algebra activities and, 87–90

Classification, in algebra activities, 31–34

"A Closet Full of Shoes" (poem by Silverstein), 175–178

Clothing, number and operations activities and, 72–74

The Cloud Book (de Paola), 37–41

Clouds, geometry activities and, 37–41

Coins, in number and operations activities, 77–79

Color
  data analysis and probability activities and, 175–178
  geometry activities and, 154–156, 159–161, 164–166
  measurement activities and, 169–172

Common good, working for, algebra activities and, 87–90

Community, individual's role in, 119–121

Connection activities
  science–mathematics, 64–65
  social studies–mathematics, 119–121

Continents, data analysis and probability activities and, 109–111

Counting. *See also* Skip counting
  in data analysis and probability activities, 54–57
  in geometry activities, 164–166